Once upon a Time

Once upon a Time

James Cullinane

To order additional copies of this book, contact:
Xlibris
844-714-8691
www.Xlibris.com
Orders@Xlibris.com
828064

Table of Contents

Why I Write

This is as relevant today as it was when I wrote it as an assignment from Professor John Herman in Manhattanville some twenty years ago. I can only add that it is as important today, if not more so, to pass on lessons learned through our life experiences in the hope it will influence someone in a positive and even spiritual way. To connect with others, to love and forgive, is, and always will be, the essence of a good and uplifting life.

"Why do you write," my professor asks? "What purpose does it serve in your life," he inquires? "It's my life, dull academic," I thunder in reply, "can you not see that? I live, breathe and bleed writing. It's as essential to my being as the blood that courses through my veins. Can you not see the dedication I bring to my writing, the passion that engulfs me as I discuss Woolf, Kincaid, Swift or Baldwin? Can you not see this? Are you blind or just uncaring?

Writing gives meaning to my life, and without it I am nothing. At times I'm plunged into the depths of hell and others lifted on the wings of inspiration to sit and sup at literatures Round Table with Herman, Edgar Allan, Virginia, and Maya. But without writing I am like a blank page, nothing. Fortune, family, and friends pale in comparison to my passion so I am a poor friend, even poorer husband and father. All are secondary to my writing, and this is as it must be.

Now, having got all that righteous pomp and hyperbole out of my system and bearing in mind my professor's admonition to be amusing, startling, profound or bemused, I will try to answer that most difficult of questions, why do I write?

Why in the latter stages of my life, have I returned to the classroom to wrestle with words, structure, and form? Why after thirty years of minimal contact with literature good or bad, and my intellect in an advanced state of rot, have I begun to read - and write, again? For if I want to write, I must read.

I've had the thought to write many times, a thought that has nagged me off and on for most of my life and would never leave permanently. I had wanted to get my undergraduate degree, and got it in August 1997, the first of my siblings to do so. When I did, my interest in reading and writing was again stimulated. I had tasted and wanted more, to explore all aspects of writing, poetry, and playwriting. I wanted, also, to find out how good my writing could become and that, of course remains to be answered.

Writing, for me, is an anxiety-laden event for I'm rarely satisfied with the outcome. So, I can't honestly say that writing gives me great pleasure. There is a certain satisfaction in completing a piece of writing that I've worked hard on and that contains most of what I wanted to say in a reasonably intelligent manner. But I usually get this achy feeling in my gut as I wrestle with words and structure, frantically arranging and rearranging. And I'm rarely satisfied with the finished product. But it's a pursuit that certainly keeps the mind occupied and hopefully senility at bay.

John Keats (1795 - 1821) the English Romantic poet and letter writer wrote to his colleague B.R. Hayden: "I have come to this resolution - never to write for the sake of writing or making a poem, but from running over with any little knowledge or experience which many years of reflection may perhaps give me; otherwise, I will be dumb." 8 March 1819. I try to remember Mr. Keats admonition.

Why do we write? I think because it helps us as humans to understand each other. If something I write strikes a chord, resonates in someone else's soul, and makes them feel less alone, then my writing has accomplished what writing should. If, sometime in the future a child or grandchild of mine will come across something I've written and be charmed - inspired even, that will be reward enough. Would I like to achieve fame with my writing? Right on, and fortune? Right on twice. Fame and fortune stroke the ego, but fame and fortune are fleeting and if you write one successful book, you'll be expected to write another and another. And writing is one lonely occupation. But if you change someone for the better through your writing, you've achieved much more than fame or fortune.

Writing does give me a better idea of who I am, 'grounds' or 'centers' - to use the in-vogue vernacular, for better or worse. I believe it reveals eventually our deepest longings and fears, and that can be scary. So, I write to find out more about myself, stripping away the layers as one would peel an onion. As humans we have an amazing capacity to bury painful knowledge and memory. We bury it so deep that we forget it's there and so long that we sometimes take it to the grave.

The world is chock-a-block with eminent writing down through the ages, enough to intimidate the bravest. And Yogi Berra's remark that "nobody goes to that restaurant anymore, it's too crowded" might well be applied to writing. But there must be a need for humans to write - and read, and every year the ranks of would-be writers, swell. And, I suppose, that is as it should be. So, I write to discover more about myself, to share my experiences in the hope that it enriches other lives and makes them feel more connected to the human, planet and universe family.

Sri Lanka Guesthouse

God, she was tired, and she had lost weight again. She checked herself in the mirror, saw that the sleeveless blouse and blue denim skirt hung on her like it was two sizes too big. Once it had fit so well.

Being a guesthouse owner was an honorable profession in Sri Lanka, but a very demanding one. If one were diligent and catered well to the needs of the foreigners, one could make money that was well above the income of the average Sri Lankan – if one could find a job. She was diligent and tried to satisfy the needs of the foreigners.

She and Katanga had been successful. They had already rebuilt the old house and had fitted out four rooms with good, strong beds, dressing table, mosquito netting round the bed, and completely tiled bathrooms with solid, very expensive shower and toilet fittings. They had installed beautiful scrollwork over each window. It was such a proud day when they had hung up the sign for the very first time – The Red Rose Guesthouse.

All the guests complimented them on the nice rooms and beautiful bathrooms. But they all haggled over the price. 2500 Rupees per night was not an enormous price in Risi's estimation. They had spent thousands upon thousands on the renovations and fittings. Were they not entitled to recover that money? Many of the foreigners were shocked when she quoted 2500 Rupees. Many said, "Oh, my friend came here two years ago and got a nice room for 1000 Rupees." But this is not two years ago, and prices have risen for everything. Also, Risi knew, they could never get a room anywhere near that price in their own country. One had even demanded hot water for the shower, and she had to explain patiently, patiently this is a hot country, so we shower with cold water. It was a demanding business.

Katanga was a good husband and handsome with a smiling, placid personality. They complemented each other. She ached for what the foreigners had. Abundance – that was the word that pingponged in her brain when she studied them. How could so much be given to them and so little to her people? Katanga, like so many of his tribe was content with how things were. She was not like that. She wanted what the rich foreigner had. She would be successful.

She had imagined this guesthouse long before it became a reality, the excellent fixtures – not like those of her neighbors. They had settled for cheaper, inferior quality and would have many problems later, she thought. She was the one who had bought the computer, had become reasonably proficient in its operation, and had put it at the disposal of her guests. She had also bought the fine china, teapots, plates, and cups. She cooked, handled the money transactions and the guests' requests – Katanga had little English so deferred to her in his deep, musical voice.

Last night she heard him sing to the Swedish couple and when she looked out – husband and wife seated at different tables, he was singing to the woman. The woman clapped excitedly and Risi felt jealousy. All the guests seemed to like Katanga, his demeanor – for he smiled constantly - and deep musical voice. He seemed more confident as time progressed. Where once he said little except to her, he was beginning to learn some English words. It was an old Sri Lankan song he had sung about an impossible love between a poor peasant and an older woman of property and money.

But there was no doubt about Katanga's love for her. They were not blessed with children, but it was not a problem for them. They had each other. Their wedding picture hung in a prominent place in the kitchen, easily seen by the guests. They were a handsome couple. It had been such an exciting time and after the wedding festivities they went for one week to the mountains near Kandy. There was a waterfall nearby and they swam every day in the cold waters and every night in the small room they had rented, they made passionate love and pledged to love each other for the rest of their lives. It was there also that Risi had told Katanga of her dream of a beautiful guesthouse.

"He-ll-o, he-ll-o." Someone was calling. It was the Austrian woman, Ulries who liked to be called Uli.

"He-ll-o, Risi, are you there?" Risi pushed the hair from her face, placed a smile on it and went to Uli.

"Can you call a tuk-tuk for me? I wish to go to Matare. How much will it cost?" Risi told her, 450 Rupees one way, 800 to stay and take her back- eight American dollars. It was so little to the foreigners. Uli agreed to the price and Risi called her friend Srip. He would pay her a percentage each week, small now but she visualized a time when it would be bigger, much bigger.

The Swedish couple, Lars and Christina had taken a rental car and driver from Bandaranaike Airport in Colombo to Mirissa. It had cost them 8000 Rupees or 80 American dollars for the four-hour journey. What wealth these foreigners had – and they would take a car and driver on the return journey also, another 8000 Rupees. How wasteful, she thought, when they could have, for the same journey, got an air-conditioned minibus for 285 Rupees. When she or Katanga went to Colombo, they took the public bus for 129 Rupees – one dollar and twenty-nine cents. It sometimes took five hours or more, it rattled, and it shook and was usually crowded so one had to stand for at least part of the way, but it was reasonable. They would never have considered the minibus.

Sometimes she wondered how her life would be when the guesthouse was running to its full capacity and successful, when she could hire a girl to help, when they had money enough to do the things they wished to do. It would be nice to travel to another country, stay at a guesthouse – have someone else cater to her needs. She smiled. Would she be as demanding as her guests, haggle over the price of the room?

The American, Stan had told her about Thailand, how wonderful it was, the food, the accommodation, air-conditioning, hot showers, how beautiful it was.

"But Sri Lanka is beautiful too," Risi had interrupted.

"Yes, yes,' he said, "but there are screens on the windows, so I'm not eaten alive with mosquitoes."

"Mosquitoes only eat Americans," she had replied. "No one else complains."

"They are too polite," the American replied. "Nobody likes mosquitoes."

She would go to Thailand and see for herself. It would be good to observe and compare. Maybe there were things she could learn. She doubted it but she would keep an open mind. She knew Thailand had many more tourists than Sri Lanka. But Thailand had never been occupied, not the whole country and not as long as her country had been. Meanwhile Sri Lanka was making great strides. It had a new airport and another one planned. Its tea was the world's best. She was very proud of her country.

Katanga had not yet come to bed. She heard the low murmur of voices from outside. It was Uli and Katanga – his low, musical voice interjecting briefly as Uli explained something or described her life. She was overcome with sleep. Later she felt him slide into bed behind her. She felt his hand on her right breast, kneading gently. This was the prelude to their coupling. She would turn around and lie on her back and stroke his penis, already hard. He would mount her. She was so tired. She felt herself sliding back into a dreamless state as Katanga's hand fell from her breast.

Mostly

When I do go out in my boat, I do go every day
I mostly have great peace there, out in that big, blue bay

But I do go because I must, for fishing is my trade
And if I don't, well on that day, I'll surely not get paid.

But I must always be afraid, for those who are not – go
Out when they should be staying home, and reap just what they sow

So, we do be afraid of sea, and mostly we survive
Except for only now and then, we mostly stay alive.

And I will always hold to that, from youth was taught to me
To be afraid, not now and then, but always of the sea.

Child of the Universe

"Atrocious, atrocious altogether." The old woman took a poker and stirred the fire. "Tis a wet one. We'll be washed away." She turned and stared at me. "Cycling Ireland, are you?"

It was a dream I had since a boy, a great curiosity to visit the country of my ancestors, see where my father had grown up, meet up with relatives I had never met, and who might, in a few short years disappear from the face of the earth. I wanted to know my tribe.

I had disembarked at Shannon three days before, mounted my trusty steed and headed for Galway and Connemara. I carefully mapped my journey staying away from the new highways that ripped through the country from city to city. I kept to the secondary roads, the old roads that wended through town and village – the main roads for ages before the bypasses and roundabouts and highways arrived.

Out the small window nothing stirred, a lazy feel to the day. The rain had subsided again, off and on all day. Earlier, I was on my way to Clifden, enjoying a warm sun between showers when my eye beheld the figure of a woman striding through a field, the field that fronted the cottage I now sat in. There was something about her that drew my attention, and I didn't know what – maybe her bearing, how she held herself, or how the sun reflected off her hair, or was it the strong legs and strong back that were evident even from a distance?

It was an urge to know her, and it was what compelled me to the door of the cottage - but why?

The door was opened by the old woman who bid me enter and who was, at this very moment, boiling the kettle for tea. I wanted to know if the woman in the field was attached to this cottage. I didn't ask, hoping she would, in time, divulge this information. She bustled about, swift and spare in her movements

"Would you have a bit of ham?"

I demurred. "No, no, too much trouble."

"And a cold spud with a bit of butter? You will."

We ate in silence, strong black tea milked and sugared, a hunk of ham and a cold spud with a good slab of Irish Creamery butter. She filled my cup twice and I finally leaned away from the table, sated and more.

"Could you not take a bus? They'd take the bike for you."

"Ah, that would be cheating. I'm well-equipped for the rain."

"Not the rain we're getting. Now the soft rain is fine."

She paused and gazed out the window. She seemed lost in thought, in another place.

"I'll take a walk in that myself, good for the complexion." She cackled. "But the other one, ('wan' she pronounced) cold and cutting, good for nothing (knottin)."

"When the sun comes out, it's beautiful," I said, "and every bend in the road a different view."

"Every bend in the road a different view, he says." She cackled again. "Sounds like your man from Bord Failte."

"I have relatives in Westport," I said. "I'll stop there."

Before she asked, I replied, "By the name of Tierney. Sean Tierney was my grandfather. I'm called after him."

She froze a second. "I knew a James Tierney from up that way. He died some years back. God have mercy on his soul. He'd be a distant cousin of mine."

"So, we could be related?" I inquired.

"We could" she said, "we probably are. Half the country is related and half you wouldn't want to know."

"My grandfather had six brothers. He was the only one who left, as far as I know, but there was a James."

The door suddenly opened, and the woman of the field came in. The old woman spoke.

"This man is from America, Deirdre, cycling the country, would you believe?"

She was even more beautiful than I imagined, a slight red to her cheeks but tall and athletic. She could have been a queen, I thought, though she dressed as a working woman, rubber boots – wellingtons they called them, I found out later – corduroy pants and check shirt. Her hair caught my attention, black, sleek and abundant and tied into a ponytail. She stared at me and spoke in a low voice.

"How far are you going?"

"The whole country, I hope, but I'm heading for Mayo and Connemara now."

"You gave him something?"

The old woman nodded, then turned and looked at Deirdre. "He's a Tierney."

Deirdre turned and stared, her eyes grown darker, greener, studying me with total concentration. Then she looked away and gazed out the window. Conversation faltered, then resumed. We chatted about the state of Ireland and the state of America and Deirdre said little, her mind somewhere else though she studied me intensely. When our eyes met, she didn't look away, her eyes now blue though sometimes shot with green as the light changed in the cottage – as the light diffused and refracted through the cottage window. Within minutes the old woman had nodded off, a gentle sibilance coming from her, and Deirdre beckoned that we should go, her finger to her lips. We left, gently closing the door and I followed her to the road.

"I have a small place of my own. We could stop?"

I nodded enthusiastically. I had an awful fear she would leave, and I'd never see her again and I'd wonder forever why I was so drawn to her, why I had this overwhelming need to know her.

"I saw you walking through the field," I said, "and I was compelled…" I stopped, unable to put into words the feeling I had. She said nothing in reply, and we walked in silence, me pushing my bicycle, my beast of burden, laden down on both sides with all I would need, I hoped, for any and all circumstances. I followed her down a narrow and overrun boreen, which led into another and then two more until we came on a cottage that I would have passed without seeing, secluded as it was and set back from the boreen. She opened a small gate and pushed open the sturdy front door to the cottage and I was standing in a room that in its simplicity and utility was enchanting. A fire burned in the hearth, two kerosene lamps gave off a soft glow that reflected off the polished wood of a sturdy table that sat by the one window, the window framed by white linen curtains. The floor was of cut stone; of a design I had never seen before though it appeared Celtic. Through an open door I saw a bed with two side tables, and I looked quickly away for fear she'd see me staring.

"You have no electricity?" I said.

"I prefer the old ways," she said, the old light. "You'll have something?"

"I'll have what you're having," I said with a smile. She brought two mugs filled with what, it seemed to me some kind of ale. I drank hungrily, the drink cold and refreshing. She sipped and watched intently. Now a bolt of lightning illuminated the cottage and thunder growled. Darkness enveloped the cottage and things became jumbled, murky as if I had entered some twilight zone.

The next few minutes – hours, what happened and in what order, what was fantasy, reality, imagination or my deepest, most secret desires, I cannot tell. She was looking deep into my eyes. She was stroking my neck and head. She was holding my hand and leading me to the bedroom and to the bed. Outside, the sky had cleared, and moonlight flooded the bedroom, lending a surreal, ghostly aspect to everything. She had shed her clothes. We were both naked. How or when I have no memory. Her hands massaged my body, and I was overwhelmed by feelings I never remembered having before – like as a child being enveloped in a loving mother's arms. I felt skin like I had never felt before and softness, invitation and yielding. It was like floating in a soft cloud on a warm day, soft and sensuous, at times grown more urgent, then heavenly release and sleep – to begin all over again.

Was it hours, days? Again, I cannot tell. I remember nourishment, oatmeal maybe with fruit, blackberries and wild strawberries and ale, this time harsh and astringent. She talked to me in a language I did not understand and held me to her breast, and I nursed like a new-born babe. She led and I, her willing accomplice, followed. We clashed bodies, kissed, nuzzled and stroked till blessed relief - where we started all over again. My last memory was of Deirdre holding a silver cup to my lips containing, I thought, an herbal drink laced with honey. By this time, I was ravenously thirsty and drank greedily. I remember no more.

When I awoke, I was lying in a grassy meadow with the sun beating down, my body reddened and bruised. My bicycle lay beside me, all my equipment intact. I could make no sense of what happened. I lay there desperately trying to recollect the sequence of events, what was real and what was fantasy, dreaming? Had I been drugged? But the eating and the drinking happened after what happened in the bedroom.

What did happen in that small, perfect cottage? How should one describe it? Was it a form of hypnosis, one taking advantage of another? Was I complicit in…whatever had happened? Was it a mutual coming together, long buried desires revealed? I only knew the experience left me shaken to my core, drained but also overwhelmed with images both sexual and sensuous. I searched for Deirdre's cottage all that day and made exhaustive inquiries. but it was as if it had disappeared off the face of the earth. No one knew though the name Deirdre seemed to spark some recognition. Neither had I any luck locating the old woman whose name I had never learned or the cottage she lived in. I retraced the road I had taken time and time again, but it was like they had never existed.

Later that night, in a pub in a nearby town, drunk and depressed I engaged an old man in conversation. "America,' he said, 'I have two brothers in Chicago and a sister in Brooklyn. They're always at me to come but I haven't. If it's as good as they say, I 'd stay. And I'd be missing this place." He laughed. "They're doing well, from what I hear." I asked him if he knew a Deirdre in these parts. He didn't. It was a name they avoided in this parish, he said.

"Why," I asked?

"On account of…," he said. "Ah, it's an old story and true or false, I could not tell you."

"How old?" I asked.

"A while ago," he said.

"How long is a while ago?"

"Ah, not too long, a hundred, give or take."

"Years?" I asked.

"Years, now will you let me tell it?" When I didn't answer, he began.

"Tis said this woman Deirdre, a fine-looking woman, they claim, was barren though it was the opinion of many that it was his lacking. Now after a few years and no child, he left her. He took up with another though he never had a child. Deirdre took his leaving very badly and, 'tis said, waylays men, late at night, wanting a child. Shure, who knows. But the Tierney name died out, at least in these parts."

"Tierney?" I said, "her name was Tierney?"

"Her married name, yes. He was a William Tierney."

I slid off the stool and staggered to my lodgings. I slept little that night, trying to make sense of what I had been told and what had happened to me. Next morning, crawsick and unable to stomach the full Irish breakfast that was set before me, I made my excuses, left that place and continued on my journey.

I met my tribe, all or most, who showed me great kindness and bombarded me with inquiries about their American relatives and how they were progressing. They were good, hard-working people, farmers mostly and I was glad to be among them and glad I had come and met them. But my heart was someplace else, and her face pursued my waking and sleeping hours. I returned to the U.S. and assured all I had had a trip of a lifetime and slowly my life returned to some kind of normalcy.

Was it love, infatuation, a spell she had cast and why? For a long time, I thought badly of her, raging at her cruelty, her lust if it was that. But over the years, I softened to her. Maybe it was how it had to be, coming from another time, a spirit who could take human form, a banshee – woman ghost? Was it because she wanted a child so badly and for years had been unable to? Maybe it was the confluence of Tierney blood, descended from her husband – who had abandoned her - and youth, me, that had solved the unsolvable, unlocked the combination that had held her.

I hoped that I had brought some balm, release to her soul and if she had yearned for a baby all those years, that she had had her baby – she would be a good mother – and that she would, finally, be content. I wished she had brought me into her confidence but if she had, then, I would not have believed or been a willing participant. Maybe how it was, was how it had to be. But I wished…it had been different, a better outcome, with more revealed. I would wonder the rest of my life.

Anniversary

Dare I say, my darling
As our time together
Grows to nineteen years
My love and affection
Grows in equal measure
Year by year, by year

I will say quite frankly
You have brought me treasure
I had never dreamed
And I hope I've given
And enriched your living
All our nineteen years

I remember, darling
Our first time of meeting
By the river gate
You were wearing mittens
And fur boots of fashion
It was bitter cold

I was, I remember

Diffident and slender

Tongue-tied by your side

You were at your ease, though

And you gave me courage

To advance my cause

And I plucked up courage

And began to, gaily,

Sing a happy song

You smiled and said 'Bravo'

I thought maybe I could

Take you for my own

It was one year later

You and I were married

Nineteen years ago

Dare I say, my darling

My love and affection

Grows and grows and grows.

Rite of Passage

"Damn," I mutter, as I hear the clacking noise my blades are making, "I need a key and soon." I'm a long way from home, don't have a key, lost it two weeks ago, before I came here on vacation to Vermont. I'm downtown West Dorset, three miles from our vacation cabin and not relishing the prospect of walking home with my blades slung over my shoulder.

My Mom and Dad keep dragging me back, though I have not made a friend in the two years I've been coming here. They coo how peaceful and quiet it is, sit in deckchairs with books open and sleep. Can't understand why they're yawning at ten o' clock and heading to bed? It's the air, they say, it's different, more bracing. What the hell does bracing mean anyway?

So, I rollerblade every day and always alone. Some vacation for a thirteen-year-old. Which brings me to my present dilemma. What do I do? There is no sports shop in town. There is no town, just a quaint - Mom's description - general grocery store that charges twice what I pay back in Long Island.

When I complained to Mom, she said, "Well, the tourist season is very short, so they charge a little more. But isn't it worth it being here?"

To which I replied, "No, and why don't we go where they got a long tourist season and charge less?"

I told her that if I had my way, they would not have a tourist season. She told me you will appreciate these times when you're older. I can't remember what else I said to her but right after that she told me to shut up, that I was an ungrateful little pup.

So, I look around and spot a kid sitting on a bench in the park. It looks like he's got blades on and as I draw near, I see that he has. He doesn't look too friendly, crewcut, earring in his left ear and leather biker gloves, the ones with the fingers exposed. He looks tough and I think about walking on by. But I say to myself, what the hell, nothing ventured, nothing gained and take a seat on the bench next to him. I let out a long sigh. No reaction.

"Hi," I say in what I hope is a cool, disinterested voice. He looks at me, checks me up and down and turns away. Next move is what?

"Been rollerblading long?" I ask. He continues staring ahead. He thinks I'm lower that whale shit. That's a favorite expression of my best buddy Mickey. I'd give a pack of Luckies right now to have Mickey here with me in this place that God forgot.

"Couple of years," he answers in a flat toneless voice. So, I jump right in.

"Would you mind if I borrowed your key?" and he says,

"No, (I'm thinking, he doesn't mind, this was easy) you're not borrowing my key. Who the hell are you, and why should I?" He turns and stares belligerently at me.

"Next you'll be looking for a couple of dollars to buy a soda and popcorn."

I started to speak but decided against it. This kid was angry over something and was taking it out on me. Gotta use your head, Benny, I say to myself and I study him carefully through lowered eyelids. There's a big Dangerous, Handle-With-Care sign hanging from him, and I have to be very careful. He's got a N.Y. Giants T-shirt on, and I take a chance.

"You a Giants fan too?"

"All my life," he replies but his tone of voice betrays nothing.

"I went to see them when they had their training camp in Pleasantville. My Dad is a big Giants fan."

"My Dad is a big vodka fan," he replies but he says it without bitterness, then "You from here?"

"This dump, God forbid," I reply quickly but stop, thinking I've made a mistake and he'll resent me putting down his town. He turns and his manner is maybe a little less unfriendly.

"I been telling my mom since we moved up here nine months ago. The place is a dump. Why do we have to stay here?"

I ask casually, "Where you from?"

"Poughkeepsie," he tells me, "Can't wait to get back there. Best town in New York. Where you from?"

"Commack," I tell him and when he answers, the hostility is back in his voice.

"One of those rich suburban kids, ha! We got guys like you in Poughkeepsie, too."

"Do you think I'd be on vacation in the ass end of Vermont if I were rich?" I demand hotly, and he replies,

"Guess you're right." So, I say, "Do you want to do some rollerblading?"

"But you want my key first, right?" he says and laughs. I laugh too.

"What's your name?" he says, and I tell him Benny.

"Benny," he says. "Can't be rich with a name like Benny."

"Got that right," I say, and he says, "Name's Mickey."

"Hey, my best friend's Mickey back home."

"How long you stayin'?" he inquires, as he takes my blades and adjusts them.

"Sixteen more days," I tell him, "Can't wait."

"Know what you mean," he says. "I been here nine months and it feels like forever. I think sometimes, am I being too negative? Then I search my brain, going over item by item for something worthwhile. Best I've come up with is that people leave you alone. They look with suspicion at strangers and down their noses at tourists. Strange class of people. And they don't like Noo Yakkers."

"Yo," I laugh, "that was quite a speech." He looks at me and begins to laugh, too and things are different between us.

"Are we rollerblading or sittin' around yappin all day like two old women?" he asks, and I reply, "Let's do it."

We spend that whole day and every day thereafter together and I have to admit it was nice. We'd rollerblade down long country lanes, having equally long conversations about life, love, and the idiocy of parents. We'd sit and contemplate the surrounding countryside, stop at a fruit, or ice cream stand, stare at the cows as they stared back and try and catch a glimpse of the native wildlife.

Discovered a nice, secluded lake where we swam in the cold waters and afterwards ran around glorying in our nakedness, hollering and screaming. We'd stop at a country store and pay their inflated prices, but it didn't seem to matter as much now.

Mickey had a job working as a busboy three evenings a week for four hours a pop. Other than that, we had the whole day to spend together. Mom and Pop seemed a little nervous about my spending so much time away from them.

"But what do you do all day, the two of you," my mother asked and when I replied "Rollerblading," she looked at me suspiciously,

"Rollerblading, that's it."

"That's it, Mom, with the odd rape and pillage thrown in just to relieve the monotony."

"Don't answer your mother like that," my father sputtered, through a mouthful of Vermont country ham and pancakes with Vermont maple syrup, "Rape is not something to joke about, son."

"I know, I know, but that's all we do, rollerblade and talk."

"No girls?" He looks at me with what's supposed to be a twinkle in his eye. And I reply, deadpan, "Not yet, but we're working on it." He looked at me uncertainly, wondering how he should take that remark, but let it go. After all, he had a plate of ham, eggs and pancakes before him and a blueberry muffin on the side.

"Dad." I looked at him with a serious expression on my face. "Are you putting on a little weight?" The fork stopped on its way to his mouth and a look that had equal parts of irritation, guilt and embarrassment all mixed together, crossed his face.

"No, Beth and I have been walking and swimming every chance we get."

"Honey," my mom interjected, "I think he's right. You have been putting on weight. Remember we talked about it two days ago. It was in the general store, and you wouldn't get on the scales. You told me I was silly and that we were on vacation. Remember what the doctor told you, dear?" I had struck gold again. It was a sure-fire attention deflector.

"Okay, I gotta go," I said, rising from the table.

"Bye mom, bye dad, see you later."

Mom turned and said plaintively,

"Benny, you're always off with your friend. We don't spend that much time together when we're at home and we should try to do it when we're on vacation. It's important for the family to spend time together. It's a bonding process."

Now it's the bonding as a family speech, I thought, as I looked at her with what I hoped was earnest concentration. You ever want to make me cringe, mention that word. Mom discovered it about a year ago and has not let go.

"You're right Mom, but I told Mickey I was meeting him at nine and it's not right to be late and keep him waiting." My mother was at least a half-hour early for all her appointments which drove my pop crazy.

"You're right, son. We'll talk again. Have a nice time with your friend, Mickey. Why don't you have him over for supper some evening?"

"That'd be nice," I said. "I'll ask him and let you know, okay? Bye mom, bye pop."

I was outta there. We had an unspoken agreement not to involve our families in our friendship. I knew he was reluctant to take me to his house and meet his mom for whatever reason. I was not sure of my parent's reaction to him and how he looked. I didn't really care how they'd react, but if they started bugging me, it was something else I'd have to deal with. So, I guess I really did care how they'd react. Anyway, things were better now, and I didn't want to rock the boat.

"Ready to meet some girls?" Mickey asked me casually one day as we sat on the same park bench where we first met.

"Sure," I answered, "why not?" I hadn't let on that I had limited contact with girls, all negative. I had tried to kiss two girls. One I ended up biting her lip and the other started screaming when I tried to stick my tongue into her mouth. Brian, my other buddy in Long Island, swore that is what I had to do to get them hot. Jerk! We almost came to blows. Then he confessed he had heard it from his cousin and hadn't actually tried it himself.

"Whaddaya got in mind?" I inquired.

"They got a dance on Wednesday nights in the church basement.

I checked it out a couple of weeks ago. The band sucks but a couple of the chicks are fine. They're not into makeup or jewelry but they got that fresh country look." He punched me in the arm and laughed.

I mumbled, "I'm not sure I could even talk to these chicks up here, they're so country."

"Yeah, but let's give it a shot. They think New York guys are where it's happening. So, we look cool and let them make the first move, right?'

"Right." But I was uneasy. I didn't want to get shot down with my friend watching. So, I greased up my hair - outside of my parents' prying eyes - scrounged up a black sleeveless T-shirt and met Mickey at our bench.

"Hey, not bad," he greeted me, "you're starting to dress better since you been hanging with me. You are gonna kill 'em." I checked him to see if he was taking the mickey, but he was serious and that made me feel a little better. We strolled into the hall, looking as drop-dead and disinterested as possible. That was Mickey's regular outlook, but I had to work real hard at it and I was beginning to sweat already. We got a couple of sodas and sat at a table just off the dance floor. There were about sixty kids there, various cliques and the band sucked. Mickey told me:

"We hang out here and see what happens. We got a few possibles already," and he nodded over to a group of girls on the other side who were looking in our direction. I resumed my sweating. Every third or fourth dance was a lady's choice, and I had a definite case of the jitters by the time it was announced.

"Ladies and gents," the announcer intoned, "the next dance will be a lady's choice where the young lady gets to dance with that nice looking fella across the hall who she's been watching and admiring and trying to get his attention. But boys being boys and not too bright" - he paused, and the girls tittered - "and having little or no idea of what's going on, this gives the young lady the opportunity to move the process forward."

"What a jerk," I thought, "only in Vermont." The music started and I intensely studied the walls and ceilings.

"Would you like to dance?" I heard someone say and I thought my pal's got someone hooked already.

"Excuse me, would you like to dance?" I looked back and into the warmest brown eyes anyone could imagine. She was nice looking, real nice looking, a brunette with blue jeans and white cotton long sleeved shirt. I started nervously but remembering Mickey's advice, checked her up and down and murmured,

"Yeah."

Well, it just got better and better. Cathy was so relaxed that soon we were chatting like it wasn't our first-time meeting. She was from Boston, here on vacation for a month with her parents and two older brothers. We stayed together the rest of the evening and danced most of the numbers. I'm not much into dancing, but that night it was fun.

She said I had natural rhythm and who was I to disagree. Maybe it was her, but I hardly put a foot wrong all night.

Meanwhile, Mickey had paired off with a skinny blonde with short hair and a half-dozen finger rings. Rings attract, I guess. We paired up for a while, but the girls didn't have much in common, so we went our separate ways. Mickey seemed to be having a good time and once, while wrapped around Annie in a slow number, gave me a big thumbs-up sign to which I replied with a large wink.

I was having a great time and for the first time enjoying the company of a female. By the end of the night, she was my girlfriend and when I walked her to the parking lot, she stopped, quickly kissed me on the cheek and ran to meet her parents. Mickey was nowhere in sight, so I retrieved my blades and motored slowly home.

From then on, I divided my time between Mickey and Cathy, rollerblading with him and meeting her later in the evening. Cathy's family were into history and monuments, so while they toured by day, we rollerbladed. In the afternoon and evening, Mickey hung out with Annie or went to his job, and I met Cathy. We were still buddies, but we were expanding our horizons, you could say, in Vermont of all places.

I was spending a lot of time in that country store too and became friendly with the owner Lorenzo O' Riley. Of course, I asked him about his name. He told me he had been called after his dad's best friend, Lorenzo, who died in World War II.

Mr. O' Riley was an interesting man, had travelled all over the globe and was originally from New Jersey. Worked a variety of jobs from welder to seaman and had settled here in the late forties for no particular reason. Now he felt comfortable here, liked his fishing and hiking and didn't mind the cold - wife dead some twelve years and his kids scattered all over the country. To each his own, I guess.

The quiet and isolation were a plus now, for it meant that I had time without interruption with Cathy. We looked for and found a great spot that we could call our own, by a riverbank overhung by a huge evergreen. Didn't even tell Mickey about it. That's where I sharpened up my kissing till, I got pretty good at it.

I remember our first one, remember thinking that it was as good as they talked about in the books. My head spun and my stomach did flip-flops. The grass looked greener, the mountains awesome, flowers more beautiful and Cathy? What can I say? When I looked at her, her tanned legs and graceful neck, impish smile, and those brown eyes, I felt like I could climb the highest mountain or swim the widest lake. Maybe Vermont wasn't such a bad place after all. It would never compare to New York, but no place compares to the Big Enchilada, right?

Mother and Child

My mother said, what ails you now?
She pulled my eye and palmed my brow
Then checked my pulse and pondered why
So seldom ailments passed me by
I never saw the like of you
Misfortune clings like morning dew
It's there and then it disappears
Again – it catches unawares
One day you're running like the stag
Soon after, you're as if in chains
You shuffle, cough, an ancient child
And then again, you're running wild
I am perplexed, as you must know
The doctor coughs and spits and blows
Consults his book and mutters low
An awful eejit, doesn't know
So, what am I to do with you?
But let you go and let you grow
And put my trust in Providence
And say a prayer, what ails you go.

Vanity

He took his usual seat in the small cafeteria on lower Broadway, Manhattan, close by the window. He loved to watch the street, the action, the characters, rich, poor, the down and outs, the unloved. Even the lowly were an integral part of Manhattan. He studied how the people moved and carried themselves, how loudly the natives conversed, the most intimate details discussed with no sense of caution or embarrassment, as the world listened.

That's how he wanted to be, bold, brash, self-assured, headlong in his ambition and damn the consequences. And he was - morphing from the cautious, unsophisticated person he had been when he first arrived fifteen months ago. Every small success spurred him. He was becoming quite the lady's man. For someone from Fallsburg, a small town in upstate New York, it was heady to be part of this broiling, bubbling cauldron of always something happening, this ceaseless exhausting but exhilarating activity, a never-ending nugget of joy deep within his being.

'If you can make it here, you can make it anywhere, it's up to you, New York, New York.' He was going to make it here; he was sure and certain of that or spill his guts trying.

'Where do you live? In the city. What city? Where?'

'The big apple, baby, the city that never sleeps.'

His job was demanding. He had to be on his toes, every minute of every day. To get to the top necessitated that kind of commitment and he was willing to make it. That's what it takes, baby. No surrender and take no prisoners. 'What city has had more songs written about it than any other? You guessed right, the one the only, start spreading the news, I'm leaving wherever I am and heading you know where.'

He whistled the tune as he surveyed the street. 'Oy vay.' He had picked up that expression, too, though he scarcely knew what it meant.

'What bodies.'

He glanced to his right and caught his reflection. Whatever regard he had for his old man, which was little enough, stemmed from the fact he had passed on to his only son some good genes, good, slim physique, and regular features. He considered his father, how drab and colorless he had always been, sometimes angry and frustrated for all his missed opportunities at success. He had also reduced Jeff's mother to drab and worn out, an exact opposite to the warm, smiling woman Jeff remembered from his childhood. They must have been happy then for a while, the first years of their married life with a new, perfect son and the future possibilities of success. When had it changed, what seminal moment had sent the first shiver of fear, the first hint of failure tugging at his consciousness?

He checked his reflection again, wavy brown hair neatly trimmed, good features, blue eyes 'to die for' as one of his ex's had described them. Which one? He could not remember. Was it Betty with the chunky body from the upstate town a stone's throw from his, or Sheryl?

No, now he remembered, it was Cheryl with a C from West Dorset 'way up in Vermont, kind of naïve and burdened with a major case of low self-esteem but with the slim, toned body he had always preferred. She sure appreciated him, hanging on his every word, often surprising him with little gifts, in the restaurant when he returned from the bathroom, or sitting on his doorstep, or arriving by mail at work.

God, he had gone through his share of women, starting slowly and hesitantly but in the last months on a very impressive roll. He was rigorous about his daily workouts, no excuses. It was something else he noted of New Yorkers, those who were on the fast track, how relentless they were about fitness and working out. He didn't do weights, didn't want to look like the weight guys at the club. Many were obsessive, weights and more weights and many blew out knees and joints. He worked to a carefully conceived program, and it showed.

He glanced around the room. At first, he didn't see her. She was bent over, sipping on a drink, or studying something before her. But then she raised her head, and he recognized that mass of red hair. He had seen her here on several occasions and she had aroused his interest. He loved the way the lights played on her hair, bouncing off mirrors and fixtures and running, dancing, changing colors across her head.

Twice he had passed by her on his way to the bathroom, stifling an urge to touch her red mass, staring intently at her and even on one occasion stumbling deliberately and grabbing her table for an instant. He had apologized profusely, she had stared at him and then turned away. He thought she must be foreign, did not understand English. He was irritated too, that she showed such little interest in him. Damn her. Then he realized she must be playing hard to get. He should have known. He had used it often enough. Play it cool, as if you have no interest in that gorgeous creature sitting on the bench. Approach casually, giving her no idea how you really feel. Engage in mundane conversation. Give her some time to check you out. Suggest coffee later or whatever. It had worked so well, so often for him.

The waitress approached, bent over, intimate. "Jeff, God, how are you? Where have you been? I haven't laid eyes on that cute face for weeks. Where've you been?"

"Hey, Cathy, yeah, I've been out of town for a little while. We had some problems in Seattle that had to be taken care of ASAP. It's part of the package. When they need you, you gotta go."

He wondered how they'd operated before he came along. But things were humming along right now, and he felt he had much to do with the transformation. Why, oh why didn't they see him as the innovator and independent thinker that he was, the future leader he could be.

His boss Donnie was a real moron, a Grade A asshole who loved to call meetings and talk about 'maximizing the potential of the company,' finishing up with his perpetual 'Who's got the power?' at which juncture we were all supposed to jump up, whistle and clap thunderously, call out 'We do' and go back to work pumped up and motivated. It was beyond his comprehension that they hadn't dumped him and recognized his, Jeff's potential.

"So, why didn't you call me? I've never been to Seattle."

"Believe me when I tell you, Cathy, all I did was work and fall into bed at night. I was damn glad to get home. Can I have the usual?"

"Sure, cutie, but I could have been waiting in that bed and *you*... would have slept like a baby when we got done. The next time, okay?"

"You got it, girl."

"Okay, your order's coming up, call me."

Damn, he thought, I should never have taken her number. Now she was going to bug him. She was attractive in a large sexual way, big lips, big breasts, and big butt. He didn't like too big of anything, especially big butts and her skin was dry, uncared for - a dollar to a dime the result of a bad diet. Why do people put up with bad skin? She must know that she has it, so why doesn't she do something about it? Does she think that people don't notice or don't care? And why is she content to be a waitress, in New York of all places, the city of limitless opportunity?

He checked his image, tossed his head and the hair settled nicely. So, what am I going to do with this mysterious stranger just three tables away? Well, as his Aunty Beryl used to say

'Strangers are just friends we haven't met.' Maybe he could use that line, corny but… As if reading his thoughts, she raised her head and stared at him, then turned away. If that wasn't a definite come-on, he didn't know women and he knew women. He wondered how he should begin.

"Excuse me, you look familiar and it's driving me crazy. Have we met somewhere before?" or maybe "Excuse me, I get a distinct impression that you're a stranger in this beautiful city and if there's any way I can be of assistance, I would be more than happy to assist you" or "Hi, my name is Jeff. I've seen you here on different occasions. You're always alone so I thought I'd come over and introduce myself. I hope I'm not intruding and if I am, just say the word and I'll slink out of your life forever and back to my drab cheerless existence." Then he would flash one of his hundred-watt smiles. It'll be easy, he thought. She won't resist. They never do.

He pushed the chair back, straightened his tie and resisting the urge to glance in the mirror, approached her. As he approached, she looked up and began to rise from her chair. She smiled, showing white even teeth. Now she was waving. He was instantly in love with this gorgeous creature. He caught her wrist and bent to whisper in her ear. She looked startled and for an instant fear flashed in her eyes. The rest seemed like a slow-motion movie. He felt a sharp blow to the back of his head and his knees buckled. He felt like peeing and maybe he had, he wasn't sure. In the background he heard a scream, his scream, Cathy's? The scream continued but was beginning to fade. He was falling but still assimilating images.

A large blonde woman comforted the redhead as they both stared down at him. The word 'schmuck' issued from the blonde as she took out a packet of gum, passing one to the redhead while surveying the room. A smile played at the corners of her mouth and a mouthful of full even, white teeth were exposed as she bent to look in the other's eyes.

They turned, glared at him again and with their arms wrapped around one another walked out the door. Random thoughts chased each other as Jeff lay crumbled on the floor: how beautiful her hair looked, how unruffled it had remained. He tried to remember if the redhead had paid her bill and was annoyed that he could not remember. He tried to remember the exact sequence of events, when it had taken a wrong turn, where he had miscalculated. He thought that he must look a total mess. He didn't even want to know how his hair looked. He drifted into nothingness as the wig settled gently over his face.

I Am Missing Ireland

In grey, damp Ireland I stand
By seaweed wall and Mussel rock
Drawn back to that amorphous place
I fled with no regret

I went to glass and steel – concrete
Relentless sun, unceasing blue
Brown earth, bright colors, garish glare
In warm seas – shed the grey

On fine, white sand, cavorted, splayed
Oh, those were happy, happy days
But paradoxically I found
That I was missing Ireland

Mysterious and unexplained
This ancient gra which has us chained
If hell was our birthplace – well then
'Tis hell we'd praise with song and pen

I lie in bed as wind and rain
Fling seagulls through the charged air

Remember times long, long ago
My mother leant to stroke my hair

I will stay only for a while
But feel a strange contentment
That I am back on ancient soil
And I'll be missing Ireland.

Teresa

A slim, erect woman strides along the crowded sidewalks of Chiang Mai, the northern capital of Thailand, a city of about three hundred thousand souls. To the casual observer, she appears to be an athletic woman, mid-fifties, with a well- toned body, thick brown hair sprinkled with grey. She will stay three months – and if the moon aligns in her favor, longer. Two years before, she had come to Chiang Mai. It was January and she stayed for three weeks. Back then she came, dejected, and exhausted, sixty years old, her body aching in a multitude of areas and in different degrees.

In the beginning she disliked Chiang Mai, the incessant traffic, the polluting tuk-tuks. In the beginning, also, she was tentative, timid about venturing out on her own, afraid of deserted streets, of eating at food stalls, drinking the water, and even taking massage. Eventually and in tiny steps she overcame each fear and grew to love this land, the people, food, the vigorous Thai massage and what, all together, they did for her body, her soul, and her very existence. Maybe she was lucky in that the first massage, and all the others to follow, that they were to the highest standards. Each one was a step on the road to healing. She wondered since, why massages were not more available in the developed countries. She thought, it seemed like a sign of a more sophisticated and forward-looking people – for it was never more needed in the modern world – and despite the obvious poverty that was here she had never met a kindlier, gentler people, never seen such industry, never experienced such a bewildering variety of foodstuffs - which made what was available in her native Canada seem at best inadequate.

Crime was non-existent, it seemed, at least here in Chiang Mai, and she took to walking where she wanted with a growing confidence. She might encounter a drunk, late at night but even they seemed gentle. Though the traffic on the main arteries was incessant, she never witnessed an accident. It was common, also to see two and three young children accompanying their parents on motorbikes or scooters. With the one precaution of drinking only bottled water, she partook freely of the food stalls.

But it was the massages that had begun the healing, the vigorous Thai massage that revealed aches and pains buried deep within her, that over time, began to dissipate those very same aches and pains– and which in turn seemed to loosen something deep within her psyche. Also, the gentler oil massage, that her skin, parched and dry, soaked up as if it could never get enough. To complement those, there were the foot, head, neck, and scalp massages. She luxuriated in the expert touch that probed and pummeled, stretched and twisted. She imagined a piece of clay shaped and stretched till it was pliant and smooth. Her body would be thus.

She relaxed for the first time, mind, and body, as if she had spent her life in some kind of rigid state, even while resting. She was opening up to a more optimistic vision of life, a more relaxed state of mind, more accepting of each new morning and its possibilities. She left the city that first time vowing to come back. She would treat herself to Chiang Mai every year.

She was a widow. Her husband Ken had died of cancer at the age of fifty-nine. It was cancer of the intestines that at first seemed easily eradicated but returned again and again more virulent than ever. In the end it had got its way. For the last three years of his life, he was an invalid, undergoing every treatment suggested by the physicians. She watched him waste away, the metamorphosis gruesome and somehow fascinating. She had done all she could to make it easier. He was a good husband and provider and a good father to their two boys.

She knew she should have loved him more and she had tried desperately. She had grown fond of him over the years, knew he deserved more but was unable to summon a deep and passionate love. He had come along when she was twenty-nine. Afraid she would remain unmarried, with a great relief and after a six-month courtship she accepted his proposal of marriage. When he was diagnosed with cancer, she thought she was somehow to blame. If he had had her unequivocal love, it might have protected him. As his sickness progressed, she fell deeper and deeper into a kind of lethargy. When he passed, she felt a great relief. She knew it was inevitable, it had taken too long and left her with little will to go on. She was as it were, bloody and bowed, edging closer and closer to serious bodily debility. Financially she was, if not well off, comfortable, the house paid for, Ken's insurance more than adequate for her needs.

One day, wandering the streets of Montreal, a poster in a travel agency caught her eye. After, she thought, there is no such thing as coincidence. It was a poster for Thailand and on the spur of the moment and contrary to her usually cautious nature she signed up for a Thailand vacation package, three days in Bangkok and eighteen touring the north of the country and based in Chiang Mai. She knew nothing of Thailand, had no idea where Chiang Mai was, but liked the name. It had saved her. Rejuvenated, she returned to Montreal. Some spirit connection had put her in touch with a place she had needed desperately. It was no coincidence. She had entered the travel agency dreamlike and was attracted to that poster. Compelled, she had cast her doubts aside and thus had been connected to what her very soul cried out for.

She relished her independence, making decisions only for her, sleeping late or rising early, taking the many tours to outlying areas, to the Akha people, the 'long necks,' whose idea of beauty was elongated necks achieved by wearing brass coils that were gradually added to as they got older. She went trekking, visited the elephant camps, rafted on the many rivers, swam under waterfalls. She went to the Golden Triangle, the center of the opium smuggling in the late 50's, to Chang Saen on the borders of Burma - now Myanmar, and Laos, took a boat to Laos on the Mekong River and was invited to drink whiskey containing serpents, snakes and a tiger's penis. She declined but bought some of the silks and carvings that were ridiculously inexpensive. She went to Mae Sai and watched the

Burmese streaming across the heavily guarded bridge between Thailand and Burma, where in the second world war the British and Chinese on high promontories with gun and radar emplacements on either side, and in close proximity to each other, monitored each other's activities.

It was exotic, exciting, preconceptions dashed, old ideas challenged. There was a great poverty, and, in its midst, there was vibrant living, strong family bonds and amazing energy. She was hooked. It was as if the bad times, the slow wasting away her husband had endured – and she had had to witness – the near depression that hovered close by for so long, the bone chilling tiredness, nightmare nights and interminable days were as if lived by someone else. They were a bad dream, a story told by someone else, vaguely remembered.

Her two sons, Ken and Michael were busy in their own lives and married – happily or relatively so – Ken in Minneapolis and Michael on the West Coast and there were four grandchildren for her to spoil if she so wished. But she wasn't intimate with them. She loved them but they were not her children, not her responsibility. She saw them three or four or five times a year – Christmas always, Thanksgiving usually and some of the other holidays. Her sons had been good and caring while their father died and after, but even they could see the change in her and satisfied, had returned to their own responsibilities.

She was always a good-looking woman though at times disbelieving and as her health returned, she had many would-be suitors. She found them all unsatisfactory, many carrying the scars

47

of previous toxic alliances, some sex-obsessed, most desperately attempting to recapture that young time of slim bodies and boundless energy, sexual and otherwise. So, she remained celibate and unattached except for one or two purely sexual encounters - for the relief it brought and the reminder that it was something she still desired.

On her third visit to Chiang Mai and soon after she came, she took a trip to Mae Sai on the Burma border. It was where the farangs, the foreigners living in Thailand went to get their passports stamped for a further thirty days stay there. It was a guided tour that took in Chiang Saen and the significant temples of that area. Their guide was a young Thai called Tom who had a great knowledge of the hill-tribes, temples, and history of the area. He was funny and easy-going and contributed greatly to the groups enjoyment of what could have been a tiring journey, a five-hour minibus journey each way, beginning at eight in the morning and returning at nine that night. He informed them he had been a monk for many years, having begun training at a very young age.

There was one member of the group with a name unpronounceable to Tom, who promptly christened him Tom Two. The driver Oom was fast and fearless, often crossing to the oncoming lane which unsettled some of the group. Tom reassured them, telling them that Oom also valued his life and had a wife and children whom he loved and wished to see again.

On their first bathroom break, Teresa spoke to Tom and

complimented him on his knowledge of the area and his exemplary English. He smiled showing strong white teeth. "Thank you, Canadian lady for kind words," he replied and when she returned "You're welcome, Tom, Thai Man," they both erupted in laughter.

He was more attentive to her afterwards. They ate lunch together in Chiang Saen and he helped her navigate the real from the fake as they shopped for some of the beautiful jade, lapis lazuli and coral trinkets available there. At the end of the tour and exiting the minibus at her hotel he approached her and asked to see her again. Surprised and unprepared but maybe with a little of the equanimity that had lately entered her life, she hesitated only for an instant and murmured yes and gave him her room number. He would call for her at seven on the following night.

After, beset with doubts, she berated herself. What a fool you are, she thought. You're maybe forty years older. He's a mere boy. What does he want from you except money? He thinks he will squeeze money like juice from a lemon. They think all farangs are rich. It was a common sight to see young, beautiful Thai women with old, Western men, one looking for youth and beauty, the other financial security for them and their family.

She slept uneasily that night and resolved to go with him but terminate the meeting quickly – she would not refer to it as a date – and leave no doubt of her disinterest in a boy lover. She thought he was attractive and funny, but she wouldn't subject herself to the stares of others and the imagined whisperings. There goes the old lady farang and her toy boy.

He was prompt. The bell rang exactly at seven. She had dressed carefully but conservatively, black silk dress with long sleeves and a bright yellow Pashmina scarf that she had purchased in Mae Sai which she draped over her shoulders. She was pleased with how she looked. He was smiling when she opened the door.

"Hmm, different outfit than bus tour."

She smiled, remembering her all khaki outfit with the multitude of zippered pockets she generally wore on trekking and tour excursions. She would not invite him in. She closed and locked the door and they walked into the warm night. He asked if she would like to eat and where and she suggested a Japanese restaurant nearby. She had eaten there before and found it good. When he suggested they walk for a while, she readily agreed. She had been thinking the same. They talked easily, revealing general information about each other but she avoided the subject of Ken's illness, merely telling him he was dead, and she was a widow. She told him her age, expecting a denial, a refusal to believe she was that age, a declaration how well she looked. He made no comment, which somehow eased her concerns, except to reveal his age in return. He was thirty-five, never married, no children. He seemed unworried that he was well past the age of marrying for most Thai men. He was unsure if he would marry. If it was meant to be, he would.

"You mean you're going to sit around and wait for marriage to happen or not. And make no effort yourself?" she asked.

"Yes, I will know when the person appears," he replied. "There is no such thing as coincidence." There was that phrase again. She thought of the day she had stumbled into the travel agency, how her eyes lit on the poster of Thailand, how she was strangely compelled to book a holiday there. She had thought then that this is more than coincidence.

She stared at Tom, studying him more closely now, his black sleek hair, his unblemished skin, faint mustache. He was maybe a little more broad-shouldered than most of his countrymen, but he had their gentleness, that serene outlook on life they all seemed to possess, their energy. They finished their meal. The evening had been much more enjoyable than she had ever anticipated. She had forgotten about the age difference, the stares if there had been stares. It was like two people bonding, two people who maybe had known each other in another time and place. She turned abruptly to him, "I have to ask you why you wanted to see me?" He looked intently at her. "I wanted to," he replied. "I wanted to know more about you. So, I asked."

"Did you expect me to say yes?" she asked him.

"I thought you would agree. I thought you were ready to be with someone, to have a friend. I wanted…" He hesitated, "I felt we could be friends, maybe." He laughed, "I know you are older woman. I just see woman, woman I feel attraction to, and hope it is like that for you. I hope" She laughed. It was like that for her, too.

They began to see each other and on the fifth night she invited him to her room. They kissed, tentative and probing. His hands explored her body and his smooth skin meshed with hers. She sighed and gave in to the warm feeling that filled her. The lovemaking was gentle and fulfilling, something she had not had in an awful long time. From then on, they were inseparable.

When they ate in restaurants, he insisted on paying his share. It was that way from the beginning. She went where he suggested, and they often ate at the sidewalk food stands that were everywhere. She wanted to advance him some money but worried it would upset the perfect balance of their relationship. Yet she knew the money he made as a guide was pitiful.

One night as they lay together, he talked again of his dream of owning his own tour company. He said he had approached the bank and had been turned down. He would need to buy or lease his own minibus. Before he asked, she had offered the money. He insisted it was a loan he would pay back over time.

From the beginning he was successful, and in a year had acquired another minibus, again with her financial assistance. He attempted to make payments on the loan, but she refused. It was a gift. She had more than enough. As the tour company took up more of his time, their time together became less. Their relationship had changed, his mind more focused on what he had accomplished and prospects. One night he slipped in beside her as he had done so many times before. He would turn and hold her, and they would begin their lovemaking. As she anticipated the pleasant prospect of intimacy, he held her momentarily, murmured how exhausted he was and promptly dropped into a deep sleep.

Maybe deep down she had known there would come such a time. She thought soon he and she would move on to the next phase of their lives. She was grateful to Tom. He was what she needed at that stage of her life. Maybe she had been what he needed also. Their relationship might - probably would – soon begin to unfurl. She would be open to the next experience, thankful for the gifts she had been given. She would stay on in Chiang Mai and see what the days would bring.

Mikeen

Every day I'd walk down to the Slip for that was where we gathered – to chat and gossip. There'd be a half dozen or more there every day – some chronically unemployed, some retired many years and the young ones finished school and waiting to emigrate. We'd sit on the sea wall and watch the tide as it filled up the harbor and later empty out. There was a drop of twenty feet or more between high and low tide.

Mikeen Kiely, a man of unparalleled knowledge was the eternal presence there with his son Jojo, working on his boat, Gusty 22. He was a yarn spinner par excellence and the way he talked, it seemed like he was on everyday terms with Khrushchev, Eisenhower and the world's leaders.

"You see, the mistake Ike made was he underestimated the power of the military-industrial complex…. when Gary Powers was shot down in his U2 plane, Khrushchev was under severe pressure to take a tougher stance ---" Mikeen knew all about everything. But he had a great way with a story and though we knew that truth never stood in his way, it was always entertaining. The boat was eighteen foot long, diesel-engine, broad-beamed, more than adequate for fishing the bay for mackerel, herring, cod, bass, and salmon in season.

The trouble was his boat, Gusty22 rarely left the Slip. Mikeen worked on the engine endlessly, taking it apart and reassembling – JoJo his ever-faithful son, silent by his side. Mikeen did all the talking; JoJo listened and obeyed. On this bright, clear morning, the boat had returned to the Slip after another failed attempt to head out to the bay. She had travelled all of ten yards - the engine rumbling ominously, black smoke in prodigious volume coming from the exhaust.

"Goddammit, what in the hell is the matter with it-- JoJo, check out the pistons, son. Then go over to the garage and get a set of gaskets. See only Pakie there – the only one of the wife's people any good." When JoJo left, Mikeen launched into another story, telling of the first time he emigrated to Wales.

"Anyway, as I was saying, myself and Frankie gets off the train in Cardiff. I says to Frankie, what's the address?"

"What address?"

"Your cousin, where we're staying," I says.

"Where?"

"You said we could stay at your cousins"

"I did?"

"In the pub, last night. No prob, you said, as good as gold."

"I did, don't remember."

"Anyway, here we are, the rain coming down in buckets, not an overcoat between us, me with my little suitcase tucked under my arm, Frankie with all his belongings in a canvas shopping bag."

"I says to him, don't you have a suitcase – anything better than a shopping bag?"

"I had a suitcase; he tells me but the brother fecked it when he went to London."

"I'm saying to myself, what did I get myself into. What possessed me to get hooked up with this man. He's the most unfortunate awlaan that ever-walked God's green earth. If the Sputnik crashed down from space in the morning, who do you think it'd land on? I'm telling you it'd be Frankie laid out on the ground when they lifted it off."

"Anyway, you don't have a cousin in Cardiff, I says. Do you, or don't you?"

"I do."

"Do you have his name and address?"

"Paul Meehan, he says. We lost touch with him years ago."

"How many years ago?"

"Thirty years or more, he says."

"Jaysus, Mary and St. Joseph, didn't you say, once we get to Cardiff, I'll take it from there?"

"I made no promises, he said."

"I was going to hit him a wallop but what would that solve? But I made up my mind, at the first chance, I'll cut away from this buck, as quick as I can. Anyway, there we are, the rain pouring down, soaked to the skin. He started to say something, and I told him, Don't, don't, just don't say a word – keep the mouth shut - tight. I'm thinking, slow it down now, Mike. We have to work it out. We must find a kip for the night. We must get in from the rain. We must have a bit to eat and then we'll look for work. Well, I'll tell you, Cardiff then was a dirty, God-forsaken town – a lot of Irish there but a lot of 'em drinking and carrying on. They'd rob their own as quick as a stranger. We goes into a little chipper we spotted. We have a bag of chips and two big sausages each – the worst chips I ever ate in my life. I had the heartburn for a week after. We're atin' the chips and sausages away, steam coming off our clothes, the oul' shop getting all steamed up, the bloke behind the counter giving us bad looks. I'm trying to figure out the next move when I hear this voice saying, by any chance would you know a Paul Meehan?"

"Frankie, the stupid bastard is asking the bloke behind the counter, does he know Paul Meehan his cousin – that he lost touch with about forty years ago. He's pushing up the daisies probably for the last twenty years or more. The bloke looks at him and says in that terrible accent they have over there, what you say mate?"

"Before I have a chance to shut him up, Frankie says again, -Would you by any chance know a Paul Meehan?"

"So, the bloke gives him a look and says, Yeah, I know Paul Meehan, he drinks at the Cardiff Arms up the street. What you wanna know for? My mouth drops open. I'm gaping at this bloke, but then I thinks, nah it can't be the same one. There's probably a dozen or more with the same name."

"Frankie says, I'm his cousin."

"I'm looking at the two of them and I'm thinking maybe we're getting a break. Then I look at Frankie and I say to myself, Mike, boy, cop on, he's misfortune from the day he was born."

"So, the bloke says, He's up there right now."

"He's looking kind of funny at us, so we leave. Frankie wants to go there right away. I want to get someplace to stay. It's still coming down, no let up. Anyway, I go along with him. Just maybe, maybe once it'll turn out right."

"We walk in the bar, ask the barman for Paul Meehan. He says nothing, just points. Way down at the end, there's a bloke sitting there, well-dressed, snow-white hair, nice suit, tie – two blokes sitting with him, one on either side. You know they're working for him or doing whatever he says. Frankie walks up and as he's getting closer; the two blokes reach inside their suits. I says to myself, Frankie's luck finally ran out. They're going to shoot the poor bastard. The bloke in the middle raises his hand, the two blokes settle back. I'm at the bar. I'm saying nothing. The bar is quiet, and I hear Frankie saying, I'm looking for Paul Meehan."

"Who wants to know? he asks in a low, soft voice, suspicious."

"I'm Paul Meehan, he tells Frankie and Frankie replies, I'm Peter's son."

"Meehan looks at him and says, Peter's son, from Ireland. How did you find me?'

"The chip shop up the street told me. Frankie tells him, 'We're a bit stuck for digs. We just got here."

"How's Peter? Meehan asks."

"He's good, retired five years. He loves the walking."

"Meehan smiles and in a Cardiff accent says, 'He loves the

walking,' haven't heard that in a long time. Then he tells the blokes to take a walk."

"He asks Frankie, how his mother is, and Frankie tells him she's dead five years."

"I met her once, he said, a nice woman, all the others dead, Ellen, John?"

"Frankie tells him, yes. He asks if he has a job lined up. Frankie says no."

"He asks if Frankie can bartend. Frankie says yes - a lie. 'How about your friend?'"

"Frankie says he's lookin' too. Frankie calls me over and introduces me."

"Meehan says, we got some rooms over the bar. You could stay there. Tomorrow we'll talk about jobs."

"Anyway, we go upstairs. There's a nice bathroom and a room with two beds in it.

Frankie is jumping up and down. I told you, didn't I, didn't I? I told you I'd fix us up- I didn't contradict him. He never had much luck in his life, so this was a long time coming.

The two of us went to work in the bar. It turns out Meehan owns the bar, and it seems a lot more too. He's some kind of bookie, illegal bets, numbers with a lot of muscle in Cardiff. I never got the whole story. He had a couple of pubs, horses too. He took a shine to Frankie."

"Right away he could see that Frankie couldn't bartend, so he put him out working with the horses. Frankie took to it. They said he could talk to them and right away they're doing what he wants. Horses giving them trouble, they call Frankie in. Frankie always brings 'em around. He had a gift."

"I worked at the bar for two years, was homesick all the time and headed home. Meehan treated me good. He was in the bar six days a week. That's where he done his business. Never traveled back to where he came from- seemed happy enough. Frankie's still over there. They reckon he's one of the top trainers in England, now. He made a lot of money for Meehan. Once in a while he'll ring over telling me to back such and such a horse. I made a few pounds here and there. He stops in to see me when he's home. I could be over in the morning working for him - making good money, too. But if fishing is your life, you're only happy fishing."

"Well, JoJo, will we go up for the tea? We did enough for to-day." He paused, "That's what I'm always telling JoJo. There's a place for everybody. If there's a place for Frankie, we all have hope."

Magic Morning

On a soft and gentle morning, I rise up from my bed

Vestige of night still clinging, I close the door and head

Into a verdant landscape, of wilderness and stone

And I am lost and found and gone to a realm of utter lone

There is no past or future, I've neither pain nor joy

Regrets nor anticipation, But just a presence – I

Family and friends, they fade from view,
lost in the moment is what I do

A gentle accepting spirit settles over me.

Filled with an overwhelming joy, the world unfolds before my eye

The majesty of planetary orbit and my –

Place in the scheme of things.

A Special Talent

"I was good, the best, they said, in that time. I got calls from New Orleans, Chicago. Most of my work was in New York, of course. A lot of action in New York, a lot of action in Brooklyn. I remember one week I had seven contracts – in one week, all clean, done exactly as I wanted. I never had a problem, y'know, about my work. That's what it was, really, really, work, my job, and they were bad guys, so…."

"Yeah, Sammy, you were the gold standard back then. I came along a few years after, but, man, everybody wanted to be Sammy 2. That time when you had two contracts and you got 'em together. Boom, boom. Some shit about an uncle dying and the other guy had to show up. To show respect, right. And he's wondering, 'Where's everybody? Never knew what hit him"

"Yeah, Richie, it was a lot of fun. I liked what I was doin.' Mighta done it for nothin.' Was always tryin' to refine, like, like my way of doin' it. To always get better."

"How about Woody? That was classic."

"So, you gotta find their soft spot. Take your time and find it. Some guys are gamblers, some guys lovers, some guys drink too much, and they's guys worship money. No good. None of those guys stick around too long. Woody loved his women, always had more than a few goin' at the same time. But Woody had a problem. He was insanely jealous of all his women. It ain't easy watchin' one, imagine tryin' to keep two, or three, or four under lock and key? So, I knew this was Woody's weakness, his soft underbelly."

"So, I got word to Woody that Sylvia, one of his bitches was, like, out and about, legs wide open, and she was rendezvousing in the parking lot in Orchard Beach. Gave him the time, too. So, Woody shows up alone, didn't want anyone to know one of the harem was strayin.' It was too easy. Walked up behind him. Put two in the back of his head. Y'know, sometimes it's too easy – and that's not good. You need difficulty, problems to be overcome. When it's too easy, you get careless. That's what happened with Fat Joe."

"Yeah, I remember Fat Joe, ran with the Jersey mob."

"When I got the contract, I'm sayin', this is gonna be too easy. I was careless. Didn't make enough inquiries. He was under surveillance by the Feds. I hit him and they were right there. Stupid me. Seventeen years in Sing Sing. When I came out, I just wasn't into it anymore. And there was competition, young guys lookin' to impress, makin' their bones. And the bosses, not like the old days, no loyalty. I got grandchildren, four grandchildren, my son works in Wall Street, for Chrissakes. Probably knows some of what went on, but we don't talk about it. But, yeah, I was good at what I did, and I have to say, kinda proud of it, too."

The Bully

He was on the horns of a dilemma, had heard that phrase somewhere, looked up its meaning and understood it perfectly described his situation. Carl Sanders, the biggest, baddest dude in East Lake High had taken a dislike to him and had promised to kick his butt all over the school parking lot – and soon. It was coming to the end of his sophomore year - he found this hard to believe, two more years and he'd be graduating, with the decisions that entailed – and if he could avoid Carl for a few more weeks, well, then he had the whole summer to figure out something. See, Carl lived in a different neck of the woods from him so chances were good he wouldn't even see him.

He was afraid of Carl, who wouldn't, but didn't really mind getting beaten. He was fatalistic about stuff like that, preferring to get it over with, rather than prolong it. But he hated the idea it would be public, and it would. As soon as the time and place were agreed, it would be common knowledge, lightning quick. Nothing stirred the juices of pubescent high-schoolers more than a good brawl – and if one or the other got their ass kicked, nose broken, bloodied, whatever, so much the better. He was no weakling, but he had seen Carl in action, and he was good – fast and strong with no mercy shown. He made up for his failures in the classroom with his poise and ability in the bare-knuckle sphere.

He was on the horns of a dilemma, no doubt about it. Maybe Carl would forget about him, move on to bigger and better targets. Maybe he'd change his mind and like him after all. Maybe the moon would turn into a pumpkin.

What if he embarked on a rigorous fitness regime, took up Karate or Tai Kwando? He really wasn't into that stuff and Carl could, would, in all probability still beat him. He didn't feel desperate – yet, but he would begin to, as summer faded and he would be heading back to school. He had to avoid this confrontation, somehow, without appearing to back down. He could inform, anonymously of course, on the event when that time and place was scttlcd. But that was just postponing the inevitable, and if he kept anonymously informing, suspicion would inevitably point to him.

After much thought, he decided his best bet was to meet Carl, accidentally on purpose, somewhere quiet with no onlookers and take his beating. He would deprive the curious, the blood-thirsty - all those who were drawn to such events for whatever reason - of the spectacle. It was a good plan under the circumstances, and he was content or at least accepting of his fate. Then one day, as he was leaving school, he saw Carl enter a room with four others. It was a tutoring session for those who were failing in various subjects. He should have known Carl would be one of them.

Carl struggled in practically every subject, and Ben had some idea why. The house Carl and his family lived in was a small bungalow on the other side of town, faded and hangdog, a front yard of straggled, suffering grass mirroring the paucity of the nurturing environment within. Carl's home life was chaotic, a widowed mother who had brought up – dragged up might be a more accurate term – six offspring, two of whom had spent jail time for various offences, drug-dealing, drunk driving, petty larceny, and car hijacking. She was a short-tempered, worn-down woman who had never come to terms with the death of her husband in a hunting accident, and though he was not without his vices, he held down a job and was a steady provider. For some years after his death, she existed in a state of listlessness and passivity, and it was then that her sons descended into willful and lawless behavior. When she tried to re-establish parental control, it was too late – at least for her two sons.

Her three daughters were relatively trouble free and the youngest, Emma was pretty but extremely shy. Ben had watched her from afar, thought her beautiful and thought of dating her, but the one time he had approached her he felt awkward and gauche, she had been dumbstruck and both, simultaneously, had turned away and fled the scene. He had put on hold any further endeavors in that direction. The lack of a nurturing home and parents and lack of discipline had sunk Carl's boat before, even, he entered high school and East Lake High was not a school that let their students slide.

Ben, himself was one of two brothers, his older brother, Tom now in West Point Military Academy preparing for a career in the U.S. army. His father had been a career army man, had retired with the rank of Lieutenant-Colonel and now dabbled in coin collecting and charcoal sketching. His mother was a secretary in the local agriculture cooperative.

When he saw Carl enter with the other educationally challenged, he decided, spur of the moment to offer his services as a tutor. He wasn't sure why, a vague idea of getting to know Carl better, finding out more about him, maybe establishing, if not some bond, some connection or relationship, so maybe, maybe Carl would cease to view him as a potential victim and turn his gaze elsewhere. He was curious about him, his need to bully, what made him tick. He volunteered and was accepted and began his tutoring career. Carl ignored him nor cast a cold eye in his direction. Ben saw no signs of hostility or aggression towards him and was perplexed.

At the end of the first week, he was assigned to Carl. He would approach this session like any other one, he had decided, concentrating on finding out where Carl's main difficulty lay and using any and all methods to resolve the difficulty. He found that Carl picked up quickly on what Ben wanted and from the beginning, he made progress. He wondered why Carl did so poorly. As they progressed, he probed as to Carl's plans after high school. After a long silence, Carl said "Navy," then "I ain't gonna make it." Ben asked why and Carl rounded on him, "None of your Goddamn business." The lesson continued, but after, near class end, Carl spoke again. "I got two brothers did jail time. I ain't goin' to college and I got lousy marks – Navy ain't gonna take me." Ben thought he's probably right but later that week checked out navy recruitment guidelines. Days later as he tutored Carl, he told him, "If you graduate high school with good marks and a letter of recommendation from the principal, you got a good chance of being accepted."

"Principal hates my guts. We bin buttin' heads forever," he said. Ben knew Principal Caulfield. He was tough and unyielding often. He was also fair. Ben said nothing. They worked well together, and Carl showed improvement.

Carl was an enigma, known throughout the school as aggressive, a fighter and if not an out and out bully, verging on. Yet, when tutored, he responded – at least to Ben's efforts – and even in a few sessions showed marked improvement. Though he was still well below class average, he was moving up. Ben realized Carl was intelligent, suffered from no learning difficulty he could decipher. The three or four Carl hung with were cut from the same cloth, destructive, aggressive, and failing. Ben seemed on better terms with Carl though still wary, and Carl had never made reference to his threat against Ben.

The day before summer recess, as he strolled home, taking in the light breeze that rustled the big oak trees that gave perfect shade as he strolled along, relaxed, feeling good about this world he lived in – feeling, even, cautiously optimistic about the future – he spied, up ahead by the next intersection and lounging against a light pole, Carl. His heart in his chest near shuddered to a stop and the day, suddenly, didn't seem so benign or friendly. Was it too late to turn around? Had Carl seen him? Of course, he had. He was waiting for him. Ben's gait slowed but he kept on going. Better get it over with, offer only token resistance – then it would depend on how long he wanted to beat on him. But something rebelled deep inside him. If he was going down, he was going down giving his best, his very best. When he was within ten feet of Carl, he dropped his bag and suddenly charged. The force of his charge bowled Carl over and they both fell to the ground and tussled there. Within seconds Ben knew he was outmatched, in a no-win situation but the blows he expected didn't come. Carl straddled him and held him, so he was hogtied, and was looking at him with a perplexed expression on his face.

"What was that about?" he demanded. Ben looked at him. Carl was in superb physical shape. He hadn't a snowball's chance in hell of getting the better of him.

"Figured I'd get a shot in before…."

"Before what?"

"Before you kicked my butt all over the school parking lot"

"Why would I do that?'

"Cos that's what you said." Carl slowly disengaged.

"I threatened a lot of guys. Don't remember you." Ben gazed at him, weak with relief.

"You mean…?"

"What?"

"Nothing, sorry." God, he would never worry again about what might or might not happen. Whatever would be, would be, would be his motto for life from this moment on. Carl put his hand out and lifted him up. They stood awkwardly.

"I did okay in my test, just got the results."

"Hey, good man," Ben told him. Carl sat with his back to the pole and Ben waited.

"That true?"

Ben was clueless. "What?"

"About getting into the Navy?"

"You mean...?"

"Yeah, yep. You graduate, get a letter of recommendation from the principal and – you got a good chance."

"Principal said I did good." He hesitated. "Would you do a little tutoring on the side? I need help bad, man."

The sun was like a golden globe in a blue, blue sky as Ben looked to the Heavens. He decided to push his luck.

"What's in it for me?"

Carl looked away for a long moment and then said, "I got your back for the next two years, deal?"

The sun shone out of a brilliant, blue sky and the birdsong he heard seemed to match the heart song deep inside him. Ben was even thinking tonight's moon might very well turn into a pumpkin.

On Getting Old

When bones do creak and fingers freeze

And movements cease and eyesight leaves

When memory old trumps memory new

When I am old and slow to do

Old friends have gone, save but a few

And they are frail and cannot chew

When time it speeds along a track

I scarce have time to pause, look back

On actions past, too late to rue

On what I was, was not to do

Then I will know that time has come

To tie loose ends and make a plan

For I am come to where we go

And no more harking to and fro

I strode decisively along.

Alas I was more often wrong

And what I did and didn't do

Is but the past, a fading brew

Of good and bad and in-between

Too late, fear bocht, the past is past

So soon, I'll lay down on my bed

And go where one goes when one's dead.

Wilma

He begs me to move in. We have three months, perfect. We do everything together.

Spend weekends upstate, red roses, long walks on the beach. He cooks dinner, candles, place settings, white wine - my favorite.

One night he asks me not to wear such short skirts. "Too provocative," he says.

I say, "Whaddaya mean, provocative, I got nice legs, I should show 'em off."

And he says, "Wilma you're my girl now." He says he's uncomfortable that other men are looking and admiring my legs.

I say, "I'm your girl but they're my legs," and he says, "That's not a good attitude."

I say, "Do I tell you what to wear? So please do not tell me what to wear."

"Well, he gets very upset. I tell you, Margie, he's your cousin, but that's a side of him I have never seen before. His face turns red and the veins in his neck bulge. He puts his face close to mine, just inches away, and he starts screaming. I 'm so scared, I near pee in my panties.

But real cool like, 'I say, now Joe, that behavior is inappropriate,' and he stops just like that."

Then I tell him, "I'm outta here, 'cause I'm an Emancipated woman, don't put up with that shit."

A Memory

I have this memory. I am five or six or maybe eight years old. I'm not sure and it doesn't really matter. I'm handed a slice of steaming fresh bread with butter thick on top and sugar sprinkled on the butter. I hear a voice say,

"Put that in your belly, young fella. There's nothing like a slice of bread, fresh out of the oven and a bit of sugar to sweeten it up. There's atin' and drinkin' in it. But it has to be fresh, and the fresher the better."

I bite into the bread and look at a perfect impression of teeth on the butter. And it all tastes so good. Mouth full, I mumble agreement to everything.

The voice belongs to my Granduncle, Augustine Flynn, who we call Gusty. I run for messages (groceries) for Gusty, a couple of days a week. When I get the bread for him,

"Fresh now, mind you, make sure it's fresh or I'll send it back to them," he cuts a slice, dresses it up with butter and sugar and hands it over to me. He has a heavy hand with the butter, but that's the way I like it. I think how lucky I am. None of my friends have a job and they listen enviously as I tell them about 'me and Gusty' and the slice of bread he gives me for bringing the messages back.

I live on a short street of mostly old cottages except for a row of four, newer attached bungalows. I live in the second of the attached bungalows, number two Saint Augustine's Terrace, called after the patron saint of the village and the reason why half the men there are called Augustine. I feel secure in the bosom of a large family and my mother is already treating me as a responsible little man. So, when she tells me that Gusty, who lives at the top of the lane in an old cottage with thatched roof, needs someone to run to the shops once or twice a week and bring him back the basic necessities, that, "'twould be a nice little job for you and 'twould be helping out poor Gusty,"

I eagerly agree, though I have no idea what 'basic necessities' meant. I feel so proud and so grown up, marching up to the cottage door. Gusty welcomes me. "So, you're Mary Anne's young fella, and a big strong man you are, too. Well, I was talking to your mother, and I was telling her that the legs are not good anymore. So, if I could find someone with a good pair of legs and a little time, to run and get me a loaf of bread, or a bit of sugar or a half a pound of loose tea, it would be a great help."

I surprise myself by piping up boldly, "I'm your man, Uncle Gusty." He smiles and say, "By God, I think you're right. Now I have a book up at Mull's, so tell them to put the couple of bits and pieces on my book. Get the bread fresh. I don't want any of that day-old stuff."

Gusty was in his seventies then, with white beard and mustache, an old seadog living on a small pension. He never married and returned to the village to live out his remaining years. He was quiet enough, read a fair bit, an odd time to the pubs. He enjoyed smoking his pipe and a walk down the strand every day until the legs got bad.

76

He didn't need much, and over the days and weeks that I got the 'bits and pieces' for him, we got on good together.

I'd watch him cut thin slices of Wills Golden Tobacco, not even looking as he cut, as he'd relate stories of his seagoing days, of rounding the Cape of Good Hope at the tip of South Africa, Cape Horn at the tip of South America, sailing through the Mediterranean Sea and into the Red Sea and of fighting a ferocious storm off the Cape Verde Islands,

"Where I got down on my knees and gave my soul to God for, I thought we were done for."

"I've seen the world," he said, "and, by God, it's worth seeing."

He paused, gazing into space. "And the women. Holy Mother of God, the women. They were like, like exotic fruit, and hard to resist, and I didn't do much resisting, until I got a bit more sense. Fine women they were and the beauty of 'em."

He paused, remembering," But I always had a yearning to come back. Don't we all, eventually – like the salmon comes home to spawn – and die." So, young fella, here I am."

I listened, ears cocked, taking it all in, like a thirsty man takes water. I determined that, some day, I'd sail the worlds' oceans, wrestle with – and like Gusty escape - the world's exotic women.

Sometimes, Gusty would have the kettle boiling when I returned. He'd throw the loose tea into the pot, heat it over the fire and pour the water in. We'd both listen to the crackle and the pop as the tea engaged with the water. He'd cut two slices of bread, put the butter and the sugar on and we'd sit and have our feast, sitting by the window and, looking out. Times were never better than then. Often there wouldn't be much conversation, for we were at ease with each other, but mostly it was Gusty talking and me, wide-eyed listening.

I felt grown-up and important, for if he didn't treat me as an equal, he didn't treat me as small boy who knew little. Gusty seemed to live on bread and tea and, of course, the pipe, though, once in a while, he'd boil up a bacon butt, cabbage, and spuds. He liked his fresh bread but otherwise gave little thought to food.

Later that same year he collapsed and was taken to the hospital. They said it was T.B. I badgered my mother to go with her when she visited him. He lingered on for four months but the last time I saw him, I knew he didn't have much time left. His breathing was fast and ragged, and he had trouble taking nourishment. When he saw me, he pulled me to him and, his voice hoarse and broken, whispered into my ear,

"Didn't we have great times sitting by the window, yourself and myself, drinkin' the tay (tea), and atin' (eating) the bread and butter, cogitatin'. Drinkin' and atin' and cogitatin.' What more could a man want, ha? I'll be back and we'll get going again, okay?"

But, as young as I was, I knew, and he knew, we wouldn't and I could only say, "Sure, we will, Uncle Gusty." He died the next day.

Once in a great while, I'll cut a slice of fresh bread, making sure it's fresh and not day old, load it up with butter, sprinkle sugar on top and sit back with a cup of tea. I'll bite into the bread and study the perfect impression of teeth on butter and I'm back again in a thatched cottage at the top of a lane, accompanying an old seadog on his travels. Times were never better than then.

My Father

By the fire my father sits
Bald head, broad frame, brown boots unlaced
Big, buckled belt secures tweed pants
Uncollared shirt sits round his neck.

Spectacles perched on his nose
He's riding horseback through the West
Single bulb provides the light
Louis L'Amour guides his ride.

All around, rain buckets down.
Small brown dog dozes at his feet
China dogs on mantelpiece
Gaze benignly on the scene.

The Fourth of July

"Honey, are you awake?" I inquired, "honey, do you want to stay in bed a little longer, or should we get up now?" My wife, Jane stirred lazily. I knew she was not awake, and this was my way of waking her.

"No honey, I was not awake," she replied, "and you knew it. This was just one more example of that cunning, conniving, scheming mind of yours at work. You wanted to get up and you wanted me to get up also. Didn't you?"

"Oh honey, how could you say such a thing," I replied, feigning a deeply injured tone of voice, but she cut me off.

"Save it buster, I know that tiny, conniving mind of yours better than I know my own."

"'Tiny', 'conniving,' darling, you have plunged a dagger into my heart. I am deeply aggrieved," I plaintively replied. She laughed. "Save that crap for your writing class. What are we doing today?"

"Honey, whatever you and I want to do, that's what we are doing. Today we will consider only our desires and wishes. Today we have no kids, have no obligations. The day is but a pup, to quote one of your gems so let us begin to plan our day." She smiled and the smile lit up her face. I still found her physically attractive after all those years. I studied her for a moment; good figure though fuller now than when we married some twenty-five years ago, thick auburn hair, now flecked through with grey and great skin.

"And there's nobody with whom I'd want to spend it more than you. Is that proper grammar?" she queried. I wasn't sure so ignored it.

"I'll take a quick shower and while you're showering, I'll pick up what we need for breakfast, okay?"

"Okay, get some corn muffins and some fruit. We have everything else." The plan was instituted.

We dined leisurely on fruit cup, hot oatmeal - which we love, winter or summer - bacon and eggs, buttered corn muffin and tea; on our deck which was beginning to heat up but was still comfortable this early. We were surrounded by the chirping and singing of thrush, blue bird and sparrow, trees gently swaying and leaves softly rustling. It was a magical moment, healing and calming to the spirit, an ideal morning, and the beginning of a beautiful day. I turned to my wife and looked deeply into her eyes.

"Happy, darling?" I inquired. We both laughed. We had watched an English movie the night before where the hero had addressed the same query to his love. It was such a distinctively English expression and so out of character when used by any other. We lingered over breakfast, reluctant to let go of this magical time but finally moved on. It was early yet, and the day was just beginning.

We set out on our walk, the sun beginning to rise in a cloudless, brilliant blue sky. We skirted our neighbor's yard and emerged on a quiet tree-lined country road. Further on, we entered a condominium development, beautifully laid out with shrubs and trees in abundance, a sizable stream wending through it and a series of attractive stone bridges. It's an adult condo development and usually very quiet with little or no vehicular traffic. It has also a beautiful clubhouse and pool. We have toured the models on display and my wife has fantasized about owning one, some day.

"Wow, imagine living here. You'd probably swim in the pool every day," she says. I murmur assent.

"And there's so much room that the kids could come and visit when they wanted," she adds.

"It sure would be nice," I say. It is too glorious a day to get into the specifics of whether we could ever afford to live here.

We continue our walk till we come to the stone bridge. We usually rest here, checking out the river and its condition. Its condition has varied from a raging, out of control monster in the depths of winter to a meek, anemic, pale shadow of its former self. We usually spend some time hanging over the bridge and the noise of the running water soothes and relaxes, almost to the point of lulling one into a trance. I think how long the stream has run here and how long more it will run, long after we're gone. We move on reluctantly.

Our house is strangely quiet recently for, finally, the last of our four children, Greg, has left and is now a college student. He is home for the summer, but we see less of him, probably, than when he was in college. It is an endless round of parties and social events, he informs us, but he does hold a summer job and rises faithfully each day to fulfill his obligations. When children leave a home, finally, there is a period of adjustment for the parents; almost like a period of mourning, for suddenly their assignment in life - which is to raise and prepare children for life - is completed. My wife and I have reached this stage with three gone, Emma, John, and Lillian, and one in the process of, and have begun to deal with it.

So, on this beautiful July 4th, we find ourselves alone, but not necessarily lonely, discussing our lives, plans and options, what we hope to accomplish in the next months, or year, or beyond. We talk of our desire to finish working in a few years, to travel more and avail of the wonderful museums, shows, sights and attractions of New York City. We talk of, someday, being able to go South for a few months in winter and visit faraway places we've always wanted to see.

"We have a lot to look forward to," I say. By now we are sitting on deckchairs in the garden, the deck being too hot at this time of the day. We sit in the shade of two massive weeping willows and no matter how hot it gets; it always feels cooler there.

"And a lot to be thankful for," Jane replies. "This has been one of the nicest Fourth of July's ever," she continues. "I feel rested, renewed and reinvigorated. We should do this more often."

"And I'm rested, renewed and reinvigorated. But I'm also bewitched, bothered and bewildered."

"By?"

"By you, of course. Your beauty, personality and presence just ..." She interrupts me, turns, and looks deeply into my eyes.

"Happy, darling?"

Momma, Poppa and Me

Growing up was a happy time. There was me, Rachel – me who's called Rachel, I mean - Tommy, two years older and Lucy, the baby and four years younger and Momma and Poppa. We lived in South Carolina, inland from Myrtle Beach on two acres in an old ranch house that belonged to Daddy's people for over a hundred years. It was never spick and span, but it had all we ever wanted. Poppa called me 'Ray' from when I was little, but Momma always said my name was 'Rachel' and that's what I should be called. I loved Momma. She was always there, always, when I come home, from school, from playin,' when I got into trouble or got a lickin.' She made everthin' right.

Once a boy kicked me and I ran home cryin.' Momma said, "What happened?" and I told her. She said, "Did you do anything to provoke that boy?" I said "No, Momma." "Then I'll take care of it," she said. And she did. That boy never bothered me again, matter of fact, walked out of his way when he saw me. Didn't never find out what she said or done to him.

I loved my daddy too, but he didn't pay much attention to me nor the others neither. He warn't that kind. But he never whaled on us too much, 'ceptin' we did something real bad and Momma was always standin by, makin sure he whaled so much and no more.

I think he was puzzled by life, didn't really know how to be this or that an' how to act when all of a sudden, he was a daddy. He dropped out or kinda retreated and got into things that took him away from every day livin'. He acted stern though his heart warn't in it - like as if he had picked up – maybe from his own pa – this was how a man should be actin' cos otherwise the world would go to hell in a hand basket. Never understood that sayin neither.

Most men are like that from what I been hearin.' They must figger thass how you got to be, stern and kinda glum like as if bad news is coming down the road and we gotta brace - though he warn't really glum, just quiet. He mostly sat there when he come home and read the paper. This was after he come home from the paper mill, where he worked.

He read the paper ev'ry day, the paper always waitin' for him by the front steps. He told my ma once if everybody bought the paper every day, he'd always have a job. He'd get upset, too if somebody said they didn't read the papers – especially if they worked the mill. Me, I reckon a lot of them just didn't know how to read. Whenever I think of Pa, I always think of him reading the paper. He was a reader.

Him and Ma got on pretty good together cos she understood him and gave him room. She loved him pretty good, too. I know, by the way she looked at him – like she was sayin' "Well, glory to God and damned if I know how I managed to catch me this fine, upstanding man and not bad-looking, neither." Once I caught Momma kissin' him on his bald head, when she thought no one was around.

His job was drivin' a truck and deliverin' for the mill. Money warn't real good but it warn't real bad neither, steady – no layoffs that I can ever remember. He was a good man – distant but good. Momma was different. She'd grab me and take me in her arms and hug me and rock me back and forth. I'd protest, like I didn't really like it, but she knew that wadn't true. I felt this was the best place in the whole, wide world, just lyin' in her arms, sayin' nothin.' Never felt so safe, then or now.

Then we all grow'd up. Tommy moved out west, got married and had four boys. Lucy got married and divorced a couple of months later – lives in Ohio. She teaches school. Me, I work in the Sleepy Inn Motel, kinda manage it for Mister JoJo Myers. He's a widower and was sweet on me but I reckoned I'd never have what Momma and Papa had.

I never did marry – got me a little house, close to Momma. Come over every Sunday. She'd cook ham butt and collard greens and sweet potato pie. Then she'd make strong, real strong, black coffee. We'd sit on the porch, Momma, Poppa and me, sippin' and sayin' nothin' – no need to. We was just contented with life. Those were good times.

Then she got old. She couldn't cook no more except small stuff like eggs and toast. So, I'd cook and bring it over. Things were still pretty good. When she was eighty-four, she got some kind of virus and died. It was quick, two days in the County Hospital is all. Poppa, he was still good, lived in the house, took care of himself, didn't want nobody movin' in, thass how he was. And one day, when he was eighty-nine goin' on ninety, he just died peaceful like, in his bed.

Warn't nothin' wrong with him, didn't sicken or nothing, best I know. I reckon he jus' got tired of livin,' lay down and died. I miss 'em.

I got money enough now, so I took to travellin,' went all over and seen a lot of places and a lot of strange things. Like to see how others spend their days and reckon the more I travel and the more I see, we ain't too much different. We all want to do right by our kids, mostly, if we have 'em, and it ain't always the richest are the happiest – though I ain't prejudiced against the rich, neither. So, I spend mostly what I make. Momma always said you can't take it with you. Don't aim to leave nothin' when my time comes. I try to live right like she would have wanted. Do right, she always said. One day we'll meet again in God's glory.

The Color of Her Hair

What was the color of her hair, that first time we met?

And all the times between.

I remember wildness and disarray and careless abundance

As if blown by gale-force winds.

But was it red, ochroid or gold, the color of golden lion?

Or all those combined.

Too, I remember sleek perfumed mass lifting gently in the breeze

Soft to the touch.

Overcome, reverential, I bury my face in and inhale its sweetness

Like new-mown hay or the sweet smell of sphagnum

Or a just-bathed baby's skin

But what was the color of her hair.

Mae Hong Son

Ben had it made. He had a beautiful wife, a three-year-old daughter, Ellen in abundant health, a house and a business, the business a used book shop on the ground floor, upstairs the living quarters. It was adequate though not spacious.

He lived in Chiang Mai, a city of approximately 240.000 people in northern Thailand. His wife, Noi was Thai. They were married four years and he was happy. Maybe not quite as happy as he was four years ago, when he was in a state of constant amazement and disbelief that this divine creature, of the flawless skin and perfect body had consented to be his wife. That degree of happiness would have been impossible to maintain.

He was of average looks, five nine in height with beginning to recede sandy brown hair. He was one of three children, and reared in Geneva, up-state New York. He had an older sister Meg and a younger brother, John. His father, Benjamin, a teacher was now retired. His mother Janet had died four years ago of bone cancer at the early age of 49 and left what seemed to Ben, a surprisingly large amount to each of her three children. His parents had agreed on this course of action as his father had a generous pension and some investments of his own. Ben had, at that time just dropped out of Ithaca College and was drifting, no clear idea of what he should or should not do. In college he was an unenthusiastic student, scraping by in his chosen major, business studies – not even sure if business was what he should be studying.

When his friend Robert suggested a holiday in Thailand he readily agreed. They had spent two weeks in Bangkok and then journeyed to Chiang Mai by night train, a trip that took twelve hours. Ben was eager to participate in all Thailand offered, but quickly tired of the blatant sex for money scene. Robert couldn't get enough, his appetite insatiable. When they got to Chiang Mai they split up, Ben to explore northern Thailand, Robert to continue his sex odyssey.

He took the obligatory tours to the Golden Triangle, Mae Sai on the Burma border, Mae Hong Son, Chan Khong, the Long Necks hill tribe, the Karen. He liked Mae Hong Son so much he decided to stay a few days. It was quiet, a village untouched by the farangs, the foreigners who invaded Thailand each year in ever increasing numbers. He read his books, walked in the hills outside the village and ate the delicious Thai food that he had grown so fond of. Here, he found a kind of peace that had eluded him for a very long time, and it was here, one early morning, the woman of his dreams materialized.

She was coming out of a small Soi or lane, and with the sun at her back, it was as if she were a sun goddess. She had long, straight black hair, flawless skin and a slim and well-proportioned body. He knew he wanted desperately to know her, that he must do everything in his power to do exactly that, that this, somehow, was meant to be. He went to her and tried to communicate but failed. She had no English, he had little Thai and she was afraid of this tall farang. But she saw something about him, maybe the yearning plainly visible on his face and took his hand. The touch sent ripples through his body. She guided him to a small shop. Behind the counter was an old woman who greeted him with a 'Sawadee Ka' but when she saw he had no Thai, addressed him in English.

'Welcome. How are you?'

He explained his predicament, how he wanted so much to know this beautiful Thai woman. He watched as her eyes crinkled and she laughed heartily while the woman by his side stood there in total bewilderment. When the old woman explained to her how the Farang thought her beautiful and wanted so much to know her, Noi's eyes opened with shock. But she didn't know this man, had never seen him before. The old lady patiently explained the Farang very much wanted to see her again. Would she consent? Well, she did, finally. There was a long courtship, chaperoned meetings, meeting her family; Momma, Pappa, Aunty Ging and younger sister Yim, fourteen years old. One year later they were married. Ben had decided to settle in Chiang Mai and Noi was amenable. That was another thing he liked about Thai women. They went where their men went.

Those first few months of married life were total bliss. He was, they were, totally unequivocally in love. Maybe the intensity of his feelings could not have been maintained, maybe it was humanly impossible. After three years and the birth of their daughter, of course he could not have been the total focus of Noi's attention. Rightfully, she gave as much attention to Ellen as the child needed.

She was an excellent mother, loving and vigilant. He felt just a little bit neglected. Their private lovefest was breached. He berated himself for his selfishness, told himself how lucky he was. He had the woman of his dreams. She was a wonderful mother to Ellen. They still made deep passionate love. And yet, yet...

By this time, he had set up his bookshop of secondhand books. In Thailand this was a very popular type of business. When the book was read and returned, the buyer got half back. It was also, a system very popular with the backpackers who thronged to Thailand. Slow in the beginning, it continued to grow and eventually yielded an adequate income. Noi enjoyed working in the shop, enjoyed meeting customers and her English was improving day by day. Ellen was a big hit with customers as she first crawled and then stutter-stepped around the shop. Ben left periodically for Bangkok to source more books and life was good.

In the beginning he travelled overnight by bus, leaving at 9 pm and arriving in Bangkok some nine to ten hours later and early the next morning. He would complete his business by early afternoon and take a bus back arriving in Chiang Mai around midnight. As time passed, he began to stay over in Bangkok. It was less stressful, he reasoned, and he would arrive back in Chiang Mai more refreshed. Noi agreed, encouraged him even. He also liked the sensation, if only for a little while, of being alone with only himself to consider. Family life was wonderful, but a break benefitted all.

On one such trip he went to a Farang bar to see an American

football game. It was the playoffs and he enjoyed being part of the mostly American crowd, loud and raucous. He had forgotten how loud they could be. The game went into overtime, and he had more beers than he normally would have. He left the bar around midnight and headed back to his guesthouse. Sukhumvit road was really starting to crank up and he thought to himself, I was part of this just a few short years ago. As he turned into his Soi, Soi 11 where the Honey Guesthouse was located, he spotted a tiny bar and decided to have one last drink. The bar was empty but as he sat down a young Thai woman came from the back and greeted him: 'Sabaii Dee Mai?' He responded appropriately 'Sabaii Dee." She was probably in her early thirties and elegantly dressed. He sat and chatted with her, no one else came into the bar and soon she was getting ready to close up. She had been married, she told him, divorced one year – her husband had left her within two years of their marriage, no children. He told her of his wife and child, his business, how happy he was. Then, when she was ready to leave, as if it were pre-ordained, she took his hand and they walked to his room. She stayed two hours and left. It was sexually satisfying for both, and she wrote out her number before she left. When he awoke the next morning, he was devastated, racked with guilt and extremely regretful of what had happened. He looked at the number she had given him and ripped it into tiny pieces.

On the bus back to Chiang Mai, he made up his mind he would tell Noi, beg her forgiveness, swear it would never happen again and take his punishment. He knew she would be shocked, hurt and angry.

She had a right to be. She was a virgin on their wedding night, a fact that greatly pleased Ben.

Why had he done this? What had driven him? It was as if it was the work of the devil, had no rhyme or reason. He could not remember looking at or observing her in a sexual way. Yet it had happened, and he had no answer why. Why was the bar empty which had given them time to establish some kind of rapport? He had never even entertained the notion of taking her to his room. Why had she been so confident? What signals had he sent that had resonated with her, that had given her the confidence, the belief that he would not refuse? He was not aware of any signals sent, yet...

As the bus approached Chiang Mai, he lost his nerve. He would not tell her. It was a once off. It would never happen again, he swore. He arrived around eight in the evening and Ellen ran to greet him. He hugged Noi. She was evidently glad to see him. Everything would be as the Thais say: Dtok long - okay. But later that night when Noi showed a desire for sex, he mumbled how tired he was and fell into a dreamless sleep. Things returned to normal. On his next trip to Bangkok, he stayed at a different guesthouse and avoided the bar where Pum worked. But on his next visit he returned to the Honey guesthouse and slipped into the bar later that night. He wasn't sure why. Had they really been so compatible? Would she still look attractive? It had a few customers, but she was glad to see him and made it evident, sitting with him at the first opportunity. When an overweight Englishman who had been pursuing her gave him a dirty look, he swelled with pride. He waited for her, and they left together. He could not find a reason why, other than she was different to Noi, different build, different in how she moved in bed and maybe a pride that he was the chosen one. Also, there had been no consequences from his first encounter and a little voice was whispering 'Why not, you're bringing comfort to this woman whose husband abandoned her?' As before, they enjoyed satisfying sex and Pum left after two hours. In some ways it was an ideal situation. She put no demands on him. Neither wanted a long-term relationship nor commitment. It filled a need in him, otherwise why do it? It was what a man did, after all, to stray sometimes. But he would never abandon his family, his beautiful wife and daughter and yes, he loved his wife very much.

For one year he went to Bangkok and saw Pum. Everything seemed fine with Noi. Then Aunty Ging came to stay with them for a few days. She was the one member of Noi's family who disapproved of Ben, of any farang marrying into their family. Noi knew how Ben felt about her and how she felt about Ben. They talked about it and Noi said it was of no consequence how Ging felt. But now Ging was staying with them for a few days. Noi explained that her aunty had doctors to see in Chiang Mai – she would only stay a few days. Ben caught them in deep conversation a few times and Aunty Ging staring at him, her eyes black and unblinking. Four days later, when Ben left for Bangkok, she was still there. She would be gone when he got back. He would be relieved.

The next night he walked into the little bar on Soi 11 and was relieved when Pum hugged him and made him feel welcome. He knew some time she would meet someone, unattached and available and their rendezvous would come to an end. It was okay, but not yet. Later that night she closed the bar and they adjourned to his room. Now they were practiced lovers and knew each other. It was slow or frenzied depending on their mood and culminating in a more than satisfactory orgasm for both. Ben felt life couldn't get much better. He fell into a deep and satisfying sleep.

He was awakened by a loud and insistent knocking at the door and some words spoken in Thai. Pum was asleep by his side. She hadn't left. Was it longer than their customary two hours? He had no idea. He left the bed and stumbled to the door, angry they would wake their guests in the early hours of the morning – though this guesthouse saw comings and goings all through the night. He opened the door to see Noi standing there. She moved aside and Aunty Ging stood there. She stared, malevolent, at him. His brain couldn't process this scene. Ging had something in her hand, and he wasn't sure what. Then he felt incredible pain in his left eye, and he blacked out.

He woke up in the Bumrungrad hospital in Bangkok the next day. He had a patch over his left eye, and it was still very painful. He had evidently had surgery. Later the doctor came and informed him he had lost the sight in his left eye. There was a remote possibility some sight might return. He didn't question the doctor and waited for Noi to visit. She came later that day, beautiful skin, beautiful body and lustrous black hair that hung to her shoulders. She bent to kiss him, asked how he was and was he in much pain. He whispered, 'I'm sorry...but she shushed him before whispering, 'No more butterfly, okay?' He knew what she meant. It was a term applied to those who could not be content with the one they had chosen and liked to stray. He gravely nodded. His straying days were over.

A week after, he was back in Chiang Mai. Now he wore a patch over his left eye. He never brought up again the events at the guesthouse in Bangkok and never saw Pum again. He knew now if he strayed there would be consequences, there always were. He thought to be blind would be a terrible affliction. Noi now accompanied him to Bangkok. As time passed, he became quite fond of the patch. Noi said it made him look like a pirate and his daughter called him Poppa the pirate. When strangers asked how he lost an eye, he would gaze into the distance with his one good eye and whisper softly, 'War is hell.' They would nod sympathetically and lapse into respectful silence.

A Time and a Place: Ciudad Colon, Costa Rica.

In Ciudad Colon there is a place
Perched on a hill of verdant green
Mango, banana vie for space
With lemon, lime, and bean.

Pass thru wrought-iron Colony gates
Family and friends all disappear
Cometh the time, the hour is near
To spread our wings and fly.

Pintor, escritor gravitate
In casas, casitas hunker down
To chase the Muse and so alone
But wind that makes the bamboo groan.

Take it as a special gift
As we pursue our lonely quest
To have this place, to be alone
Submit, oblit, repeat and hone.

Tropical plants unceasingly
Give forth their fruit prodigiously
Hummingbirds sip and boas slide
Unearthly quiet where writers write.

Coconuts crowd high in the sky
As rain relentless passes by

Worker ants unceasing toil

Cut pathways in the verdant soil.

Go now to another plain

Heed not hunger, thirst or pain

Be thou creative with pen and brush

Waste not this time bestowed on us.

Nire Valley View

There was a line in a song, "The sea oh the sea, gra geal mo chroi (bright love of my heart) She had altered that line to, "The view oh the view, gra geal mo chroi." Without fail, this line popped into her head whenever she sat where she now sat, at the small table in her upstairs bedroom before the window that looked down on the Nire valley. It was a scene that settled her, that she never got enough of, no matter the seasons. She was convinced this was where she was meant to be, in all the planet. Of all the places she might have gone to, she had been directed to the one spot that brought her total contentment. God was good.

Once it had been a small window looking out of thick walls, hundred-year-old walls – the original walls from when it had been built somewhere in the latter part of the last century - Jack thought maybe around 1890. When she first moved in, in nineteen thirty-five, it was as a new wife coming to another family. She expected some resentment, a begrudging towards the usurper, the stranger in their midst. But no, they were as Jack had told her. They welcomed her and from the beginning - she fit in and loved this house and where it was situated.

They had reared four fine children here. They were all gone now, scattered to the four winds, Jim in England, Paddy in New York, Moira in Sydney and Anne a nurse in Dublin. Jack too was gone and above all she missed him. When they met, it was as the old folks might have said 'weren't they meant to be.' They were best friends and lovers for all the time they were together. They had celebrated their fiftieth wedding anniversary, all the children home. One month later almost to the day, Jack was dead. He was found in the top field by a neighbor, a probable heart attack, the doctor said. The doctor had never called back to verify that, but she thought it was probable. He had had a touch of high blood pressure in his later years.

She looked at the picture by the bed, their wedding picture – God, who was that slim auburn-haired girl with the shy smile by his side – a smile tugging at the corners of his mouth, the light bouncing off his bald head. He was bald in his twenties. He never stopped smiling, good times or bad and they had some bad times. The winter of sixty-two they were snowed in for four weeks and lost near sixty sheep to dogs, cold and starvation. Always, Jack was by her side reassuring, soothing. "We'll get through it, girl, mark my words." She marked his words, and they got through it. She was proud of what they, together, had accomplished, over two hundred acres now of mostly good land. It was leased for now. Jim was talking about coming back but he had the wanderlust. She wouldn't put any pressure on him. It was his life.

The window she looked out of was five feet tall, almost to the floor and three feet wide. It was the one change they had made to the house. She wanted a big window so she could take that view in, all of it, every day she lived there.

Jack protested. "Goddamn it, the house might fall down. 'Tis old, you know." She was adamant and she got her way as she knew she would. She asked for little over the years but what she wanted, she fought for – and got.

It was dusk now, the light beginning to fade from the sky, but she still saw the outlines of the valley spread before her down to where the river cut its way through field and gorse and hedgerow and on to the village of Fourmilewater. She thought herself privileged, blessed to live in such a place and though mostly on her own now, relished that, too. She *liked* being on her own, liked the solitude, sounds of wood and field coming from the outside, a fire blazing in the cold evenings. Children and grandchildren came to visit at regular intervals – they could not comprehend her relishing the solitude and she pictured them plotting their visits, 'If you take July, I'll take September and Jim will come for Christmas'- and played along though sometimes she heaved a sigh of relief as they exited the yard, waving furiously.

Thanks be to God, she had good health, in her eighty seventh year now and mostly sound. There was a twinge of arthritis in both knees now and then and especially in the cold. 'Arteritis' as her neighbor, Mary Hickey two miles down the road, called it. "How's the arteritis, Anne girl? It's playing the divil with me."

Three weeks before, two young bla'guards had broken into Mary's house and stolen money. What was even worse, they had deliberately beaten her when there was no need. Anne thought of what Tom, Mary's husband would have done to them, all six foot two of him and hands like ham hocks. A gentle man but God forbid you got him mad. She remembered him years ago at a match in Dungarvan. A bunch of bla'guards had attacked him as he was leaving the field. He had flattened three of them and the other three hadn't stuck around. He would have done awful damage to anyone who would hurt Mary. But he was gone these past eleven years.

How could any man who called himself a man, and especially an Irishman do damage to an old woman living on her own? Whose son was it who could do such a thing? What rearing had they gotten? It was beyond Anne's comprehension. She sighed. They'd have to answer to God – and Tom might have a few things to say and a few blows to deliver. The thought made her smile. She believed we all had to answer for our actions, wherever, whenever.

It was dark now outside and still. Another day gone, swallowed up in that amorphous mass called the past. She had only the present and her present was not such a bad place to be.

Physical Reality

There is, was always, and will always be, a purpose to each life. Find that purpose, follow that purpose and your life will be one of achievement and a deep personal satisfaction, and this throughout the life that has been bestowed on you.

Find your Divine Purpose and follow it in accordance with the Source. Therein lies the path to true happiness. The problem for many is the difficulty of finding that purpose.

We must meditate, empty our minds of all distractions, maintain a serene countenance, look deep inside our core and wait. Wait, be patient, believe, and the path we are meant to take will appear.

Repeat the age-old mantras: I honor the Divinity that resides within me. I place myself in Your hands, do with me as You will.

We often ignore the obvious. When our better instincts are telling us, this is the way, this is the path we must follow, we ignore this instinct and out of a sense of rebellion or pure cussedness – or a destructive tendency often contained in our tribe, we embark on a directionless pursuit of 'highs' or 'fun' or sexual activity, sometimes involving drugs or alcohol, which always leads to disappointment and lack of fulfillment. When the God-connection is weakened, it is more difficult and often impossible to identify our Divine Purpose and follow the path to the Source. That path is the one true journey we must take to fulfillment and happiness.

You have to have a vision of victory, of accomplishment on the inside before it manifests on the outside. You are the master of your own destiny. You are the one who brings it to fruition.

Now, we all have periods of lethargy and even depression. When we're passing through this time, stumbling through life, often merely existing, accepting what life has handed us, neither the good or the bad exciting any great emotion, it is difficult to see or find the way out. But maybe this time is needed, a time of reflection, this standing still for a time, this time of processing all that has happened to us, what we had or hadn't done, opportunities lost, times where fear had dominated and influenced our decisions. Fear often does become a dominant factor in our lives and what should be clear and compelling becomes murky and fearful. In these times, we must turn to the Source and ask his help. Ask and you shall receive. God wants to give all that we need, if we but ask.

We are meant to achieve our potential, to realize that unique, God-given gift in the service of humanity and the betterment of the planet. That's when we're realizing our potential and fulfilling our destiny. That's when we live a life of abundance.

We will die only a physical death. We will leave this three-dimensional physical reality. This physical reality is only a small part of our total existence. We are magnificent, eternal beings. We are God-connected. We are eternal. We will live forever.

Soul

If I could only know the soul,
Its rhythm and its lie
The things I do that make it sing
And those that make it – cry!

Or rage or hang its head in shame
Or cry out in despair
Or drop on knees already scarred
And besiege who? with prayer

If I could only know the soul,
And open wide its door
To gaze upon its beauty pure
And understand its core

To know it's each and every want
To be in harmony
Then I would know the universe
And finally, be free

Perfect Punch

The complexity of it all – he couldn't get it right – how we should live here, here where we had been placed. Had we – been placed, by who or what? How was it we ended up here, on this spinning planet, one of how many? They say millions, billions even. So why was it not one of the others? Who decided? A random event? Billions of planets spinning with exquisite balance – at random? He thought it highly unlikely. And this thing about all being equal – unique but with varying characteristics, abilities that we were meant to utilize.

That's why we were given, gifted them. To use them and be exalted, all of us using and exalting, this sea of humanity, this multitude as one lifting, elevating to a higher plane, a higher consciousness so we'd be better, more serene, cerebral, accommodating, loving – yes, so we'd love each other more, be more forgiving of each other's foibles, bad deeds.

The two great emancipators of the soul, love, and forgiveness. When we had each in abundance, we were on our way to touching that which lay beyond the randomness, not just touching but communicating with, strengthening ties with, enlarging presence – in our lives – of that which lay beyond.

The question of gifts, 'God-given ability' was the term used, was a complex one. If one were a great warrior, if this be your gift – in service of the righteous and just – and your services were no longer needed. War was declared obsolete, unnecessary. You were told to put away your weaponry, learn a new trade. What then? Though maybe this was a bad example, ludicrous, for war would never be obsolete.

He thought of his friend, Jake, his best friend all through the years as they grew into manhood. Jake was kind and good and proper – respectful to his elders. But to some this was a weakness, a sign of non-aggression, timidity, even fear. Jake was none of those. So, he was picked on by those who saw in him an easy mark, a validation of their toughness, proof to the world they were to be reckoned with – with a 'Do not disturb' sign stamped on their chests – for fear of swift and terrible retribution.

Jake was slow to anger, able to reconcile and forgive those jibes and so walked away – in this imperfect world, a mistake. Maybe there was something about him that made them uneasy, an untouchable core, something. So it was that the neighborhood bully, Jesse, developed a deep dislike for my friend – he who respected all and challenged none. Jake was quiet and serious, even as a boy, less boyish maybe, than a boy his age would normally be. But what's normal? We all try to be normal, fit into a mold, act boyish when boys and more mature, serious as we progress through life. It was what was expected of us, and we acquiesced – most of us. Maybe it was this characteristic, his gravity that 'offended.'

When Jesse the bully challenged, it was total destruction or nothing. He was strong and quick and mostly fearless. His reputation was well-deserved. All who stood before him had fallen. When he picked his fight, it was, as it were, to the death. He didn't challenge lightly, confront haphazardly. So it was, he confronted Jake, my friend, on a clear summer's day as we walked along the strand that lapped the village. He had his crew with him, his hangers-on. But they would not interfere. When Jesse fought, he fought alone, and he alone would savor victory. I stood helplessly by. It was Jake's dilemma. If others jumped in, I would also but I knew my impact would be less than adequate.

"Something about you pisses me off," he told Jesse as he approached. "Any idea what it is?"

I watched Jake. His total concentration was on Jesse. For a second, something passed across his features, maybe a fight-or-flight reflex, a million calculations being processed, and the flight option instantly rejected. This, he knew, would have to end here, whatever its outcome and the odds seemed stacked. Yet, as intently as I studied him, I sensed no fear.

There is an aura – joy, timidity, hate, fear that surrounds us, especially in intense moments. His aura was of complete and total concentration. The obvious lack of fear incensed Jesse and he struck out viciously, catching Jake in the chest and he stumbled back. Jesse's cohorts oohed. If anything, Jake's intensity increased, and he began to move slowly, warily around his opponent. Jesse flung two more vicious blows that were easily countenanced by Jake then, as Jesse lunged again, Jake caught him in the throat with a roundhouse left.

He stumbled back and looked at Jake as if he was seeing him for the first time and his stance changed.

No more was he cocky, challenging, overbearing. Now he was hunkering down, aware it might not be as easy as anticipated – though sure he would emerge victorious. So, it would take a little longer. He would not lose; he had never lost. He would beat this boy who had pissed him off, he knew not why, who walked through his life as if being nice was enough, who was not aggressive, wary, hating enough to live in this world. Jesse would administer the first painful lesson in how it had to be.

They circled each other, cautious, respectful and little happened in the next few minutes. I watched my friend intently, mesmerized by his total concentration and even more so by his total lack of fear. He showed no fear, had none as he jousted with the town's most notorious bully.

He was becoming more adept, too, in anticipating his opponent's blows and most arced harmlessly through the evening air. Jake's cohorts were quiet now, aware that this might take longer than the norm but all the sweeter for it. This was war and their warrior leader had an exemplary record. The end when it came was vicious, unexpected, shocking and I saw it as if through Jake's eyes. While his concentration, was, if anything, more focused, his opponent was beginning to show impatience. He was not used to long fights. His forte was quick, vicious, and deadly, and by now the fight had entered the eleventh minute. He wanted to end it and end it dramatically, proof to those assembled that he was king – for by now a crowd had gathered, silent, intent, breathless as if they were witnessing history or at least an event that would be talked about for years to come.

And then it happened. Jesse saw an opening and maybe wanting this to be the blow that would end it, he took a milli-second longer to put it in motion. It was a vicious left hook to the body and in doing so he left his jaw exposed. It was as if Jake had anticipated this punch since the fight began. While Jesse's blow was beginning, Jake, my quiet, serious friend came over the top with a left that landed high up on his opponent's jaw. I can still see Jake poised like a gladiator who has discharged his spear, head upright, back arched, eyes focused and balance exquisite, every ounce of muscle beautifully coordinated as he smashed his fist into Jesse's jaw.

I knew it was over, even before his knees buckled, his eyes glazed as he pitched back, and his head hit the ground with a sickening thud. There's an artist who paints primarily fight scenes. This was a picture to be painted. No one moved, barely breathed as the wind rustled the nearby trees and the waves bumped gently on the strand.

All recorded the scene for posterity, the unbeatable vanquished, the victor standing, looking down, composed, inscrutable. It seemed like forever as we held our breaths, stared, and recorded the images, Jesse on his back, arms splayed helplessly above his head, nose leaking lightly, away in another place, his face oddly composed.

My point being, was this Jake's gift – that he could throw a perfect punch, beautiful to watch, deadly in its execution? Was it his destiny to fight, where I had no illusions but that he would be extremely successful? Or had he other gifts, did we all – to be honed and exploited – for the good of mankind, you see. Jake never fought again that I know of, at least not with his fists. Soon after he was drafted and sent to Vietnam. Within two months he was dead.

Cruise Ships

We cruise, plied and pampered

Sit naked, cooking in the sun.

We lift a finger, beckon

And smiling staff indulge us

Do our bidding

And answer silly questions.

Does the ship have its own power source?

Is it fresh or salt water in the toilet?

Does the staff live on board?

We doze overfed and bored

Our veins course with Tequila Sunrise

Bahama Mamas, Rum Punch

And Mango Coolers

We eat: Continental Breakfast, Breakfast Buffet,

Main Seating, Second Seating, Sun Worshippers Lunch

Hamburger, Hot Dog and Chili bar

Self Serv Frozen Yogurt, Afternoon Snack Service and

Don't forget the Midnight Buffet.

Waiters stroll throughout

Serving Canapés and Petit Fours.

We stagger off, overweight and liquored to the eyeballs

Can't wait till next year.

Fantasy/Reality

I always loved her, even when I said otherwise, when I acted like I didn't or when I yelled at her like I hated her. I loved her from the moment I first set eyes on her. I remember the first time I saw her. I was sitting on my favorite bench in the little park directly across from the building where I worked. I worked as an accountant for Smith and Klein, a large accounting firm in lower Manhattan. I was relaxing, eyes half closed but also taking in the changing scene before me.

Manhattan on a summer's day, you're going to see some of the most beautiful women on the face of the planet. And that's what I was doing, checking' out the scene. Suddenly she passed by. I thought she was the most beautiful woman I had seen in an awful long time. But it wasn't just her looks. It was something else, and whatever she was projecting was overpowering, major medicine having maximum effect on me, and leaving me weak, disoriented and gasping on the bench. I was literally vibrating to whatever she was emanating.

She was wearing a dress, a simple summer dress. Nobody could have worn the dress any better than she did. The most expensive designer in the world could not have created a better fit than that dress to that body. But it wasn't just the body, it was the whole package; how she held herself, how she moved. I never understood the term 'poetry in motion' till I saw her. Yet she seemed unaware of how beautiful she looked or how men turned to look at her.

Most men have a vague fantasy of their ideal woman buried deep within them. If asked to describe her, most could not. For it's not necessarily the color of hair, how tall or how small she is, how much she weighs. It's a thousand different intangibles in one package. Our subconscious knows this ideal woman and will recognize her immediately, sometimes in direct contradiction to our conscious preference. I had had my fantasy woman tucked away, deep inside for many years and had begun to seriously doubt that I would ever meet her in the flesh. Until now. When I saw her, my inner self, my center, my core cried out yes, yes, yes - bells rang and whistles blew. My fantasy had materialized.

She was about 5-7, around one twenty pounds, not fashionably thin. I do not like that skinny, emaciated look that some think attractive. She was healthy looking, looked like she had been involved in sports for a long time, light brown hair, blue eyes, good legs, little makeup. She would probably be described as trim, athletic build in a brief description, but she was more than that, much more. She projected an air of independence, and a sense of ease in who she was. As if she had come to accept the world on its terms, instead of tilting at windmills. Centered, I think, is the new way of describing this kind of person and she was centered.

She had stopped walking and was sprawled on a park bench nearby. She had hiked her dress above her knees and had opened the top two buttons. I sidled closer and could not help staring. I was

117

mesmerized. I have no idea how long I stood there, how long I stared. Without moving, she spoke in a low tone so only I could hear.

"It's not nice to stare," she murmured and "you look kind of silly, too."

I mumbled something and slunk away, my mind a welter of conflicting emotions. I had found the woman of my dreams and because I had never really believed it would happen, I was dumbstruck, tongue-tied with no idea how I should proceed. I considered going back and engaging her in conversation but decided that I had looked stupid enough for one day. Yet, I felt that this woman could be something special in my life.

There's a force that lies dormant in every man -- and woman, and when conditions are right this force comes alive. It must do, maybe with choosing your mate, with moving on to the next stage of your life and settling down. My conditions were right, my force had come alive, and I wanted to do my part in choosing my mate and moving to that next stage. But she had given me no indication of attraction or interest, and it takes two to tango. I met her again, two days after. She was working for the same company, different department and had been transferred from Chicago, two weeks before. She nodded, said "hi" as we passed in the hallway, and I thought I detected a slight smile touching the corners of her mouth. It might have been a smile of contempt. I wondered how someone so beautiful might fall in love with me. Maybe I was overreacting. So, I donned my cool and distant persona and tried to let go. It was not going to happen, and I would not let myself dream.

Consciously or unconsciously, I was meeting her more often, in the cafeteria, elevator or passing in the hallways. She kidded me about staring at her in the park and I blushed appropriately. I was surprised that she had remembered. We'd go for lunch once in a while with a bunch of others. Because I had banished any idea of a relationship with her from my mind, I relaxed and enjoyed her company. then one day, out of the blue, she asked me why I had never asked her out. So, I asked her out and weeks later, she told me that she loved me.

Without thinking and with my defenses down, I said "'' I've loved you from the moment I first set eyes on you."

We had weeks of such perfect happiness. We went everywhere and did everything together. We strolled on hidden beaches, took bicycle rides through the surrounding hills and valleys. We would pack a lunch and when the fancy took us or when we came to a particularly beautiful spot, we would stop and picnic there. We seemed to be able to talk on any subject for hours and it was amazing how alike we thought on so many subjects. It was a case of compatible rather than opposite attracting. We liked a lot of the same things, too. We both liked the summer, beaches, long walks, Broadway shows, Ray Charles, 100% cotton and casual dress.

There's a tree in Woodstock, near Max Yasgur's farm. We had taken a ride up there to see the site of the Woodstock festival. On the tree it says, 'Jo and Joe 4ever.' Josephine was my love's name, and I called her Jo. She carved it. I watched her that day, how she moved, long legs, hair catching the rays of the sun reflecting different colors. There at the end of a perfect summer's day, when I knew we were both ready, it was time and this was the perfect place, I laid her down under that great old oak tree and we made love, each to the other.

I had thought about this moment, when it would come, and I imagined myself nervous and unsure. But it was so natural, so good, both of us knowing this was the right time, the right place and it was as if we had done it a thousand times before. We lay in each other's arms and watched the golden orb of the sun sink slowly in the multi-colored sky and wished this day would last forever. I thought I'm the luckiest man on the face of God's green earth. I thought that I would never be happier than I was that day, that this must be how heaven felt.

And in spite of this great feeling of happiness in both our cases, a distant voice inside my head began to be heard and repeat - Is it too good to last? Over the next weeks and months, the voice kept getting louder and louder. The voice said she'll see through you, find out who you really are, how imperfect and unsure you are, how fearful and indecisive you can be. I felt somehow guilty that I had all this happiness.

I met my friend Mike for a few beers and laid out the whole scenario for him.

He told me "I hope it lasts but it ain't gonna last. When it's extremely intense like this, it burns out quickly. Believe me, I been there. Enjoy it while it lasts, walk away when it's over and don't look back." I asked him "What makes you such an expert on love and relationships?" and he turned to me with an exasperated look on his face and said, "When it's over, call me and you can cry on my shoulder, okay?"

"Some goddamn friend," I told him, and he said, "I'm being your friend by telling you what I told you." I tried to dismiss his words from my mind, but they kept coming back at odd moments. Inevitably, his words and my own feelings of doubt and fear began to affect the relationship.

Jo didn't seem to pick up on my mood swings at first but as my frame of mind became more somber and my silences longer, she could not help but notice. She asked me what if anything was the matter and I kept telling her that nothing was the matter. How could I tell her that I feared losing her, that there were times when I thought that I was unworthy of her. She begged me to talk to her, but I wouldn't or couldn't and I began to berate her for harping on it. That was the beginning of the end. I began to find fault with her and with the relationship. I tried to minimize her virtues and magnify her faults. On one level, I could not believe what I was doing. It was like one part of me watching the other set out to destroy what we had between us. But I was just doing it before she would. She would eventually want out. Wouldn't she?

I stopped off for a drink one evening and forgot about our date, got the dates mixed up. When she found me in the bar draped over some nobody whose name I didn't even know, I knew it was all over. She stood there as if frozen, about five, six feet away, and the look in her eyes and on her face, I will never forget. It will be forever seared into my brain. My God, how could I have done this to her?

I knew at that moment, that she loved me unequivocally and had from the beginning. I felt too ashamed over the next few days to try and get in touch with her. When I did, she was gone. She'd left her job and her apartment was empty. Her friends avoided me, would give me no information on where she was, what her plans were – but it was obvious she had warned them. She didn't want to know me or be in touch with me for a very long time, if ever.

I think about her constantly, curse myself for being such a fool, so timid, so wrapped up in my own inadequacies. I pray that she'll somehow return to me, that there's a merciful God somewhere who will give an idiot like me a second chance. If I get a second chance, I will open my heart to her and reveal my deepest feelings, and how empty my life has been without her. I will beg her forgiveness for my terrible past behavior and pledge my love forever. I will plead with her, please, please just give me one more chance.

Lizzie Molloy

We all loved Lizzie, all eight of us. We were all on or about fourteen years old and we were all obsessed with the mystery of women and under fierce attack by biological urges and raging hormones. We were all, also, very aware of the shame attached to masturbation and all things sexual as dictated by the Church. We were a sorry bunch. We were lost in a world all to do with women. We had no interest in games or sports or any kind of physical exercise. Our bodies were calling out for a different physical exercise, wet dreams and sexual touching. We ached to touch - skin, lips, breasts, arse and that mysterious region beyond the thicket of dark hair that guarded its entrance. That was the ultimate touching.

And why wouldn't we love Lizzie. She was a woman in every which way to our concept of woman, experienced, tantalizing, sexual – like forbidden fruit and confident in her womanhood. She was as different as night and day to the girls of our age. They giggled and blushed and ran away at even the thought of our approach. She was broad of hip and solid of breast, fine strong legs and a way of walking that made us uneasy. She wore large, hooped silver earrings to set off dark, unruly hair that hung below her shoulders. She wore revealing sweaters, the top two buttons always undone, ankle-length skirts that somehow seemed to promise more than skirts tight and knee-high. The undone buttons showed the beginning sloping's of healthy brown breasts and everything she wore seemed made just for her.

We hung out in front of Burkie's house. Their wall was low and wide and comfortable to sit on. Mrs Burke didn't seem to mind us being there, or said nothing, unlike most every house in the village. They guarded their front walls like they had money stuffed there, or the family jewels. It was as if they lost ownership of the wall, their world would collapse. It helped too that Burkie was in our gang, was one of us. But she said nothing anyway. The real reason we were there was that all of Murphy Place passed there on the way to the shops and town – and Lizzie lived in Murphy Place. She passed by there, three or four times a day – that was before they returned to England, where they had been before the Glue factory job took them home.

We'd watch her coming out her gate up at the top of the street and were instantly on the alert, all eyes riveted on that swaying, rhythmic figure that proceeded slowly, pleasurably towards us. I wondered then if she knew. After, I realized she must have. Women know these things. Some have what turns men's heads by right of birth. Lizzie had it in abundance. We shifted and muttered to each other as she approached, each in our own exquisite tableau of 'Lizzie and me.'

"What are ye doing, hanging out by the oul' wall every day? Aren't ye bored to death?" she inquired.

"Not at all, Lizzie, there's a great burst of sun here, a sun trap," Burkie told her, and Jeff asked, "How are you getting on yourself?"

"Ach, I'm all right, what's the good of complaining." And she laughed that laugh of hers, rough and full-throated.

Once she hiked herself up on the wall, the rare short skirt she wore riding up, showing fine legs and shapely ankles. We sighed and exhaled, slowly and audibly.

"Nothing right now" Micko said, "the oul' town is dead."

"'Tis a shame we can't get another factory. 'Twould make a great difference. Sure, wouldn't it benefit the shopkeepers and everything – a bit more money circulating."

There had been rumors, whispers about Lizzie, that she entertained a visit or two from young men when Mike had returned to England - the Glue factory had lasted only two years. Such and such got the ride, it was said or such and such was seen leaving in the early hours of the morning - but such and such never admitted to anything. The rumors remained rumors. But there was something about Lizzie, the way she looked at us, the way her eyes squinted that hinted at invitation, challenge. We felt it and were aroused by it but ignorant in the ways of seduction or courtship, were helpless to act on it. Yet we were tantalized by the idea of sex with an older and more experienced woman. Wasn't that every boy's secret wish, dream, fantasy - someone to take his hand, someone who knew how and what and where, who would guide him in his first faltering steps to full, carnal knowledge?

But if the others were taken by Lizzie, I was in love. She came to me each night and tormented me, and I woke, moist and trembling.

The more exotic my dreams became, the more rigid a demeanor I maintained to my friends. I was petrified that my secret would be exposed, and I would be ridiculed. I spent hours outside Burkie's, much of it on my own, waiting for a glimpse of her and when she came, I barely acknowledged her passing. As she cut down the railway tracks, I wanted to run after her, confront her and declare my love. But what would I say? Where would I find the proper words? Where would I find the fortitude? I visualized standing there, mouth dry and heart pounding, chest heaving and wild-eyed as croaking, unintelligible sounds issued forth. She would look on me with pity, shake her head and continue on her way. If only I could still my beating heart, tell her how I felt, how I dreamed of her every night, then maybe, maybe…. At least I'd have some relief, be unburdened, and whatever would happen, would happen.

I kept my lonely vigil to the mystification of my friends as they came and went.

"Do you want to go to town? What's the use of hanging around here, there's nobody around?" But there was and I wanted to mark her passage.

Then – one night as I maintained my unhappy vigil, one wet and miserable night, all the cares of the world seemed to weigh on my shoulders. School had started up again. My mother was unhappy with my progress. My father would be notified if…She warned me I'd have to do better. I was lazy and had developed bad habits. I did little around the house to help my father. The fact she was right didn't make it easier. I didn't like school; didn't like this place I lived in and mostly didn't like myself.

There was no sign of Lizzie and I thought she was in for the night, as miserable as it was. She wouldn't stir out this night. I was ready to turn in, bringing another dismal day in this dismal time of my life to an end. As I turned to go, there was Lizzie coming out of the railway cut, carrying two shopping bags and soaked. Without thinking, before paralysis set in, I went over and took the bags, and we walked up the road together. We exchanged no words. For once, it seemed, the weather had overcome her natural exuberance. I sat down in her kitchen as she put on the kettle, excused herself and went to change her wet clothes. I had pulled off my raincoat and cap and was drying myself by the fire when she came back out in addressing gown, drying her hair with a towel.

"God, an awful night, depressing," and I replied that it was terrible.

"You'll stay till you dry out; we'll have a cup of tea." I nodded in assent. I watched her as she bent over the stove, barefoot, and I fantasized being married to her and spending every day and night with her, watching her going about her business, laughing, bending, stretching.

She turned and started to say something and stopped. Something about the way I was staring at her held her attention. Years after, I thought, my need, yearning must have been as obvious to her as if I gone down on bended knee and pleaded with her to take me out of my misery.

She laid out the tea, slices of bread and butter and jam and we ate. She was quiet, not talking, and I stayed quiet. I was conscious of every movement she made, and I sensed a turbulence in her. She asked me how old I was, and I told her I was seventeen – a lie. She said she was often lonely in the house with Mike on the buildings in England. And then she said, "We'll go to bed." It was said quietly, not a question but a declaration. I nodded and I remember saying her name. She touched my face and smiled.

I had my first initiation, step by careful step. She was all I had fantasized and more. She was kind and considerate and passionate – and skilled. My mind opened and my heart expanded, and my body picked up the rhythm. All the images that had tormented me on so many nights were bleached away into nothingness. Her skin was smooth as rabbit fur, her hair was like wind-blown grass, her shape was firm, muscled in places, deceptively strong. I thought this is how it should be for everyone, the first time.

When I left her bed, she cautioned me this would be the one and only time, our secret - and I nodded and promised yes. And it was. We said hello and smiled at each other. I never approached her, and she never invited. I kept that promise for truth be told, I wanted it for me and me only, savoring it for a long time after.

Things got better after. I was easier with the women my age. My grades improved. I helped my mother more. Once, even, I put my arms round my father and hugged him and he didn't know what to do but after, we got on better. Soon after, Lizzie left for England and never came back. I never saw her again. Now I'm married to a good woman and happy, I think. We have three children. I kept Lizzie my secret. She'd be old now and I wonder, maybe, I wouldn't want to see her old. But for me, always, she'll be that fine woman with skin as smooth as rabbit fur and hair like wind-blown meadow grass.

Inevitability

Mesmerizing is how I would describe
Falling unequivocally under your spell
But retrospectively, how could it be
Otherwise – I will explain.

A vision of the one for me
Was in my head, how she would be
As time marched on irretrievably
And then and then, she stood before me.

How could I not fall hopelessly in love
She was my Mona Lisa come to life
Unerring image, dominant in dreams
The stars aligned; the God of Love loved me.

I wallowed in, drank copiously of this brew
My self-esteem gained stratospheric heights
My goddess strode imperiously by my side
Was it not as it should be – my due?

Grandiloquent endeavors filled my brain
I was God-like, and she was by my side

Imperiously I viewed all with disdain
Then she was gone – despair unending void.

Dejected, downcast, mewling here I sit
Digesting, disassembling all that passed
And feeling sorry for myself, I do admit
Love pressed me to its bosom then out cast.

World's Oldest Divorcees

Have you read the story in the papers recently about the world's oldest divorcees, a 99-year-old man, Antonio divorcing his 96-year-old wife, Rosa after he found out she had had an affair in the 1940's? The Italian man, Antonio was going through an old chest of drawers a few days before Christmas 2011, when he discovered letters, she had written to her lover over seventy years ago.

He could not, would not forgive her and said he would file for a divorce. She confessed everything but was unable to persuade her husband to reconsider his decision. They have five children, twelve grandchildren and one great grandchild. They're now splitting after nearly eight decades – seventy-seven years married. Of course, we don't know all the circumstances of their relationship. People change over time. Maybe he was looking for an excuse. Maybe he had his eye on an eighty-eight-year-old down the block who had been giving <u>him</u> the eye, a widow who was being very friendly and who had kept herself slim and trim and he imagined, full of vim!

Maybe they had a fight. Maybe she was feeling lonely, put upon. But she wants to stay in the marriage, he doesn't. She could make some concessions. Ok, it was her indiscretion that precipitated the breakup. Maybe now she needs to make the first move but, it was, seventy years ago.

So how did this indiscretion come about? A possible scenario:

She had asked for a floor mop with a long handle so she could mop the floor standing up. He said "No, mop the floor on your knees like my mamma always did, still do."

She said "But Antonio…" He said "No buts, you a woman, you mop floor." Then for good measure he kick her up a the behind. Then he leaves to meet his men friends in the piazza and drink wine.

So, she's feeling sorry for herself as she sits dejected on the floor rubbing her sore behind and it's just at that moment the postman Giovanni walks in with the post. When he sees her on the ground, he exclaims loudly and kneels to comfort her. When she explains through a flood of tears what happened he is indignant, outraged.

"No man should strike the woman he professes to love."

He asks to see where her husband kicked her. He lifts her summer shift and gently slides down her knickers. When he sees the red and bruised area, he is even more outraged. He asks her permission to massage the damaged bruised area. He lovingly applies salve. He shakes his head at the cruelty some men visit on their loved ones.

She asks, shyly "Are all men as uncaring as my husband?"

He emphatically shakes his head and cries 'No, no, there are many men - like me – who value women for all their outstanding qualities, their beauty and ability to complete a man's life."

She gazes up at him in open admiration. He gestures towards the bedroom, and she shyly nods her head. He offers his arm as they slowly make their way from the main room to the one bedroom in the house. He asks if she'd rather be on top, considering her bruised buttocks. She murmurs, yes. She assures him her husband will be late. He has gone to the piazza and will drink wine until the café closes. They make tender and satisfying love, unlike her husband's, which was neither tender nor satisfying. She has her first orgasm, which solidifies the affair. It continues for many months until Giovanni is promoted and transferred to the main post office in Palermo. What woman, in that time and place, expected tender and satisfying. Thus, the affair began all those years ago.

Hard Times

He was riding on my shoulder, He was nipping at my heels
And no mind how I maneuvered, I just couldn't get him peeled
And I worked all of the hours, that the Man would give to me
But it didn't seem to matter, I was stuck in poverty

Yeah, I fought him to a standstill, And I ain't no weak-a-ling
But he matched me blow for blow, at the end was standing – still
Was close to capitulating, tellin' Hard Times he's the man
Then I looked at wife and daughters, and
their look said yes, you can

And a fierce determination, overtook me there and then
So, I doubled up my efforts, did the work of two strong men
And Hard Times, he shook a little and I knew I had a chance
And I vowed to God in heaven, Hard
Times wouldn't make me dance

Not long after, turned the corner, and he faded out of view
And the future, once so dreary, was a future all brand new.

Hard Times 2

He was always our companion, as we stumbled on our way
Choleric breathing close beside us, other times seemed held at bay
Claiming kinship most intimate, like the blinking of an eye
Dank and drab and cold and clammy,
stretched beside us thigh to thigh.

Time and time I heard my mother, with a mumble and a sigh
God and His Blessed Mother, will he ever pass us by
God Almighty, give us respite, for a little while at least
And it seemed her plea was answered, he retreated, heartless beast

Then one long and brutal winter, seemed like he was everywhere
He harassed and hurt and hindered, till we turned again to prayer
And we cried to God almighty, give us succor from this load
But He clearly was distracted, for He paid no heed at all.

Hard Times cracked the whip and rode
us, like the cotton fields of old
And we sang to ease the burden, like the
slaves, them bought and sold
And they say that there is a Heaven, and they say that there is a Hell
We been stuck down in the bad one, first we stumbled, then we fell

So, we keep on keepin' goin,' till we just can't go no more
And one day, we'll stop movin', and the nightmare will be o'er
Though faith in God diminishes, as He slowly fades from view
Still a tiny flame still burns, still despite this hellish brew.

The '56 Chevy

They were pathetic, all four of them. They never did anything original or fresh. They avoided sports – or maybe sports avoided them. They had tryouts but failed miserably so lied to each other that 'sports suck.' They went to the Palace for the double feature on Saturdays, laughed too loud and made a show of themselves. They participated as little as possible in school activities, spent hours on the stoop, lethargic, dazed. Next morning, they stumbled out of bed and started all over again.

Mikey was almost eighteen, lanky, not bad looking with wild, black hair and a lazy dresser. A senior in High School, he hadn't dated in six months, and he was worried.

Danny was lanky too, uncoordinated with self-esteem issues. Years later, he found God and became a reasonably successful motivational speaker with a beautiful blonde wife and two gorgeous kids.

Ralphie, deemed the most unlikely to succeed, was small and neat and shy and would go on to be a millionaire with a string of delis strategically placed on busy corners.

Johnny was good-looking but a dreamer. He was going to be an actor, or an airplane pilot, maybe a screenwriter and possibly a businessman. He was mulling over what businesses. He ended up his days a bartender at the local watering hole, silent and introspective.

There was a time when they were younger, when they had ambitions and did things that bonded them – like smoking, petty theft, finding and perusing dirty magazines and righting wrongs visited on them by other gangs from adjacent neighborhoods. Once they had flattened all four tires of Georgie Tynan's Belair. He went around the neighborhood smacking kids and dealing marijuana. He fancied himself a big shot until he got plonked in the face with a baseball – and screamed like a baby, thereby destroying any credibility he might have had. He had pushed them around and they had flattened his tires. It had done more to bring them together that summer and they were close, real close for a while.

Mikey slumped in the back of Danny's Datsun as they rode down South Broadway in Yonkers, the Datsun – Danny's pride and joy - rattling and wheezing. The exhaust, a mixture of grey and black was a perfect match to their mood.

Mikey spoke, resignation edging his voice, "Our youth is slipping away." Danny had heard it all before.

"We do nothing, go nowhere. We don't date. We don't party. What's wrong with us?"

"Listen, our time will come, Mikey, I'm telling you. Hey, check that ass out."

He considered not looking but force of habit prevailed. Yeah, the ass was nice, but she was overdoing it, slinging it all over the place. He turned away but something caught his eye. In a used car lot, a 1956 Chevy Belair, looking like it had just rolled off the assembly line, sat glistening in the sunlight – a beautiful combination of chrome and red paint. This was what he needed to achieve all he craved – power, confidence, girls, and good times.

"Pull up," he instructed Danny, and his friend, uncharacteristically, immediately pulled to the side.

"What's goin' on, Mikey?"

He was already halfway to the lot, drawn to that lethal combination of color, chrome, hood ornamentation and leather. It sat there, outshining all the others and years after, he swore he heard it whisper, "Buy me, buy me, and I'll change your life."

The first faint stirrings of possibilities were lapping at the edges of his mind, feelings like he hadn't felt in a long time, a sense of urgency, overwhelming desire. He must acquire this Chevy Belair ASAP and all else would fall into place. A new life would begin, a life of endless promise, of exciting times and of growing and maturing into the person he always felt he could be. He put his plan into action, hunting down every possible source of cash, driven by that vision sitting in the lot on South Broadway.

He went to see his Uncle Larry in Bronxville, a stockbroker on Wall Street, the shining star of his extended family, and his Godfather. He earnestly related to him his success in school, how he would be graduating in June, that he had seen this wonderful car that he wanted so badly, so if he could have his gift a little early, he would appreciate it so much and never forget it, ever.

His uncle arched his eyebrows and stared incredulously at him but impressed by his naked resolve or remembering <u>his</u> first car, wrote out there and then a check for $150. His parents, overwhelmed and impressed by his fervor ponied up and two weeks later, Mikey walked into the lot and bought it.

The car lived up to its promise. *Buy me and I will change your life.* Picking up girls got easy and easier. His life was turned around. Now there were girls everywhere, he was in demand, the bad old days were gone. The car was an attraction, he had to admit but he was convinced his change of attitude had a lot to do with it. It was his negative attitude, their negative attitudes that had isolated them. Problem was, Danny, Johnny and Ralph still had that bad attitude. They were still stuck in a rut. He had talked to them, earnestly, seriously detailing why their lives hadn't turned around, why his had – and it wasn't just the car - but they were baffled, impenetrable. What was a fellow to do?

He drove out to Jones Beach on the Long Island Expressway, top down, radio blaring, arm 'round Angie, his latest, the wind blowing through their hair while she gazed adoringly at him. He watched his friends exit the bus at Orchard Beach, while he parked and exited with Carol Anne, a brunette with athletic build and great legs. He blew past Danny, Johnny and Ralphie with a casual wave and a long toot on the horn, Margie giggling by his side. He even passed them on the stoop one evening with a "How y'all doin,' fellas? Gotta go."

He noted their looks of bewilderment, but he just didn't have time to chat. He knew he was neglecting them, that Danny's Datsun was no more, a victim of escalating costs and old age, that maybe he was treating them shabbily, that he should be staying in touch, but he loved his new life. He didn't want to look back or go back or want anything to do with how things had been. He had been deprived for too long. The past was too recent, too fresh and too painful. He had broken from the pack – and the past - and he wasn't going back any time soon.

Danny came by late one evening as he sat on the stoop outside his apartment. "What's goin' on, Mikey?"

"Hey, Danny, where you been, I haven't seen you in a while?"

Danny, puzzled, looked at him. "Are you kidding me, where have I been? Where have you been? I been here but you're never nowhere no more."

"I been busy, school, girls..."

His friend looked at the ground, hands deep in pockets and without looking up, said "We used to be close, Mikey, pals, close pals. What happened, what went wrong?"

"Nothin', nothin's wrong, Danny," he said, defensive "we're still pals. But I don't wanna hang around and do nothing and be bored, no more."

"Whaddaya mean", Danny said. "Are you saying it was boring hangin' around with me and Ralphie and Johnny? "Is that what you're saying?"

"Mostly yeah. You only got one shot at it, Danny. We're only eighteen once. You gotta live. That's what I've been tryin' to tell you. That's all I'm tryin' to do."

"So, you're livin' and we're dyin'."

"Tell me, Danny, when's the last time you've bin with a girl?"

"None of your Goddamn business." Mikey got up and stretched.

"Case closed, Danny. I rest my case."

He had changed. He dressed sharper now and he was dating some fine chicks. He had picked up a nice little job - down at the pool hall on Saturdays, where some heavy hitters hung out and tips were good. Frankie the Felon had taken a real liking to him and used him as his runner all day.

"Mikey, run out and pick me up a couple of cheeseburgers, double order of fries, heavy on the catsup."

"Mikey, how about a couple of milkshakes?"

"Mikey, you wanna go to the Donut shop for me?" Frankie, it seemed, ate constantly - but he always tipped, and he had taken a shine to Mikey.

"Mikey, you're all right. You're a good boy, you know that. You do what you're told, and you never give me an argument. You take care of me, and I take care of you, capiche?"

His grades were falling, but he was eighteen, money in his pockets and he deserved to have a little fun. He never wanted to be out of the action again, like - he had to say it, Danny, Ralphie and Johnnie.

He had a new girl, Diane, and she was a knockout. She was two years older than he, had got some kind of an equivalency diploma and had a job. On their first date, she told him she was a Package Expediting Specialist, which sounded impressive, but later he found out she sorted packages at the U.P.S. company. She was a party girl, and he was in party mood, and all should have been right with the world but... Reality was rearing its ugly head and - there was a problem. His grades were sliding. His teachers were circling.

"Your grades have deteriorated to the point where we are very concerned. You're a bright boy, Michael, consistently in the top one third of the class. Now you're getting C's and C minuses. Is there something going on in your life that we should know about?"

He hated when they called him Michael and yeah, there was something going on in his life. He was having fun and he wasn't going back. Sometimes he looked at his convertible and imagined an air of arrogance about it. He wondered if some of it had rubbed off. His attitude <u>had</u> changed, dramatically. When he got his first speeding ticket, he laughed as he took it from the officer.

"How's your day been, officer?" he had inquired breezily, and the officer, suddenly hostile, put his face up close to his and fixed him with a hostile stare.

"Son, I can't say I like your attitude much and I would advise you to not say another word, or you'll have tickets coming out your skinny little butt. Do I make myself clear? Just nod your head if you agree with me?" He had a reply ready in his head.

"A little grumpy today, Officer? Momma's not treating you well. I'm not your son 'cause <u>my</u> Momma was always a one-man woman and that's my Daddy. Your job, Officer is all about communication, communication, communication and you are failing miserably."

But he didn't. He gave him a big, shit-eating grin and nodded energetically. The cop stared suspiciously, turned abruptly and left. Miserable poor bastard, he thought, probably hates his job. When he was in his Chevy, he was brand new and fancy free. Away from it he tended to revert. But he didn't want to revert.

"Diane, how do you feel about me, me sans the car, the good times?" he had asked her in a rare moment of introspection. She looked at him blankly.

"I mean without the car, if we couldn't afford to go out as much, if I didn't have money? Would you still want to be with me?"

She laughed throatily. "Mikey, you think I want you just for your car." She leaned closer to him, her left breast brushing his arm. "I want you baby, just you," she whispered, low and husky-voiced, "but I like goin' places and doin' things with you. We have so much fun together."

It was the wrong answer; not that she would have known. She was what she was, sexy and not too complicated. She had decided somewhere way back to dress, talk and act sexy. It was her best shot at getting somewhere in life and she was good at it. When he watched her enter or exit the Chevy, he could only stare in unrestrained admiration. She had more moves than a snake, a very limber snake. Men ended up in jail for women like her. He thought about dropping out of school, getting a job, gettin' a place and movin' in with Diane.

But he was having too good a time. Such a good time that he had already used up more than a hundred of his thousand-dollar stash, which was earmarked exclusively for college expenses. If his parents found out, they'd have a shit fit.

He pulled up in front of Diane's apartment house and beeped. He had stopped going up to the apartment after the first date because frankly what he saw depressed him. Her father was foreign-born; he wasn't sure where, one of those Soviet republics maybe, Albania or Yugoslavia maybe, or Romania, and had eyed him suspiciously as he stood nervously inside the door. The father slumped in an armchair, with a tray of food in front of him and the television blaring. He grunted something unintelligible when Diane introduced him. He was large, overweight and beetle-browed. That one so ugly could produce something so beautiful. Her mother was a shy gentle woman who smiled and bobbed her head at Mikey and then disappeared. The apartment was a study in bad taste; yellow shag rug, yellow bulb hanging down naked, Formica furniture, sagging couch and peeling paint.

"Done anything with the apartment?" he inquired as she slid in next to him. God, she was beautiful. She was wearing a yellow turtleneck sweater, tight, black, silk mini-dress, black nylons and black high heeled shoes. Her blonde hair was piled on top of her head and held there in some ingenious arrangement that was a total mystery to him.

"Nah, that's the way they like it. They haven't spent a dime on that apartment in twenty-five years. They're saving, that's what they tell me when I ask. I think the old man has some idea of returning to the old country when he retires. Look, if it makes them happy... I'll be outta there in another six months. So, how you doin'?"

He was doin' fine. As soon as he got behind the wheel of that Chevy, he was doing fine. He made a fast U-turn and headed out for Throgs Neck. There was a new club out there they heard was hot and they were going to check it out. He was feeling it tonight. The car was purring, and the slightest touch of the accelerator sent it leaping forward. His baby was lookin' dyno-mite and he had to confess, as he checked himself in the mirror, he was no slouch either. Life was good.

They were cruising along in the middle lane of the Cross Bronx Expressway when suddenly a black Firebird pulled alongside of them. Four mean-looking punks looked over and eye-balled the Chevy. He knew exactly what was going down. The Firebird was challenging, and he knew his baby wasn't backing down. Suddenly, both cars surged forward, and the race was on. He felt powerful, confident. This was what it was all about, he thought, as he skillfully guided his baby through the traffic, jumping from lane to lane, the Firebird in hot pursuit. He glanced at Diane, and he realized she was turned on by the whole experience. She moved closer and her soft curves caressed him as the car swayed. The Firebird began to inch up and was less than a car length back.

Suddenly a hole opened and both cars surged forward. The race had come down to this. Whoever hit the hole first, would win. He floored the Chevy, the Firebird hesitated for an instant and he was gone. The hole closed as quickly as it opened. The Firebird, forced to slam on its brakes, lost control, hit the curb, balanced delicately for an instant and flipped over. It landed upright, slammed into an abutment and came to a halt, windshield shattered and badly damaged. He quickly pulled to the side and ran back. He glimpsed a young mother clutching a tiny baby with a look of absolute terror on her face. He reached the Firebird. Four scared kids stared out at him. Had they really seemed so menacing, minutes before? When he looked at that terror-stricken mother with her baby, then thought that one of those kids might not have walked away, he began to shake violently, and fell to his knees on the graveled ground.

"Mikey, Mikey, where are you, honey?"

He lifted his head as she raced up, bubbling over with excitement and adrenalin. "Honey, wow, you were unbelievable. You made shit of those punks."

He rose to his feet and walked slowly back. If for once the car seemed subdued, Diane

"That was so fun, baby. I was so proud of you. You were like some gladiator killing off the bad guys."

She was all over him, stroking and petting, and it seemed the whole episode had charged her sexually. But it had changed him in as yet, some indefinable way. He dropped her off outside her apartment and for the first time she sensed something.

"You aw' right?" He nodded slowly and looked away.

"Okay, call me," she said as she slid off the seat and headed up the street. She glanced back and waved, and he was struck again by her beauty. He thought of calling her back, then drove away, slow and careful. Two days later he took the car back to the same dealer he had bought it from, what seemed like a lifetime ago. He handed in the keys and accepted the first offer that was made.

Weeks later, as he was walking back from school and feeling kinda low, a car passed. It was a top-down Caprice convertible, a hard-looking guy driving, with black, slicked back hair and a white shirt with turned up collar. He was smiling at a blonde sitting close by his side. The blonde was wearing a yellow turtleneck. She was sitting close, real close and her breast was brushing his arm. Her hair was piled high on top of her head in some ingenious arrangement that was a total mystery to him.

Good Parent

Parents, nowadays, are confronted with such a bewildering array of information and advice on bringing up children and being a good parent that it is inevitable that confusion sets in. The latest bestseller trumpets a breakthrough, sure fire method of dealing firmly and fairly with all the problems of parenthood. This advice may range from tough love for children to parental authority so diluted that we might refer to it as non-authority. I, with the invaluable assistance of my wife, having raised four children whose ages range from eighteen to twenty-nine, all of whom are good and productive citizens of this great country, feel that maybe I have something to contribute to this discussion.

My experience has been that there are no hard and fast rules in being an effective parent. Each child is different and unique, and an approach that works for one may not work for the other. I do not believe that there is a one hundred percent, can't-miss method in existence and there never will be. As stated, each child is different. As the tailor must adjust his cloth to the fit, so the parent must adjust his methods to the child. Having said that, there are certain essential ingredients that must be present in a successful parent-child relationship. The primary one is love. The child must be loved and whether by word or deed must know that he or she is loved. And love does not necessarily mean that the child is showered with material things. Sometimes it means the opposite. If this love is in place, then there's a good chance that other issues can be worked out. You may feel anger, frustration, and irritation at various times with your child's behavior and vice versa. This is normal and need not trigger feelings of guilt. It is important to talk about the cause or causes of friction, listen to the child's side, and state your position clearly. After stating your position, you must hold to your position, as children do not respect equivocation.

The next essential ingredient is discipline. Children need discipline, whatever form it may take, and order in their lives, though they may rail against both. They need to know that you love them enough to make unpopular decisions, decisions that may not be met with easy acceptance. I have a problem with parents trying to be a buddy to their children. Children don't need their parents as buddies, but as protectors who love them, make them feel safe and let them know when they're out of line.

I recently read a letter written by a teenager whose mother was so involved in her daughter's life that she picked out what her daughter would wear before a date and waited up for her return so that she could find out everything that had happened on the date on a blow-by-blow basis. The daughter felt strangled by her mother's need to be involved in every detail of her daughter's life and was beginning to feel angry and depressed. Children need their privacy, and there has to be an element of trust between both. So, another important element is trust.

You cannot live your child's life. He or she must make mistakes as you have and learn from them. As the world is perceived as increasingly more dangerous, there is a tendency to try and micromanage a child's life. Don't talk to strangers, don't leave the group, the mother constantly admonishes the child, and sometimes the child's life becomes filled with fear and distrust. It is right that a child is warned of possible dangers, but trust is the glue of civilization and if it breaks down then civilization is doomed. We trust the policeman to patrol our streets, the garbageman to pick up our garbage and the fire department to come if our house is on fire. We must trust each other and our human instincts, helping the less fortunate, looking out for each other's welfare, looking out for our neighbor's children, and reacting if we see a crime in progress.

There is one other essential ingredient and that is the ability to laugh and see the funny side of things. Life is not all about being serious. A sense of humor is imperative if we are to survive reasonably intact. This trait can be passed on easily from parent to child and is invaluable in countering the pressures of our modern world.

Do these four elements guarantee a successful parent/child relationship and the title of 'good parent'? No, for there are no guarantees in this life. But if they are present then there is an excellent chance for both. These four elements, with some luck and many prayers will, in most cases, be enough.

End Out of Sight

I stagger on, end out of sight, not knowing where it leads

Or what I'll be, when I get there.

But I said, finally, I must pursue it.

When I read: What a person really needs in life,

Is struggling for a goal that is worthy of him,

That each man knows in his heart, what his assignment is.

Frankl's words set off a light in my brain,

Made crystal clear, what I had and had not done.

I had run away, circled and avoided, lied and cheated

And made believe, I need no more.

While, deep down, I was not pursuing, what I really wanted.

If I fail, at what I really want, I will fall so long, and so hard,

That I will never recover. So, I tackled lesser things,

Persuading me, it matters not.

So, have fun, don't push, all comes to those who sit.

I sit, dissatisfied, empty husk, hollow,

I smile, converse, exist. I am nothing, going nowhere.

But now, fire in my eye

Tho' anxiety's icy fingers clutching at my innards,

I set my sights, chest out and firm of step,

Not knowing where it leads, or who I'll be, when I get there.

Life All Day

She sipped her coffee and faced the long morning. The house, remnant of another era, with too many windows, corners and small spaces, echoed with its emptiness, her loneliness - a house too big for two people, even more so two who led separate lives.

Who was she? She was Grace Cahill, wife of Dr. George Cahill, both respected citizens of the small community of Glenbeg, a village overlooking the Atlantic perched on the Southeast coast of Ireland. She was childless, too, had lost two children in difficult pregnancies. It was like a dream now, long, long ago and she rarely thought about it. She was forty-eight now and even to her critical eye, looked younger. If she wasn't beautiful now, she had been, many years before. But she was, still, well, arresting, skin good, hair the color of wheat, the color needing minimal upkeep, and legs, well maybe her best feature, long and well-toned, the legs of a walker. Yes, she was still trim, and ate sparingly but well and proper.

She knew all about nutrition, that's what she had studied, that's what she had been, a nutritionist at the regional hospital, where she had met George and what? Fallen in love? She never remembered *falling* in love. She liked him, at times quite a lot – other times found him incredibly boring. She was of middle-class background, her mother a teacher, her father - retired and now deceased - a salesman for a printing company. She had loved her father, his energy and drive. But he was also, the gentlest man she had ever known and missed him, achingly. Her mother was now on the verge of retirement and had moved to Dublin to be near her daughter, Grace's sister, Mena. Her mother had always been distant, and more so when she entered widowhood.

She had one other sister, Greta, the youngest, who was in Africa – she thought Uganda - who worked with an international aid agency and whom she hadn't seen in more than five years.

Then there was her brother Tom, who was studying finance and working in New York. She had been close with her siblings. They had all been distant from their mother who considered affection or its display unseemly, a useless emotion and who spent her time reading voraciously. Grace's enduring image of her was of being engrossed in a book, sitting upright, straight-backed, spectacles perched at nose end.

She had no memory of being held in her mother's arms, nose wiped, or tears dried. They pecked each other when she left for university and then, later, for marriage. She thought the emptiness she felt years later had begun then from the lack of touching, intimacy between daughter and child. Her sisters hadn't seemed to be as affected as she – or hid it better.

She considered what else she was – or wasn't. She had never been in love – or at least felt the kind of all-encompassing emotion her fellow-students had proudly boasted of. There had been Michael Porter, whom she had dated for a year in Trinity. But they had broken up and she could not remember being devastated or even regretful; especially when she had been more at fault for the breakup than he. She had cried hysterically when, a year later he died in a plane crash in India and was depressed for months after. But it was more to do with the impermanence of life - how slender the thread of life was – rather than the love they had had.

She had drifted into this marriage. George was available and he pursued her. She resisted appropriately and then accepted. She was an efficient hostess and a good cook. She was good-looking, appropriately educated. There was that word 'appropriate' again. He was dull, would never be considered handsome but he was a doctor, so had excellent prospects. She would have a comfortable lifestyle and more than sufficient finances for a lifetime. She dressed stylishly but spent only modest amounts on clothes. She liked accessories, brooches, pins and earrings, loved scarves and had a drawerful. In the beginning they entertained regularly but that time was gone. Then she had taken up golf, had been passionate about it for a time. That passion had evaporated. Now she drank too much. She and George were practically strangers, had sex infrequently but were civil and respectful to each other. Every morning George read the paper over breakfast, they made small talk, George brushed his teeth, kissed her goodbye, and departed. He had just left.

She wondered if George had ever enjoyed, really enjoyed sex. There was always something furtive about the way he approached it. It was done in darkness or near darkness. He would tentatively kiss. She would reach for and stroke his penis. She would discard her panties and he would climb on top. In later years, but early in their marriage she took the dominant role, rolled him over and rode him – not just out of frustration with his efforts, more so she could dictate events and achieve climax at least some of the time. She thought George might have been surprised, shocked even at her aggression but she felt she was entitled to at least that, and felt no shame for wanting it.

They were reasonably well off, took a two-week holiday on the continent every summer but she wondered, more and more as she got older, about the lives others her age lived in other countries around the globe, and couldn't help but think their lives were more interesting, challenging, fulfilling, stimulating. Her life was none of those. They attended golf club functions where the same individuals strutted, the same few drank too much, talked too loudly, and proclaimed what a great party it was, and what a marvelous time they were having. The same fools flirted with her, surreptitiously stroked, and danced too close. It was like a reel that repeated itself, function after function, year chasing year. Now here she sat in her big, tasteful house and the morning - and after, the evening – stretched endlessly before her.

She considered having an affair but with whom, and was it worth the trouble? Anything happening in this small community was public knowledge sooner or later – and she was fond of George and didn't want to cause him embarrassment. Still… It just seemed too much trouble with no guaranteed results. What were the odds of meeting someone discreet, who would be an exceptional lover? She didn't want average – she had that already – or even good. She wanted someone who would love what she did to him and who would, in turn, bring her to a slow, steadily-building, totally satisfying orgasm. She wondered if such an animal existed.

She sipped on her first vodka of the day – vodka and orange with a dash of soda water. That was her drink. She hadn't realized she had poured it. She had wanted to hold off till midday. Here it was just past ten and she had started. It had happened and she wouldn't berate herself. By the time midday rolled by, she was on her fourth and she knew she would have to exercise some discretion. George was home most evenings by six though sometimes he stopped for a drink after work, and it might be as late as seven thirty – never later. She knew that George knew she drank but he had never brought it up and she had never tried to explain it.

She wished sometimes that George would have an affair. It would release her somehow to become promiscuous and have a series of sexual adventures. She would inform him that she was taking vacation – on her own and more than one a year – in Morocco or Bali, someplace exotic-sounding and mysterious, where the sun was hot and the cocktails cool and she ran on the beach, topless. This is where she would meet the mysterious stranger who would slide into the seat next to her as she sat at the bar just inches from the beach, as she sipped on her vodka and orange with a dash of club, as the silken shawl draped carelessly round her shoulders billowed in the warm tropical breeze. He would look into her eyes, and she would know. He would take her hand, guide her to his room, lay her on the bed and make gentle, thrilling love to her. After they had both climaxed, she would climb on top and they would begin again, only this time slower, as the waves crashed outside the window and the wind rattled the shutters. She would rendezvous with him at regular intervals. He would be one of many.

She took her drink and climbed the stairs to her bedroom. A beginning rainstorm spattered against the windows. She undressed and lay naked under the covers. Eyes closed, she began to bring herself to orgasm as she rode that mysterious stranger, as the tropical rains increased in fury outside.

Pat O'Dwyer

Pat O' Dwyer was a small trim man, serene, untroubled, 52 years young and rarely seen without a tweed cap on his head, brim to the front and a pipe, often unlit, stuck in his mouth. He had fourteen of the finest children any man or woman could want, his face as unlined as a man half his age.

Pat O,' as he was known, worked in the shipping section, in the chocolate crumb department of the local creamery, known as the Co-op. Here he bagged and labeled the huge slabs of the dark, sweet substance that was shipped to England and the continent of Europe. He considered himself a small but important cog in the chain of events that produced what he always proclaimed was the best chocolate crumb this side of the U.S. of A.

Emily, his wife, was blessed with many talents and besides producing healthy, inquiring children, knitted, and crocheted and baked. She was not an unfriendly woman but reserved and where he tended to indulge the children, it fell to her to maintain order. So, the children naturally gravitated to Pat O' and climbed all over him and ran to meet him as he walked up the road from work. Often also he came with pockets filled with chunks and sweepings of chocolate crumb which he duly distributed to the children; a practice frowned on by Emily. If it were he they favored, it was she who rose in the middle of the night to soothe fevered brows, administer lotions and potions and dissipate bad dreams while he slept the sleep of the unencumbered, the innocent.

When they met neighbors or friends, Pat was the talker, while she waited patiently as he comforted and reassured them. Healing and bone setting had been in his family for generations and though Pat had never pursued that path, people gravitated to him. Many still remembered Pat's mother dispensing mysterious brews and concoctions from the little cottage she lived in, two miles outside the town – concoctions that more often than not, healed and renewed.

Unlike many of his co-workers, Pat O' rarely took time off from the job and was punctual to a fault. His one indulgence, if it could be called that, was that he liked to stop off at Doocey's Pub after Mass on Sunday.

Dooceys on Sunday morning and after a work-filled week was the perfect ending - not just an ending but a renewal for the coming week. He'd meet up with his mates, Dinny Brien, Joe Egan and Rush Kiely there. They'd have their pints of Guinness, rehash the happenings of the past week, laugh and joke and slag each other. The four worked together and had bonded over the years. All looked forward to this weekly get-together. There was something special also about the way the barman, little Mikey Troy immediately set about pulling four pints of the creamy, black stuff. Mikey pulled the best pint in the town, and though scruffy in appearance, of indeterminate age and rarely spoke, this talent, in a town where pulling and drinking pints were considered exalted occupations was a rare gift. Also, he had the uncanny ability to anticipate exactly when one needed a refill, so that as the pint was drained the next one was settling, this no matter how crowded or noisy the pub.

They all had their different ways of attacking the pint, Dinny, small and compact and powerful, with an eye withered and scarred from a youthful encounter with a mad cow, offering a muffled 'Slainte' as he dived into his. Joe, slim like a boy though he was the oldest, and sipping like a bird made quick work of his. Rush, solemn and overweight, and Pat O' taking the first long copious pulls that reduced the contents by half. Joe, a sprinter of some ability in his younger days was the talker, a voracious reader of newspapers and magazines and frequenter of the local library and he entertained the others with happenings from all over the globe. Rush, who had spent years in England, made judicious comments, to clarify a point raised or question a particular situation. Dinny, who had never been farther than Cappoquin and professed no desire to do so, was the listener and in every group a good listener is indispensable. Pat O' was the entertainer, the spinner of yarns, the singer of songs, reciter of poems and ballads. Dinny's comment after that first long swallow was an unvarying "Better than mother's milk," whereupon Rush proclaimed solemnly 'the nectar of the Gods.'

All were married with children with Dinny having eight, Rush six with one on the way and Joe practically childless with two. Their wives were glad to see them heading to Dooceys and the couple of pints. This respite from responsibility, this reverting to the boy in them – for there they were like little boys - invariably softened their disposition and made life more palatable for those around them.

So, for the wives, after the pub session was a good time to bring up delicate matters to do with family, recalcitrant in-laws and childrens' indiscretions and which in the afterglow of good conversation and good drink were easier resolved. Emily should have been glad, too, but for reasons unknown, she resented his having his few libations. Because she wasn't one for confrontation, Pat noticed nothing wrong. It wasn't that he came home roaring drunk either. He had his four pints of Guinness and headed home, always in time for his dinner. He walked, though he owned a bike and was back inside his own door at five or ten minutes to one. But resent it she did, and Pat finally sensed something wrong. He also surmised that it had to do with stopping off at Dooceys. 'Dallying in Dooceys' was the one reference she had made some time back. Half listening then, it hadn't registered until weeks later but now that it had, he was bound and determined to continue. This was his reward for his diligence and hard week's work. The craic, the slagging, the company was respite, too – though he would admit to no one -from his wife's more austere nature.

He was a storyteller, it too, with the healing, ran in his family for generations. Hadn't his grandmother told the stories and history of the Seana Pobal, the Old Parish - passed down from generation to generation - to a man from the Department of the Gaeltacht from Dublin who had recorded and archived it. The copy, a source of great pride, was in the local library and he had many a night perused it. Maybe Emily felt left out. She had never touched alcohol in any form and didn't like pubs or the pub culture. She confided to her neighbor, Mrs. Burke that alcohol had diminished the Irish drive and initiative and if they had never found alcohol, they would have rivaled America in industry. To which Mrs. Burke replied, "they didn't find it, girl, is it codding me you are, they invented it." Events proceeded unchanged. Pat went to Dooceys on a Sunday and Emily maintained a calm exterior. But change was on the way.

On a carefree Sunday morning, Pat and his butties settled themselves comfortably in their favorite pub, the black lady with the blonde head sitting dutifully by elbow and anticipated a pleasant hour or three. Joe brought them up to date on local, regional and world affairs, Pat O' spun some yarns as only he could, Rush kept the dialogue brisk with some judicious comments and Dinny listened with rapt concentration – very gratifying to the others. Then in milliseconds, all was changed. The door opened inward, and Emily entered.

If a picture was taken at that very moment, it would show four open-mouthed, middle-aged men, two with pints in hand on way to or from aforesaid mouths. With a nod of her head, she acknowledged Pat O,' sat herself down in the corner opposite to him, pulled her knitting out, and proceeded to knit away. Sensing all eyes gauging his reaction, Pat O' gave a nod in her direction and continued with his yarn. The noise level returned to normal and the three listened intently.

But it was not as before. As hard as Pat O' and his butties tried, this foreign element in their midst, this alien presence robbed ribaldry and rhythm. Intimacy shattered, they were left bereft and floundering. It was as if they had been thrust on stage, a microphone stuck under their noses, a powerful spotlight trained on them and ordered to perform. They all made valiant efforts to continue and for a while conversation continued in ragged bursts but finally it ground to a halt, a knitting needle through its heart. Silence reigned. Pat O' sighed and made ready to leave, bidding the others a strained good day, the wife gathered up her knitting and walked out before him. Neither made mention of the incident.

On the following Sunday, Pat O' and his butties again entered Dooceys. There was no sign of Emily. She had made her point; he would be firm and make his. The drinks were served and after an appropriate wait, he breathed a sigh of relief and settled in. Soon, the good times were rolling, repartee sparkling, Joe educating, Rush commenting, Dinny doing his usual excellent job of listening and Pat O' in a nice rhythm of song and story. Then the unthinkable happened – again. Drinks stopped in midair, and all eyes riveted as Emily nodded to the assemblage, took out her wool, took her seat and, with sure and skilled hands, proceeded with her knitting. Again, the group made heroic effort to continue, but just as before, they were soon mumbling their excuses and stumbling out the door. This time as they patted his shoulder, there was a finality about their departure and they left as they would leave a wake, knowing they would never mingle in quite the same way again. Pat O' sighed deeply and with as much dignity as he could muster, pulled on his tweed cap and made his way out the door, leaving – sitting on the chipped and battered table - a half-pint of Guinness, a transgression never before committed and eloquent testimony to his inner turmoil. The dinner was late that Sunday, but it was the last time.

Pat O' never graced Doocey's again. The lads carried on for years after, but it was never the same. The perfect combination had been shattered. Even if Pat O' had made his way back there, it would not have been the same and they all sensed it. Something happened the day Emily walked into Dooceys and took out her knitting, something ancient shattered. If she noticed any change in Pat O', she never made mention of it. He seemed the same, still made himself available to advice and comfort. But if one knew him well, or studied him closely, there was a hint of sadness or melancholy, a tiny dark cloud in a cobalt blue sky.

Rush, Dinny and Joe rarely made mention of Dooceys now and if they did, it was to disparage it as if to suggest to Pat O' that he was missing little. When he didn't reply, they dropped it. It was as if it had never happened. At times they'd forget, and one would say 'D'ye remember that day in Dooceys when Mikey wouldn't serve the Bull Maher or bring up one of the many occurrences that had made it memorable. Then they'd remember and there would be silence. They'd spit or clear their throats, get up and stretch, quickly changing to safer matters like the game just played or the latest political developments.

Sometimes Pat O' would make oblique reference, like 'you have to keep the women happy' or 'there's no doubt they have their ways' or 'tisn't a lot to ask, when all is said and done.'

He never confronted Emily and they never discussed it and for their remaining years she was a good and faithful wife. From the day of the second knitting needle incident, Pat O' made his way straight home from Mass, avoiding passing Dooceys premises entirely. On any Sunday morning, he could be found sitting by his own fire reading the paper, having his few pints, poor imitations of Mikey's but graciously provided by Emily.

Jane

You left your man, abandoned child
Moved somewhere where the weather's fine
Now you pole-dance with little on
I'm asking, Jane, are you insane?

You husband grieves, your daughter cries
You walk the beach, gaze at the skies
You smile with white and even teeth
And sit with drunken, loutish beasts

This dropping out, forsaking all
Is but a temporary pall?
You will come back to kith and kin
Or conscience will make such a din.

You married Tom, you had his child
And then you leave and leave a void
Not even for another name
I'm asking, Jane, are you insane?

The Drunk and Redemption

He was sick again, his love of alcohol dominating/destroying his life, a pattern repeating itself with monotonous regularity. He returned home after work to his small, one-bedroom apartment. He cooked some eggs and toast and drank two cups of coffee black, no sugar. He tried to relax.

He watched TV, aimlessly flicking channels. Tonight, he swore, he would stay home and just take it easy, his body needed rest and recovery. He surveyed his accommodation and felt depressed at how it looked. He took a shower and soon after, a second. He checked his CD collection, checked his bookshelves. He checked the refrigerator, made a list of what he needed to get. He kept no beer or liquor here. Alcohol was meant to be imbibed in company, convivial company, and appropriate location. Friends or acquaintances had never seen the inside of his apartment. As time progressed, he became more and more restless. He did some stretching exercises, sit ups and pushups. Then, as tension heightened and as if he had received urgent instruction he dressed quickly and left.

A minute and thirty seconds later he was among friends, belly-up at Mac's Place just around the corner from his accommodation. A minute and forty seconds later he was sipping on his first Screwdriver, dispensed by John, the bartender in his usual heavy-handed manner.

Four Screwdrivers and an hour later, he was where he wanted

to be, feeling that minute glow in the pit of his stomach as it slowly, luxuriously expanded. It would soon suffuse his whole being and he would feel benevolent, sensitive, and understanding of all the world's inadequacies and disappointments. He listened intently as the poor soul by his side unburdened himself, and he, to the very best of his ability, dispensed nuggets of wisdom to soothe the confessor's soul. He now felt worthwhile, fulfilled. Later, events and occurrences would grow dim and disjointed as the clock climbed to midnight and beyond.

The next morning, to the harsh clanging of the alarm clock, he struggled out of bed and to his job in the august Continental Savings & Loan Bank. After three or four coffees, some on the way, some when he arrived at his desk, he began to feel somewhat revived and endeavored to immerse himself in bank business. In the mornings and for some few hours after, he wished to be invisible. He buried his head in ledgers and accounts. He would not engage in long conversation with any of his fellow-workers.

He was petrified someone would pick up some clue, some slight indiscretion of his - a hand that shook minutely, eyes still bloodshot, a not quite normal voice, scratched, raspy – that would give the first clue, begin the first faint whisperings of gossip detrimental to his prospects at this great institution of finance. At his best, he was an excellent employee of this great institution, at his worst he was still, for now, competent.

As morning turned to afternoon he relaxed, his voice returned to normal, color returning to undercut the pallor that was always companion to his hangover. If he lunched with his fellow-workers, he stuck to coke or soft drinks, firmly declining any offer of alcohol. It was his policy to abstain during his working day – in the evening only occasionally. He was, as he projected, serious, dedicated, and sober. They perceived him as he wished they would, maybe even envied him a little for his strength of character and his principles. Later that evening, he would hurry into Mac's, where without asking, John would prepare his potion and within minutes, set him up again.

Mark loved the ambiance of this place, benevolent bartender who catered to his every wish, dim interior, the serious drinkers who inhabited it. Occasionally a patron collapsed; it had happened so regularly that it barely interrupted the commerce of the place, John tut-tutting, quietly and efficiently lifting the fallen comrade, draping him or her – for there were many of the opposite sex who loved this place too – in one of the leatherette booths where a cold compress was applied, and sufficient time given for recovery. Some elected to return and continue at the bar while others decided a timeout was needed, a brief absence, sustenance, and a good night's sleep. Mark had never seen an ambulance called, all believed - had total unequivocal faith in the magical ministrations of John. He was batting a hundred, had never lost a patron – some banged up and bruised, maybe, but soldiering on. This was Mark's world and he loved it.

His immediate boss was Joe Larkin. Joe had two years seniority on him – not that seniority mattered that much. But Larkin had ambitions far greater than Mark's and though not that bright, he was punctual, eager to please and his one redeeming feature; an excellent dress sense, always a crisp white shirt, dark pinstripe suit, expensive dark, leather brogans – not flashy to outshine his superiors but subtle and proper. He had been Joe or Larkin for ages, a fellow employee you could punch on the shoulder, arm wrestle and banter with, insult, make fun of. That was before. Now it was 'After.' He had made it clear. No more Joe or Larkin, it would be Mister Larkin.

He had also developed, to Mark's initial enjoyment - enjoyment that had, later, turned to irritation - an unblinking stare which was meant, Mark presumed, to intimidate. Whether this was something learned from a bible of managerial protocol - how to establish and maintain control, keep employees on their toes, 'a little fear is a very good thing,' or some recent seminar he had attended – no one knew. To Mark it was childish and immature though he had known of some who were intimidated. Little by little, Larkin was – a coarse expression - feeling his oats, flexing his power. He ordered his morning coffee in a sharp, demanding voice with little or no please or thank you. He would run his department on fear, not encouragement or praise. He was becoming more and more obnoxious to those in his department and Mark was finding it more and more difficult to hold his tongue and temper. He avoided him as much as possible but Larkin, sensing his antipathy and reacting to it, seemed to find more and more reasons each day to require Mark's presence.

That morning, Larkin had called him to his office. Mark knocked and entered to find Larkin gazing out his window with hands clasped behind, surveying the city below him. To Larkin's murmured request to sit, Mark took a seat while Larkin continued to survey the scene before him. For several long minutes he remained unmoving then suddenly turned and fixed Mark with his stare. Mark, knowing what was coming, looked away and was gazing round the room in apparent relaxed curiosity. He did not want to engage in dueling stares with Larkin. He was afraid he would do something frivolous like stick out his tongue or slow wink.

When he did engage with Larkin, he inquired in a polite but impersonal tone, "You wanted to see me, Mr. Larkin?" Larkin continued to stare but sensing Mark's indifference, he took his seat and steepled his fingers.

"Are you content in your work, Mark?"

"Yes, yes, I am."

"Do you ah…resent my promotion? I know you were considered, and I assume, wanted it?"

"No, no, I know I was considered but would not have accepted,' - which was true. He was happy in his work and content – up until Larkin had taken over. Mr. Allen, who had preceded Larkin, was a wise and unobtrusive supervisor. All were sorry to see him retire.

"Your work is more than adequate, more than adequate, I might say. But I sense a…a…discontent, disillusionment maybe… resentment might be too strong a word."

"No, no, I'm fine, Mr. Larkin… I'm sorry you've got that impression. Was there something specific?'

"No, nothing I can put my finger on." He hesitated. "I know you all admired Mr. Allen as I did. He was a good man but apt to be taken advantage of. There was some slippage there that was of major concern to management, (in Mark's estimation, this was a bare-faced lie) so the decision was taken. I was chosen to…ah…reestablish… order and efficiency and this is what I've endeavored to do over these last six months. (Mark knew for a fact the department was not more efficient and that, indeed, upper management was dismayed at Larkin's roughshod style and was keeping a close watch on his activities) This is a business. We are all adults. It is in all our best interests to advance the company. The more successful we are, the more benefit we reap. Is it not so?"

"Of course, Mr. Larkin, we are on the same page."

"As I said, I sense a disillusionment…that…seems to deepen as time goes on. It would be incumbent on me to address that situation…" And then Larkin uttered the word that would change their relationship forever, "Dismissed." He wasn't sure he had heard right but Larkin was shuffling papers on his desk and generally looking busy. Not alone had he made a veiled threat, but he had treated him as a schoolboy. Mark was furious. He stared at Larkin for a long moment, then quietly rose and left the office.

He resolved from that moment on to do everything in his power to derail Larkin. It seemed clear to him that both he and Larkin would not prosper in the company. It would be one or the other. Mark was a very likely replacement if Larkin screwed up or earned the displeasure of management.

There had been rumors, whispers through the years of Larkin being less than loyal to his fellow-workers, a tendency to carry tales, all in the cause of furthering his own career. Now he had one more reason to work towards his elimination. Larkin's 'dismissed' remark was burned into his soul. Not 'glad we had this chat', 'thank you for your work.' I appreciate all your efforts. Dismissed – the fucking moron.

He would bring him down, humiliate him, find his weakness, and exploit it. For the first time in a long time, he had purpose in his life, a goal to be achieved and a changed outlook. Over the next weeks, as his resolve hardened, he drank less. Now he had to be more on top of what was happening day to day. He would give Larkin no excuse to criticize or reprimand.

"More like your old self, what, Mark?" He didn't reply. Larkin was the enemy – two gladiators in the arena fighting to the death. He smiled at the idea of Larkin dressed in gladiator armor wearing his perfectly polished black shoes.

Each day he studied Larkin assiduously and his interactions with the staff. He took to writing a report each evening of Larkin's activities. His visits to Mac's Place grew less frequent. Now, incredulously, reluctantly, he saw it for what it was, a haven for those who had given up hope, who were involved in the process of terminating their lives.

They were drinking themselves to death and however long it would take, it would happen – the law of inevitability.

They were hastening the natural aging of the mind and body, the deterioration of the myriad, interlocking and interdependent functions, injecting a slow, creeping poison that would cause the kidney and liver and intestinal system to work ever harder while depleting and depriving the life-giving nutrients. (He had been reading a lot of health and vitality books lately) More stress and less support to fight it would bring failure and shutdown. He visualized Larkin failing and shutting down, but how? What lever, switch could he engage to begin the deterioration? He reviewed the situation. Larkin was overbearing and ambitious, even more so since his promotion. He was competitive also but not likable. So, Mark had some potential allies.

The one person Larkin seemed to treat with the utmost respect was Martha, Mr. Bogle's personal secretary. Mr. Bogle was Larkin's boss, a competent, well-educated, and securely placed upper management type with as many as six titles and chair of various departments. He was rumored to be connected to the chief honcho himself, Brad Perrin through marriage, though no one seemed to know the exact connection.

Martha was competent and discreet and believed to be held in extremely high regard by Sam Bogle, so much so that in his absence, she handled all routine matters that came to his desk, her actions, and decisions in total synch with Mr. Bogle's management style. She was attractive, in her mid-forties, married and divorced, no children.

Larkin's interest in Martha was, Mark felt, for one of two reasons – or both. He was attracted to her and believed he could score and/or she was a confidant of Mr. Bogle so a valuable ally to have in the treacherous waters of office politics.

Mark was on friendly terms with Martha and had been for many years. It was known but to a very few that Martha had, after her divorce, battled alcoholism. Mark had attended AA meetings infrequently and they had met. She had been successful in her battle with alcoholism – Mark was still at risk, but they respected each other's confidentiality and supported each other. Mark now found a pretext to visit Martha.

"Hey, stranger,' she greeted him, 'we haven't talked in months. How are you?"

"Like we worked on opposite sides of the planet. I'm good, you?'

"Great, great. Mr. Bogle's away for a few days. It should be quieter, right, but no, it gets busier."

"You can handle it."

"I guess."

Mark knew he didn't have much time. "Hey, is it my imagination or is Larkin, Mr. Larkin being much more attentive to you since his promotion?"

She sighed. "He is so…crude. He's actually flirting with me. His head has grown since that promotion. He would not have been my choice."

"He's impossible to work with."

"Just be careful. He can be devious and ruthless and will do whatever it takes – to advance his cause."

"He sees me as a potential replacement if he screws up, so he'd be happy to see me gone, I reckon."

"I'd be careful. How's life otherwise?" Mark knew what she meant.

"Better much better," he told her. "You?"

"I'm fine. It's been like eleven years now."

"That's wonderful. Okay, back to the coalface."

She put her hand on his arm, "If there are any developments, I'll be in touch." Mark left her and walked down the long corridor. Martha was on his side and was a valuable ally. He felt more secure, much more secure.

Time proceeded uneventfully over the next few months. Mark was winning his battle with 'demon alcohol,' feeling better, more energetic as time passed. He had finally done what he had been threatening to do for a long time. He had joined a health club. As he participated in calisthenics and yoga classes, it seemed the better he felt, the more he wanted. He thought ruefully, it was a relationship not unlike that with alcohol in that the more he got, the more he wanted. He thought he might have an addictive personality.

Now the May monthly conference was upon them, where goals and results were discussed, and initiatives put in place to hopefully boost profitability. Mark was required to attend with other department heads and their assistants – as was Larkin.

The meeting was chaired by Martha's boss, Mr. Bogle and each person, in turn was asked to give a brief presentation of his department's results, expectations etc. Larkin seemed ill at ease and impatient and when his turn came, jumped up and, monthly report in hand, expressed his disappointment to all at the less than stellar numbers for the past month. He berated his employees for their lack of initiative and threatened dire consequences if there was not an improvement in the month to come. He promised that next months would be much, much improved. When he was finished, Bogle looked at him and quietly asked why. For a long moment Larkin pondered the question with a perplexed look on his face and repeated Bogle's 'why.'

"Why,' Bogle asked again, 'is it disappointing? What are the reasons?' Larkin looked as if he had been asked how the earth was formed. He didn't understand the question and had no answer.

"I haven't had time..." Bogle cut him off. 'But the report was in your hands a week ago.' Bogle looked at Mark and Mark nodded. He had prepared the report and submitted it to Larkin a week ago. Larkin caught Bogle's inquiring look and Mark's nod of confirmation and his face reddened. One could almost read his thoughts. They are plotting against me.

"As you know,' Larkin began, "I'm in charge of preparations for our annual conference...."

Again, Bogle cut him off. "You're not able to deal with both matters simultaneously?"

Mark looked round the conference table. Most were enjoying the public humiliation of Larkin. The bully was taking some punches. "Of course, Mr. Bogle."

Now he knew he should keep his mouth shut for he had no idea what was occurring. Mark realized instantly that Larkin must have picked up the wrong report, the month-old report instead of the most up to date one, which was positive and showed improvement over all the indices. Mark knew the appropriate step to take would be to excuse himself and go and whisper in Larkin's ear that he had picked up and brought to the meeting, the wrong report. But he kept quiet.

"Mr. Larkin, would you verify the date of your report? The current report is more positive."

Larkin looked at the report and realized his mistake. He had not bothered to check the current report, busy as he was with annual conference matters and writing his own speech to the conference – the speech which would announce his coming, his ascent in the company, the speech which he had strenuously lobbied for in the months previous, (He was the conference organizer. Why shouldn't he give the opening address to the annual conference?), the speech on which he had spent countless hours to the detriment of all other business.

Mark could read his thought process. Is there any way I could foist this whole mess on Mark – and rejecting it. It would be too obvious. He muttered an apology, excused himself and left the room to return minutes later with the current report. But whatever was in this report and however positive, it would not change Bogle's perception of him. He had missed a golden opportunity to expand on his leadership qualities and wax eloquent on the positive monthly report. At meeting's end, Mr. Bogle signaled for Larkin to remain behind. When, at last he emerged, he was ashen. As soon as he returned to his office, Mark was summoned. This time the stare was missing but he was ready to explode.

"Enjoyed that, Mark?"

"Excuse me, Mr. Larkin?" (Mark could barely suppress a smile. He would exploit this situation.)

"Excuse you for what, Mark?"

"I don't know, Mr. Larkin."

"You are enjoying it, aren't you?"

"Excuse me, Mr. Larkin."

Larkin exploded, "Don't you keep saying that, Riordan."

"Saying what, Mr. Larkin?"

"Goddamn you, Riordan." Mark knew the whole office was listening. He could push it just a little more.

"I, I don't understand, Mr. Larkin."

"Oh, you do, Mark, you do, you devious, scheming, back-stabbing…"

"Excuse me, Mr. Larkin."

"Goddamn you." Larkin was out of his chair, coming around his desk, his face redder even than many of the denizens of Mac's Place. Mark smiled and again said, "Excuse me, Mr. Larkin." Larkin face turned a darker red. He emitted a gurgling noise and rushed at Mark with outstretched hands. Now, with exquisite timing, Mark tipped over his chair and as Larkin's forward momentum landed him on top, Mark began screaming in a high, falsetto voice, "Help, help, somebody please help."

It was over in minutes, Larkin led away by two burly security guards, Mark being tended to by nursing staff for minor cuts and scratches. Larkin's employment was terminated, ending up with a more generous termination package than he probably deserved.

Mark was offered his job and accepted with alacrity; he didn't want any more Larkin types messing up his life. Martha winked and whispered, "Great job," as she passed by and when he stopped at Mac's Place one evening on his way home from the gym – he would proselyte there at times with John's blessing, John knowing there would be few if any converts there - who did he spot ensconced at the bar, all the way to the end, staring morosely into his drink, but Larkin. He thought life does take some funny turns.

Assignment #6 - Happiness

We had discovered Lake Welch early that summer, a lake in an area of many lakes and breathtaking scenery of evergreens and low-lying hills. It was situated in Rockland County, off the Garden State Parkway. It was our little secret and we returned there every weekend throughout the Summer of that year. We lived in Mount Vernon, then, near the Bronx border, in a house we had bought in 1969 and 'we' consisted of my wife Anne, Patricia 10, Catriona 8 and Christine 5.

Someone had told us about this sea-blue lake, where families spent their time far from the congested beach areas of the metropolitan area, in an area of peace and tranquility that even on weekends remained relatively uncrowded. And we had found it so. To us it seemed like Paradise.

So, each Sunday morning, we rose soon after dawn, attended early Mass, packed our Volkswagen Bug with our day-at-the-beach necessities and away we went. Our children loved going there, for to them it seemed like a magical place. There, they could run, play ball, build sandcastles, bathe, and make new friends. In truth, it was also how my wife and I viewed it. It seemed to all of us, then, a long ways away, 'upstate', and we anxiously scanned the directions and studied the signposts as we made our way there.

There was always a feeling of tension, suppressed excitement and my youngest daughter, Christine could not refrain from rising up and down, unable to sit still. "Daddy, I think we're near, are we?" she inquired, her blue eyes wide, willing me to answer yes. "Yes, not too long more," I reassured her, then added mischievously, "but maybe we'll just keep driving and get home early. It would be nice to spend a quiet ..." I was interrupted with shrieks of "No, no, no, we want to go to Lake Welch," from all three, and my wife looked at me with mock disapproval and stated, "You're outvoted four to one, so we're going to Lake Welch." I sighed and muttered "okay" and everyone cheered.

I sat on my beach chair later that day and looked out over the wood-fringed lake. I looked at my wife, humming contentedly to herself, busy with the task of feeding five hungry people. I looked at my children, playing at the water's edge and I thought about me. I was thirty-six years old, then, a bus mechanic for the Transit Authority for eight years, with enough seniority to workdays and have my weekends off. It was a decent job with plenty of overtime and I liked the job. I worked with a good bunch of guys, and it wasn't all work and no play. I was one of the 'hungry' ones, a term they used to describe those who worked a lot of overtime. But I was healthy and in good physical condition and overtime did not bother me.

In fact, the whole idea of overtime delighted me. I had come from a culture where to have a job was special but where overtime was frowned on. Working overtime prevented someone else from working and was equated with greed. A woman was discouraged from working outside the home if her husband also worked. That was the attitude of Church and the work unions. So, for me, to be asked - and sometimes begged - to work overtime, to be paid time and one half, meant that I could, that much more quickly, acquire the material things that seemed the right of every American, even newly arrived green-card Americans.

I remember, when I was younger, my best friend Blondie asked me what would make me happy. I didn't have to ponder too long, for I had often thought about it. "I want to be married," I remember saying, "I want to have children. I want to have a house and a car. It doesn't matter if the house or car is paid for, as long as I'm seen to have both. And I want my wife to love me." As I looked out over the lake, I felt that I had realized my dream and a sense of peace and accomplishment settled on me. There was contentment there and happiness, finally.   I am, by nature, wary of the world and believe we're all destined for mischief and misfortune at various times in our lives. But the feeling I had that day, I can still recall. I felt all the things a man should feel when he works hard and has some luck in his life. I was providing for my family. We were living our version of the American dream. With the loving environment that my wife and I were providing, the possibilities for our children were endless in this, the greatest country in the world. I believed in America. The boy of twelve had worked towards this goal, consciously and unconsciously, all those years. I had come to America and realized my dreams.

I have never been sure what happiness is, but that day and that time I felt that I got as near as I'll ever be to that elusive, amorphous state - happiness.

Journey

From mud and mist,

We grunt and shuffle to higher ground

Eat berry, root and forage

Discover stone and fire and sharpened tool

Hunted becomes the hunter and we discover meat.

Ankles locked; we walk upright.

With no respite, drawn and driven

We journey on

How long will it take, how far have we come?

Will we know when we get there?

Where's there?

Who or what is waiting?

Who or what are we?

Does the journey end?

Jackie Maher

Jackie Maher, he lived in a barrel, a tar barrel, a fifty-gallon drum that once held tar used by the County Council to tar the roads. On top of the tar, they poured crushed stone. That's how roads were made, then. Still are, I think. So, I asked my mother, I was about six, then, could I see Jackie Maher's barrel. It's only a barrel, she said, But I bothered her until she took me out to see it. I was taken by the whole idea of living in a barrel. Life couldn't be any simpler than that, I thought.

He didn't really live in it. He slept in it at night. But there it was, some straw and a couple of coats thrown in. He'd be off around the countryside in the daytime, begging. He didn't really beg. People gave him things, bits and pieces of food and he'd do an odd job for them, cut some wood or watch cattle, a bit of digging, mending a fence. He had good hands on him, took his time and did good work. He had a nice way about him, too. Many a farmer offered him steady work, but he was restless and after a while, moved on.

He always returned to the barrel in the evening. You could see him, cooking a bit of grub or boiling a kettle for a cup of tea. In the winter, when the days were short and 'twas cold and damp, he'd sleep more, his head to the inside, curled up. Nobody bothered him. They tried to move him to better accommodation, the people who felt it was wrong for him to have to live in a tar barrel, but he said no. That was where he wanted to be and that's where he stayed. He became a bit of an attraction. People would walk up quietly and take a look at him sleeping, warning the children to be quiet or they'd get a clip across the head. But they were just as curious and watched him, wide-eyed, and had to be dragged away.

To my mind, he had everything you'd ever want. He lacked for nothing, went his own way, wasn't a burden on anybody that I could see. He wasn't one to mix or carry on a conversation but seemed happy in himself and people left him alone, other than a "Hello, Jackie. Are ye all right?" or "Bad day, Jackie boy." He'd nod his head or wave a hand and continue with what he was doing. He had a way with birds too, and they flocked around him. He fed them bits of stale bread and stuff that he found in his pockets.

He was there in the barrel for years, about a mile outside the village, a nice location, under a big oak tree. He had picked the location well. I suppose you get a good sense after years on the road. He hadn't put the barrel there. The Council had, empty on its side. Once in a while, they kept a little gravel there, but mostly it was empty. I suppose Jackie spotted the possibilities and moved right in. The Council workers didn't object. They were mostly country men who worked on the roads and had known all their lives men like Jackie who moved around. You'd wonder what started them off to that life of wandering and imagine a great tragedy or a lost love.

The world is a frightening place for a lot of people. Others could care less. But as someone said, there's no two of us born the same.

We fight our own little wars every day. A funny thing about Jackie Maher, nobody knew when he left or if he died. People would say, "I haven't seen Jackie lately, have you?" or "Any word of Jackie Maher, at all, at all?" It was like he disappeared from the face of the earth. The barrel was there for years after.

Absent Father

He remembered everything about her, all these years after, the comfort of her, the sweet anticipation of coming in the door knowing she'd be there, seeing the way she turned, a smile touching the corners of her mouth and her greeting.

"You're home." Not a question, he was obviously home, but a declaration of satisfaction. He was home, they were together, she was complete. To him, she was beautiful in every way. He didn't know the classical definition of beauty. But she was perfect, the way she wore her hair carelessly brushed but abundant and shining, the beautiful smile that dimpled as it grew, the silver cross and chain that forever circled her neck, the dress she wore, apron, soft shoes.

The front door opened onto the kitchen, and she invariably stood by the sink or the small space by it cooking or washing. She liked to keep busy, and she baked constantly, breads and muffins, delicious pies – blueberry her favorite, because it was his. Occasionally she would surprise with an exotic creation, a chocolate cake beautifully sculpted or a peach meringue. He thought it was more to challenge her cooking skills than any other reason. He would come and bury his face in her, smell her smells, feel her arms tight around him, her hands stroking his head. She would turn his face to her and kiss his forehead. He would be complete, loved, at peace.

And the thought would come to him again, why, why had she

married his father? He wondered always why? He had never seen tenderness between them, never seen his arms around her, holding her, loving touch, a smile. He came and he went, silent, watchful when he was there, head sunk in shoulders, hidden behind the newspaper usually, a non-participant in his wife's and son's life.

In the beginning, when he was younger, before the teen years, Alan had tried to engage him, desperate for his approval, for a relationship like he had with his mother, where he could easily nestle up to his father, feel his hands holding him, his head stroked. But it was as if this kind of behavior was alien to his father's nature.

Why had she married him? He could not comprehend. Were they in love once? Did she feel obligated, though knowing it would be devoid of tenderness? And why would she feel obligated? She wasn't pregnant when they married. He had checked. So why? Why had she consented, knowing how hard her life would be, bereft of the intimacy a kind and loving husband should provide? Had he been – kind and loving once? And if so, what had happened? What had changed? And why? When? It was an enigma, a mystery, two people so unlike, coming together to spend their lives together. In married bliss? In marriage, yes but there was no bliss. But why? Was his mother happy? What was her degree of happiness – or unhappiness? What was the equation? Mostly one or the other or neither? Which? He put it from his mind. He spent too much time and energy, way too much on this question.

He was twenty-seven now, outwardly successful, making a very comfortable living in banking, international banking. He dated steadily but never committed. He had met some wonderful women but lacked the courage – or was it hope or faith or optimism – to commit. Always he thought about his parent's relationship and felt a chill. How could his mother have been so wrong?

Yet, he was the product of that union. But he had this lack of faith in his own ability to find his ideal mate. What if she changed after the marriage, became someone different, mean and grasping, or worse, empty. How could his mother have been so wrong, so misled? How could she have not seen the shadow on his soul, the gaping emptiness that was hidden inside him; she who anticipated Alan's every mood, who quieted his fears before even he could articulate them, who was good in every way – good neighbor, kind and generous to those less fortunate, involved with clothes banks and food banks, who delivered meals to the homeless, who had such an empathy with all. She had failed in her choice of life partner, failed miserably to choose wisely, to make a determination as to the character of the man she would marry.

When Allan was fifteen, his parents split up or to be more accurate, his father walked away – he was there and then he was gone, taking most of their savings with him. He had also cleared out their joint checking account. He had gotten a transfer to Minnesota, leaving a two-line note. He was leaving. He would file for divorce. His mother never contested the terms and against her lawyers wishes, signed all was put before her. Anne, his mother, was an only child and her parents, Mike and Sally stepped in and took over all financial obligations that had accrued.

Allan was glad his father was gone, a source of stress and tension removed from his and hopefully his mother's life. He did not miss him. He had always watched his father closely. Now, he began to see an increase in his father's erratic behavior. His mother seemed not to notice or chose to ignore it – the two great enigmas in his life, his father's behavior, his mother's seeming acceptance of it. He had expected something bad happening, something that would fix in his mind forever, the dark void that lay inside his father. He was angry when he found out about the checking account and ashamed. He was his father's son, and this action was reprehensible to him, craven and cowardly. He wished for the day he could provide for her. Now, it was just the two of them and they were at peace.

So, he could be close to his mother, he attended a local college. He had offers from more prestigious colleges but chose the local one so he could live at home. He brought up his father's leaving, but she didn't want to discuss it.

"It's in the past, darling. Leave it be. Aren't we well rid of him?"

It was the only negative thing he had ever heard her utter about his father. He had so many questions, but he held them. Maybe, some day, she would talk about him, their relationship, the beginning and all that came after.

Life continued in a good way. Thanks to Mike and Sally, they were financially secure. Neither he, nor his mother, was extravagant.

Neither one desired fancy vacations, or, indeed, fancy cars. They lived soberly, Allan studied, Win, his mother, baked. They watched a little TV in the evenings, went for long walks by the lake nearby, which was part of a state reservoir system. They went to Mike and Sally's for Thanksgiving and Christmas. If he expected Win to be changed after his father left, she was disappointed. She seemed the same, seemed set on a course that brooked no deviation for joy or sorrow. She was loving to him as always. But he wondered and wished he could see inside her soul – or mind. Was she happy? She seemed so. Or was there a great boulder of sorrow, regret lodged deep inside her?

She never dated, had some woman friends through their church and other charities. Once he had gone to a restaurant where they were meeting. He wanted to see her in a social setting, how she acted. Was she different to the woman he knew, the kind, smiling woman who still ruffled his hair as she hugged him? He stood outside and watched her. She was composed, sociable – yet he got the feeling that she was not fully participating, aloof but not so that any of the group noticed. He looked at her and his love for her was all enveloping. Oh, if only he could make her laugh. If only she would unburden herself to him. He would move heaven and earth to bring her peace and happiness. Because of her, he knew love. She had buffered him against the trials and obstacles he had would meet in his life. But she hadn't coddled him.

He thought of the time J.G. the school bully had given Allan a black eye. Bully might not have been the correct designation. He loved to engage in rough house play and inevitably, kids got hurt. But it didn't seem to bother him too much either. His mother had studied his face and given him specific instructions. Though shocked, he determined to follow them. Two days after, he watched J.G. go to the bathroom. He followed him inside. J.G. was urinating and as he turned, Allan struck him with all the force he could muster in the face. He staggered and collapsed against the bathroom wall. They stared at each other. Allan saw something change in J.G.'s eyes. He was not sure what it signified. Was it one of puzzlement as if his original diagnosis was flawed as to the character of Allan? Now Alan waited as per his mother's instructions. He was giving J.G. opportunity to continue the battle. He rose, nodded to Allan and left. Now they both walked around with face bruised and turning various shades of yellow and purple. Classmates looked and puzzled over this oddity. As his mother had cautioned him, Allan never spoke of this encounter. Neither did J.G.

No one ever bothered Allan again. Somehow, all knew he was off limits to would-be bullies. It was another instant of his mother's wisdom, and it drew them even closer together. He wondered what his father would have done, counselled, if he had been in their lives, and somehow, he knew the outcome would have been different.

Because he lived with his mother, he passed up more than one opportunity for advancement. These promotions entailed much more travel and in one instance, entailed moving overseas for a time. His mother was aware of this and gently chided him.

"Allan, you should consider these offers. I'm fine. I'm in good health. I can come and visit. Matter of fact, I would love to travel more. You're young and should be looking to your future. Opportunities have a time frame. As you grow older..."

"I'm fine Mom. I like my job. I like being with you."

"I know, love, but what if you leave it too late?"

"Ssshh. Aren't we happy as we are?"

"I want you to live your life to the fullest, see wonderful, inspiring places, meet wonderful, unique people."

"Not yet, Mom, but some day. I promise."

"I feel like I'm holding you back. I've never coddled you, Allan, so please don't coddle me."

She had a point. He was twenty-nine now and had turned down some opportunities – Zurich and London specifically – that would have been valuable impetus to his career. There would come a point, inevitably, where he would be viewed as a mid-level executive with little ambition. Offers of advancement would dry up. He had influential allies in the banking business, but they would grow old, retire. His time frame was shrinking.

He wondered about many things, the different lives lived, different outcomes from identical or near identical situations. How different we were - our differences forged by events, situations, incidents of varying importance we encountered as we progressed through this life. Maybe progress was the wrong word? Yes, we grew into adulthood and, hopefully, knowledge, and yes, many of us did progress in good and positive ways, searching for answers to all the ancient and forever questions – how and why and where, how we should live our lives, why were we here, where had we come from, where were we going, what was this life's purpose, how should we relate to God, what should the relationship be? Implicit trust, awe, fear? Was there such an entity?

But there was regression also, unfulfilled ambition, disappointment, addictions, anger, frustration, sense of hopelessness, criminal behavior. His life hadn't been such. Yes, his father had deserted him, but he had the unending love of his mother. He had a good job, good prospects – unavailed of to this point and at this time in his life, a degree of financial independence. But his mother was all he needed, his rock, his connection to all that was good and worthy in his life. Sometimes, he wondered, could I have made it without her? Could I have emerged whole and unscathed? What if she had been ordinary, lackadaisical in her love for him, her devotion? He would never know. He didn't need to know. He had her, her devotion, love like a bottomless pit, no end to it, encompassing and fierce – that brooked no interference. I was and am so lucky, he thought. How many others were loved so? How many loved as she did?

There was a time when he entertained thoughts of revenge, retribution towards his father, when he thought over his father's treatment of his family, his lack of responsibility, fiscal and otherwise, his callous disregard for their welfare – total absorption in his own. But he knew instinctively his mother would not have approved and he knew, she was right. There were too many good and positive things in both their lives to wallow in the irrational and selfish actions of his father. Still, still. There was something unresolved. He had given up trying to resolve their relationship. Had he ever loved his mother, ever? Then why had he married? What compelled him to commit to marriage, knowing as he must have, it was doomed to failure? It was an enigma. But had he not felt some degree of wonder, if not love, when he first beheld his son, held him in his arms, gazed on his wrinkled countenance? There was something unfinished in their relationship, questions to be answered, mysteries unfolded.

So, he passed his days and weeks dismissing his father, pushing him from his thoughts and dreams and then, when he finally felt rid of him, banished from his life – he came creeping back. Why, why, why? There would be days, months at a time, when he was focused, sure, and if not happy, then content. Then an image, a father and son passing in the street, arm protectively, lovingly round the boy, man and small boy sitting side by side, feeding the ducks, man and boy sitting in restaurant, the boy reciting some incident, secure in his father's love, while the father listened intently, his head nodding from time to time, a hand clasped firmly, hair smoothed, head kissed. Then it all came rushing back. Why, why, why? What manner of man was he? Finally, it came to him that he would have no peace until he delved deeper into his father's life, the life he was leading now.

Without informing his mother, he hired a private detective to find his father and find out his present circumstances, what and where he was. Within days he found out his father was dead, a possible suicide some six months before. Allan was able to obtain his father's few belongings. He had left little, his driving license, expired, a bank statement with the princely sum of twenty-one dollars and seventy-three cents, a wedding picture of he and his mother, both serious and concentrated – as if both knew there was much work ahead. Also, his wedding ring, surprising to Allan that he had not disposed of it. Also, a letter, envelope unaddressed. In it he had written:

My life has been one of total and abject failure. Whether it was humanly possible to change the arc of my life, I don't know but doubt it. All my life I carried rage within me, and all my life I lived afraid I would damage those around me. One time and one time only, I thought I had a chance at redemption, a life of consequence. It was when I met my wife, Win. She was the most loving, forgiving, 'good' human being I had ever met. When we began to see each other, I unburdened myself and confessed to her, the rage, emptiness, at times desolation I carried within me. I believed she would walk away as she had every right to. She said let us try to work it out. So, we married and had a beautiful son, Allan. For a while, rage diminished, and desolation was replaced with a kind of contentment. But always, always, I knew my demons lurked in the background, leering, drooling, waiting for the opportunities they knew would come.

As my son grew tall and strong, I imagined love would blossom, but it did not. I berated myself for this lack of love, seeing the need in my son's eyes and countenance. But I could not, I was incapable – and the demons howled ever louder.

Now, desolation returned ever stronger, and anger settled in my being. And as it grew, and as the demons howled, I feared for my wife and son's welfare. I would do everything in my power to protect them. It was then I knew I had to leave. I took our savings – to damage my family's regard for me, if there was any left, so they would not pursue me, so I would be left in peace? No, never peace – so I would be left in my rage and desolation, away from them and so unable to cause them harm. May God have mercy on my soul.

Now, all was revealed. Now I could understand my father's actions. If he was incapable of love, there was, without doubt, a kind of love in his determination to not cause harm to us. When my mother read the letter, she sighed and nodded her head – as if it had been as she imagined. We held a small private ceremony for my father's ashes. Now we could proceed with our lives. I felt a sadness at my father's burden, at what he had to carry all the days of his life. And what had happened was what had to happen. As I folded the letter, I offered up a prayer that he would finally find peace and contentment. I believed he would. The God I believed in, would surely acknowledge the trial he had endured. Now I had closure. Now I could live my life with a burden lifted.

Years later, I would imagine my father's presence near me, guiding and protecting me and I found it of great comfort. Maybe that was his reward. He was finally able to accomplish in another dimension, what he could not in his physical time on this planet. Life surprises in unexpected ways. We are meant to carry the burden we've been assigned – or assigned to ourselves. We are given the means to overcome those same burdens. We don't always succeed.

Little Darlin'

Lovin' you has been the cause of all my pleasure

Lovin' you has been the cause of all my pain

You been messin' with my feelins'

Till I wanna hit the ceilin'

And you may succeed in drivin' me insane

But I keep on comin' back and keep on tryin'

Tho' I sometimes think, it may be all in vain

If you'd just commit, my darlin'

Settle down and quit your wanderin'

We could build a life together, Little Jane

And I know I love you only, little darlin'

And I know I'll never find another you

And I know you love me, too'

But it's difficult for you

To forsake your to and froin' and be mine

Lovin' you has been the cause of all my pleasure

Lovin' you will be the cause of no more pain

We can build a new tomorrow

Full of lovin', no more sorrow

You and me together ever, Little Jane.

Old Sea Dog

The debate raged anew. When he reviewed his life and the choices he had made, in particular, one choice, the choice that had changed his life. It had changed his life for the worst, changed it to a gradual, downward spiral. Now he was an empty husk, empty of optimism, hope, energy, conviction. Still the debate raged on.

Maybe I should have, maybe? But I wasn't ready. It would not have been fair to any woman, let alone Moira. Oh Moira, Moira, she was everything a man could want – if a man wanted to settle down, have children, live a normal life.

Go to Mass of a Sunday, a walk out the country on a summer's evening or over to see a match at the Gaelic field, then home for the tea. He had the job offer, driving for the Creamery, steady, a paycheck every week. She wanted him to take it, but she wouldn't ask, tell him to – take it. But he knew. And she knew he knew.

He rose from the flat rock he was sitting on and stopped at window of the cottage. A bearded, weathered stranger stared back - a full head of grey hair, wool shirt and corduroy pants shoved into worn black boots. Who *is* that old man, he thought and where did the young fella go, the one who was going to go deep sea and come back rich to settle down?

He turned abruptly away. Settle down, you old fool, he had argued. You'll never find a better woman. If you go, you'll lose her.

Somebody else will snap her up, as fine looking a woman as ever lived around here and a long ways out besides. But he couldn't. He was afraid, deep in his bones, afraid the sea would call him back.

"Tis like a virus," the old man in the Azores told him years before. Only he had said Wirus, unable to pronounce the V. He had laughed then. What did that old man know? He would use the sea and when the time was right, he would abandon it. Now he knew what the old man knew.

Also, he didn't want that life for his family, away two, three or four months at a go, missing out on the children growing up as his father had done. He remembered the aching loneliness as his father left, the slow getting to know when he came back and then the going away again – the emotional seesaw. But he also knew, deep in his bones that after a while at home, he'd be restless and want to be away and away he'd be missing her and the children.

The evening he told her he was going – it was away out on the strand, the tide flat out, a still summer's evening - would stay in his mind forever, a dull aching presence that never completely left. He would always remember the way she stopped, bent a little, her face suddenly pale, bloodless.

"You're entitled to your dreams," was all she said but he knew, then, he was destroying her dream. He told her he'd be back when he had some good money made, hoped, and prayed she'd be there, but wouldn't hold her to it. After all, he was doing the leaving. He believed then he would come back but she knew better, and she was right. When the sea called him, he went. It was as simple as that. The call of the sea was a drug, a Wirus, stronger than any woman.

Now these last few weeks he'd been uneasy, dissatisfied with how his life had evolved, decisions made, careless unthinking choices. I was selfish, damn selfish, he thought. I should have committed myself, asked for her hand in marriage, fought for their happiness, the children they might have had.

The sea would have called. He would have had misgivings. But who doesn't? Life is never all good. He could deal with adversity. If doubt entered the equation, all he had to do was look at Moira – and count his blessings. After all, into every life a little rain must fall, someone once said. But was I not entitled to my dreams? And so it went, back and forth and back again, the constant battle that never left. Now he was all alone, in a small cottage, with a small pension and small dreams, by the side of the ocean, in the very spot he had dreamed the big dreams.

He was, finally, finished with the sea – or the sea had finished with him. It had beguiled him, fed his dreams and ambitions, broken him and cast him aside. He was old now and he limped - a series of accidents caused by carelessness and a liking for Wild Turkey Bourbon.

When he returned, she was gone. To the North of England, they said. Some said she had married but divorced. Some said she had no children, as far as they knew, but others heard she had a flock of children. Nobody knew too much. She returned twice for her mother's and then her father's wake and funeral, but gave no information out, even to her own. He had missed her both times.

He wondered how she looked now. He thought she would always look good. She was prideful always about her appearance. He imagined what it might have been like, Moira sitting beside him, the children away to school. He looked across the small field next to his cottage and heard the shouts and caffling of children on their way home from school. He watched as two – or three – broke away and came up the lane to him. The wind coming over the fields, chillier now as the sun dropped, assaulted him. He shrugged and rose and entered the cottage. The door closed quiet behind him.

Regrets

(Old man sitting by pier, young man comes up and sits by his side. They gaze out over waters, seagulls swooping, waves breaking, nets piled nearby)

Young Man (YM): It's quiet and peaceful.

Old Man (OM): Aye.

YM: You don't have the boat?

O: No more.

Y: You got rid of it?

O: Aye. (Long silence)

Y: After the….?

O: Aye.

Y: Do ye want to talk…...?

O: (interrupting) No.

Y: But…

O: No. (long silence)

Y: If you talk about it, it'll help.

O: Did I not say 'no.'

Y: Sorry. (Long silence)

O: You're like your uncle.

Y: What?

O: He only hears what he wants to hear.

Y: He was deaf in one ear, y'know.

O: Hmmm.

Y: So....

O: Will it bring him back? No.

Y: No.

O: Well then it can't help. Talk! The world is full of talk, every fool spouting off. Maybe that's what's causing the global warming we're hearing so much about. All that hot air.

Y: You might be right there.

O: More silence is what we need – and quiet. The world needs to take a rest. It needs a rest.

Y: He's in God's hands.

O: (Long silence) I wish, oh how I wish....

Y: Don't torture yourself, Gust.

O: It was so stupid...

Y: But it wasn't your fault.

O: It wasn't his. He was a boy, adventurous, up to mischief like any ten-year-old. And a smile on him that'd light up the worst kind of day.

Y: Ye were a pair.

O: Ah sure, he loved the boats, like myself. Never happier than when the two of us were together. As nimble as a goat he was.

Y: 'Twas a weekend morning.

O: We'd go down of a Sunday morning, this one the sun splitting the stones.

Y: But a bad forecast.

O: Aye. A storm approaching but a ways off, we were told.

Y: And….

O: I left him down, John, I didn't protect him.

Y: You can't watch 'em day and night. Things happen.

O: Things happen if you're careless.

Y: You cared, you cared. Gust. He was your golden boy.

O: I fell asleep, John, I fell asleep.

Y: And he took the boat.

O: He took the boat.

Y: He wanted her on his own.

O: He was always wanting to have a go, to go on his own, that's what he wanted to do. But there was something out there that frightened him too, and I could sense that. So, I held off.

Y: And he wanted to confront his fear. Don't you see, Gust, that's why he went.

O: Who knows?

Y: He would have found a way.

O: I don't know what came over me that day. 'Twas the heat of the sun, maybe, or the fact that I'm getting older but the sabhan came over me and I couldn't keep my eyes open.

Y: Aw, Gust.

O: I couldn't, I couldn't, I tried. It was like some malignant force, whispering in my ear. Ah, go on, take a rest. Ah sure, what harm is in it. And I dropped off, as deep a sleep as ever I had.

Y: He took off in the boat.

O: When I woke, I was all alone. He was gone. I never held him again.

Y: They mounted a mighty effort.

O: They had the lifeboat out seven days. The boat or what was left of it was found abroad in Ballyvoile.

Y: The body…

O: Oh, the sea took him, boy, and still has him. We couldn't wake him proper, the poor devil, only say prayers in the chapel.

Y: Nobody's blaming you, Gust.

O: And if they did, what matter? He's gone and won't be coming back. Poor Peg is withering away. I think she wants to go to him. When he came, late in life as it was, it was like our prayers were finally answered. God was good. Is it the same God that took him away or another God, a meaner vindictive one?

Y: But ye had him for a while.

We had him for a while, I suppose – on loan from God, Peg says. I suppose that's the best way to approach it. It's hard to get the head round it.

Y: No more fishing?

O: No more boats, no more fish, no more sea.

Y: The world is a sad oul' place.

(Silence. They both gaze out to sea.)

On the Silver Sprinkled Sand

On the silver, sprinkled sand
As I strolled along the shore
Lay a pulsing, speckled trout
Fighting for its precious life

So, I lifted, and I cradled
Carried carefully to lay
In the limpid, lazy waters
Of the languid blue-black bay.

Saw it slowly start to circle
As revival fought decay
Then it flipped its speckled torso
And proceeded on its way

On the silver, sprinkled sand
As a breeze traversed the bay
I skim stones and dance with wavelets
Spirits lifted; I feel gay.

Nasty Divorce

So, she had come to Chiang Mai and there she had found respite. Not peace, she thought, she might never find peace again – not after what had transpired. The divorce had changed her perception of people, life – everything. She had seen an ugly side of life, a side she never knew existed and she had survived, but barely.

She was not entirely blameless; her actions, reactions were not above censure. But her faith in humanity, in decency and fairness had been shattered and she, too had been diminished, her integrity shaken, her core breached. She had been so unforgiving of those women she had heard or read about in unhappy, abusive relationships. They had persevered in the relationship, often blaming themselves for – everything, whatever happened, mental or physical cruelty, financial ruin or near ruin, the loss of love, good will, good manners, the emergence of vulgarity, the sins of the other, offering up excuses for the inexcusable behavior of their partner. She now knew it was not such a black and white picture.

She sat and sipped her cappuccino, an attractive woman – few would say otherwise, five foot eight, good cheekbones, brown eyes, hair dark and sleek with just a touch of grey showing. Early forties, one would say but she had just celebrated – not celebrated, there was no celebration, no one to celebrate with – observed her fiftieth birthday in a small café in Chiang Mai where she had made a wish, a fervent, heartfelt wish for better times ahead.

She watched the unending backpacker traffic on Soi 7, young, confident, believing. She sensed their sense of invincibility, their ability to handle any and all difficulties, their utter certainty that they would overcome any and all obstacles. They would live long and productive lives. They perused maps and Lonely Planets, just arrived from Laos or Cambodia or Myanmar and already planning further explorations to parts still unknown, roads less travelled, where paradise awaited, golden sands, cheap food, cheap beds – and for those so inclined cheap reefer and booze - a place yet undiscovered by those overweight, moneyed tourists who would, sure as God made little, green apples, ruin it if and when they did.

It was late November, and the weather was perfect, mid-seventies, blue cloudless skies and cool at night and as she sat under the shade of the old fig tree, she felt grateful she had discovered this place. She knew Bangkok, twelve hours by bus or train to the south was hotter, more humid, crowded, noisy and open twenty-four hours. She had spent time there and disliked it. Here it was slower, cooler, would stay comfortable until the end of January and into February.

The day lay ahead of her, a long walk, a Thai or oil massage maybe, a Singha or glass of wine later in a bar she had discovered on Soi 9 by Ratpakinai Road. It was run by an old Thai woman with no English but who she understood perfectly, no jukebox, no raucous farangs or their stalkers, no TV even, an oasis. She would sit there and read or fulminate – on all that had occurred, the good, the bad and a lot of ugly.

She was a Butte, Montana girl, and her Irish forebears had flooded into that mining town at the turn of the century to work the copper mines though her coloring suggested someone somewhere had spiked the gene pool with some Mediterranean color. She liked Butte, didn't love it. She loved to come back and visit family and friends. But she was glad to leave too. It was a blue-collar town, hard-working and much hard drinking.

Her father was a steady man, her mother down to earth and unflappable. Elaine was one of three children, a brother Ben, two years her junior and finishing up a career in the navy, her sister Libby a policewoman in Denver, Colorado. For some reason, her father had insisted that Elaine go East to college. She had attended and graduated Manhattanville and it was there she had first met Robert Newsome. They dated intermittently, drifted apart, and went their separate ways.

Years later and now in her thirties with a marriage and divorce behind her – a brief three-year affair that both she and a mister Jamie Denning realized from the get-go, was a mistake, and both were for a long time too embarrassed to broach.

She and Robert Newsome had literally bumped into each other on a crowded subway platform in Manhattan. At that time, she believed it was meant to be. There was no such thing as coincidence. They were meant to be together. (But the pain, what about the pain that came later?) She was pushing her way onto the train, he was on his way out, the platform and train crowded with rush hour traffic.

They recognized each other instantly, amazing considering it had been all of ten years since they had last seen each other. He had promptly stayed on the train and after an awkward moment they were babbling excitedly to each other. He was so different then, Elaine thought. He was easy-going and down to earth. She was cautious in the beginning, not wanting to repeat the mistakes of the past. They dated for four years before she was convinced, he was the one, and accepted his proposal of marriage.

They had married in a small church in the village of Garrison, situated on the Hudson River, fifty miles north of Manhattan, a small wedding but relaxed and enjoyed by all, none more so than she. Robert – he had never been Bob - worked in the IT business, generally small, start-ups and his income was never regular and often minimal. She didn't mind. It was what he loved, and he was happy. They had a small apartment on the upper west side of Manhattan. Elaine worked for Columbia University, a brisk walk from their rented apartment. Looking back, she thought it was the happiest time of their marriage. They lived frugally and were content. She found to her amazement that Manhattan offered an incredible variety of free and inexpensive options in entertainment, parades, festivals, street fairs, conferences, concerts, and recitals.

They had both decided children were not in their future. They had tried, in the beginning and when it didn't happen, had pursued it no further. For eight years they had been happy with no dark clouds on the horizon and Elaine could envisage growing old gracefully with Robert by her side, strolling into middle age and beyond, hand in hand. What was about to happen, happened quickly, breath-takingly and in the beginning thrillingly.

Robert had moved on to another company, a startup called Tech-Up, the brainchild of a man called Harold Shipp. He had got in touch with Robert, whose skills were just what his company lacked at that juncture. Robert had eagerly accepted. If the company were successful, he would be handsomely rewarded. Harold Shipp was personable, persuasive and on his third marriage. Elaine hadn't liked him from the beginning, but they rarely met so it wasn't of great concern to her. Robert had been impressed with Harold, his contacts in the IT business and his fund-raising skills. Harold had launched a half-dozen companies. All had failed – not necessarily that they did not have potential, but competition was fierce, and investors were impatient and constantly being bombarded with the next great invention, innovation, idea, concept.

Things would be different with Tech-Up. It was successful from day one and Robert's remuneration was handsome. Elaine shared in Robert's excitement and was happy for him. Suddenly they were better off, financial worries reduced, and for a while, it was overwhelming. The quiet quality of their lives disappeared. Robert was on the road constantly with Harold. She could have accompanied him, but she did not want to lose her sense of worth, validation, maybe, in what she was doing. She was as entitled to her dreams as Robert was to his.

She wanted to continue working. She derived great satisfaction from her job assisting students with financial loans, grants and scholarships, accommodation options and the myriad problems that new students encountered – many from rural backgrounds, in the huge, sprawling metropolis that was New York.

They, Robert and Elaine, began to drift apart, as they spent less and less time together, Elaine desperately trying to maintain a semblance of continuity and togetherness, happily greeting Robert as he returned from longer and longer, always necessary business trips. He was changing, had changed, babbling on about stock options, prospects for growth and what a genius Harold was.

Harold too, was changed, the harried look replaced by a look of confidence bordering on smugness. He seemed to Elaine to have changed into something alien, puffed up with self-importance, with expensive clothes, shoes, haircuts and all the accessories of the newly rich, Rolex, cufflinks and all accoutrements that would set him apart as a man of consequence, substance.

Slowly, inexorably, with Harold as his model, Robert too, was changing, buying into the affluent lifestyle more and more. He was mimicking Harold in dress, accessories, facials and high-end haircuts. When she queried him, he replied, "It's just part of the process. Harold says a look of affluence reassures the client, especially when you're pitching for funds. Results bear him out. Don't worry, honey, I'm still the same steady guy you married."

(But he was not.) "I'm not changing. Harold says…" She was hearing this more and more as time progressed. Harold says, Harold thinks, and Harold wants. Harold was changed, utterly and Robert was in the process. The company had been written up in various financial and IT publications and though Harold garnered the major plaudits, Robert had been mentioned and quoted also and to Elaine's utter surprise was not immune to ego inflation. Now Robert was asking her to accompany him to a four- day seminar in Miami.

"I can't, honey. I'm already committed to working this weekend. We have conferences going on all this weekend. I marked it on the calendar a month ago."

"Couldn't you cancel out?"

"No, I can't and it's unfair to ask."

"Okay," he sighed, "I guess I'm going alone."

"Last thing I want, is to listen to Harold expound on his genius."

"We owe it all to him, honey," Robert replied, "without him…"

"We were doing just fine," Elaine interrupted. "I wish sometimes we had that time back."

"It's only going to get better, honey, I promise." He took her in his arms and kissed her. "Wait, just wait."

But it didn't. Elaine couldn't be certain, but she thought that Miami was the beginning of the unraveling, that something happened to trigger a major change in Robert's behavior and personality.

Maybe he was seduced. Maybe he seduced. Whatever happened, he liked it and wanted more. If she thought it would eventually quiet with a gradual return to normality, she was mistaken. If anything, it grew more frantic, Robert constantly working late or attending conferences, seminars throughout the country and more and more overseas. Now he rarely asked her to accompany him. He knew she disliked Harold and Harold was part of the package. More and more she detected a distancing in him, a casualness in his contacts with her, a reluctance in sharing details of what was happening in the company and how it was progressing. Their physical relationship, too, was fast disappearing.

She broached the subject with Robert, and he reassured her. It was a critical time for the company. He was pouring all his energy and effort, alongside Harold into establishing the company as a major player in their niche. This was their time, their window of opportunity and they had to grab it with both hands. There was cutthroat competition out there and today's new idea was obsolete next year. She knew that what he said was true. It wouldn't always be like this. He was securing both their futures. The time would come when they could relax, marvel at what had been accomplished and how their lives had changed, where they could travel and enjoy a fulfilling life together.

She was reassured – but a month later discovered evidence of his infidelity. It was a room paid for in a hotel in Atlanta, a hotel he had not stayed in. When she made inquiries, her suspicions aroused, she recognized the name of the young woman as an employee of the company. She kept quiet. Robert could justify it. She was a valued employee of the company and accompanied him to many of the conferences, seminars etc but why had he charged her room and why a different hotel.

Discreetly she hired a private detective and within a week had all the proof needed that Robert was not just engaging in an extra-marital affair but more than one. Where was the relaxed, easygoing man she had married? She was stunned. Though she knew things had changed, not just in how they lived and what was now available – they had moved to a much bigger apartment, leased for now, with magnificent views of the Hudson River – but also in their relationship. She had never believed Robert was involved with another woman – or women. She felt angry, humiliated, betrayed. He was her soul mate. They were soul mates – or had been.

Maybe it was partly her fault. She had been selfish in not participating fully in his triumph, in the incredible turnabout that had occurred in their lives. She had clung to her career - yet she was entitled to that. But she could have made more of an effort. There were times she could have accompanied him but the thought of Harold's overbearing presence, his latest trophy clinging to his side with her perfect skin and perfect teeth and perfect body, his air of superiority and triumph. Also, in Harold's presence, Robert changed, took on the persona of an acolyte.

Maybe she could have done more. She had no children to dilute her love. She had only Robert. She loved him and determined she would fight to hold him. But it was he who had betrayed their love, marriage vows. She would confront him, listen to him, and decide.

The meeting didn't go well. He had promised he would be home by seven at the latest. She had taken a leisurely bath, had studied her image carefully in the full-length mirror and had been reassured. She was within a pound or two of her mid-twenties weight. Her skin was excellent as had been her mothers. Thanks Mom, she silently mouthed. She dressed carefully, blue jeans and a white silk shirt with mid length sleeves and what used to be called a Nehru collar. She wore a silver necklace and matching bracelet, a gift from Robert years before. She laid out prosciutto and melon – he rarely ate on arriving home. He liked to eat earlier and would grab something at work. She opened a bottle of red, Merlot and a Sauvignon Blanc. Robert liked both. Seven o' clock came and went and by eight o' clock she had finished her second glass of wine. She was irritated and slightly inebriated when he finally pushed open the door at 8.25. All her good intentions flew out the door.

"Where were you? How could you do this to me?"

He took off his overcoat and scarf. "I'm sorry, hon. It was another of those 'Way Forward' sessions that Harold loves so much. It doesn't end till he says so."

"Fuck Harold."

"What's the matter, honey? You know how it is."

"You've been cheating on me."

He was in the process of removing his shoes. He stopped, was still for a moment before straightening up. "What are you talking about?"

Suddenly all her anger evaporated, and she doubled over, huge sobs wracking her body. "How could you? How could you?"

He went to her and held her. "No honey, that's not true."

Her anger flared again. He was lying, barefaced. If he had admitted then to what he had done, Elaine thought, months later, they might have had a chance. She raged at him, throwing out names and dates.

"Where did you get all this information? It's garbage."

"I hired a detective."

"You hired a detective to spy on me?" Now he was trying to turn around the confrontation. Demonstrating love and support for her hard-working husband, she hires a detective to spy on him.

It just got worse from there. He admitted to nothing. She ordered him to leave. The husband she loved and trusted had been replaced by an alien, who cheated and then lied about it, who seemingly had no regrets in destroying a marriage he had seemed so happy in, not so long ago.

She knew not this man. Robert left the next morning, and her nightmare began. She hired a lawyer on the recommendation of her friend, Beth who worked with her in Columbia and who, herself, had gone through a divorce five years earlier.

"He's good, he's thorough and he's kind. He's a gentleman."

His name was Michael Ferders, and she saw him a week after Robert had moved out. He was tall, somewhere in his fifties, married happily, it seemed for over twenty years, just beginning to lose his shape – thirty pounds overweight, she thought. He was still distinguished looking – and he was kind. He listened silently to her story without interruption. When she told of hiring a detective, he raised his eyebrows. When she was finished, he was silent, deep in thought.

"The detective, he has photographic evidence?" he asked.

"Yes." She took a large manila envelope from her bag and placed it on his desk.

He didn't open it. "You want this to be amicable, as much as possible?"

"Of course," she replied.

"Has he contacted you?"

"He tried, left messages, but I didn't call him. I didn't know what to say. I'm angry, sad, outraged, sorry for myself, sorry for this mess, on some level sorry for him. It was too much for him… everything. He wasn't… able to…process it…in a positive way."

"I understand your confusion," he told her. "Has he hired a lawyer?"

"I have no idea," she said. "If he had just opened up to… his affairs?"

"He had more than one?"

She nodded silently. "Okay, leave it to me. I'll make some calls."

They agreed on a fee structure, she signed some papers and, it seemed like nanoseconds, she was out on the sidewalk, walking down Broadway. She hardly believed what was happening to her. She remembered a remark a colleague of hers had made. It was the annual Christmas party and he had said, 'Life has a way of kicking us in the teeth.' She was flabbergasted by the remark.

"Isn't that being rather harsh," she had challenged him. "Isn't life what we make it?"

He had shrugged and turned away. His remark had more relevance now.

Things were eerily quiet over the next weeks. She shared her distress only with Beth. Robert didn't call and she heard nothing from her lawyer. Maybe this would be a quiet, uneventful divorce, a fair sharing of assets – and they would go on with their lives, separate, apart. A small voice inside her whispered, maybe they could reconcile, commit to counseling and slowly build up a loving relationship but now on a firmer foundation. But the voice grew dimmer.

She read of Tech-Up's triumphs, occasionally, and saw a picture of 'Harold and Robert' with briefcases, serious and determined in a financial journal. Robert looked good, prosperous. She had not thought much about the money, the financial aspect of the separation and divorce. She did not need a lot, but she wanted her fair share, and it would be more than adequate. Robert's compensation from the company was enormous. As little as she knew about the company and his benefits, she knew that.

She began to think that it was just about inevitable it would be divorce – it was heading in that direction rapidly. She had heard nothing from Robert. She had called his cell and left a message. Could they talk privately, just the two of them? She heard nothing. Then she got a call from her lawyer. Would she schedule an appointment to discuss the case?

She met with him on a raw November day, grey clouds scudding across a dark sky and rain coming and going. He was as direct and as kind as ever and, after inquiring of her health and well-being, provided tea and biscuits. She sipped her tea as he unfolded a large sheaf of documents retrieved from a filing cabinet.

"Well," he stared at her intently, "it seems we're in for some difficult times. Your husband maintains you were having an affair – with a colleague at work. He's hired a very efficient, very expensive lawyer and he's tied up the bulk of his compensation: stock options, deferred compensation etc., that won't be realized for years to come. Both he and Harold are foregoing serious compensation – and according to these papers are practically living hand to mouth," he smiled, "until the company is on a sounder footing. He's filed for divorce, citing your affair, your lack of support as wife and partner and lack of interest in his efforts to put you both on a sound financial footing. You've refused all entreaties to be with him at important functions and he's had to employ surrogates in situations where it's imperative he has a partner."

She was stunned, speechless, the statement of her supposed affair blocking out all the other issues. How could he? She didn't know this man. Where did he come up with this preposterous idea of an affair? She struggled to express herself. He threw some pictures on the table. It was a small function at Columbia.

She had listened patiently as Ben Coachford had poured out his heart at the breakup of his relationship with his girlfriend of eight years. She drank more wine than she normally might have, as he poured out his tale of woe and hugged him more than she normally might have as the evening progressed. Ed Long, the insatiable amateur photographer had given her the pictures days after. She had thrown them carelessly in a drawer in their bedroom where… Robert must have come back to their apartment. Then she knew. Harold was pulling the strings, using lessons learned over three marriages, Svengali to Robert, his pliant acolyte.

Finally, she asked, "What's the next move?" He remained deep in thought.

"This is looking like all-out war. His lawyer has resources than I have not. I can hire a temp to help with research, leg work etc. but it's going to be expensive. I will continue to represent you, if you so wish – and I will do my very best to obtain an equitable settlement. It's clear he has done well. It's also clear he seems unwilling to be fair.

Whether it's his lawyer playing tough initially and possibly, possibly backing off later…"

"It's Harold."

"Harold?"

"Yes. Harold, his partner, his three times married partner, his Svengali. He's pulling the strings. Robert was never like this. He was a good and decent man. We dated for four years. I wanted to be sure."

Michael swung his chair and gazed out the window behind his desk. He stayed quiet for a long time until Elaine was ready to ask if he was okay. Then he spoke.

"What exactly are you hoping to get from this divorce settlement? We've talked in general terms about an equitable division of assets. But you live in a leased apartment, correct? A sum of money in your name from before your marriage – which will quickly dissipate as this situation progresses. So, what exactly…?"

"I would like to be able to buy my own apartment, preferably in Manhattan, otherwise in the Bronx or Queens. I would need a lump sum, for a deposit, a hundred thousand plus or so. Otherwise, I'll be fine. I have my job which I love, and which gives me health coverage. That's it."

"Doesn't sound like an awful lot. Okay. I'll approach about a settlement, ask for a sum much more than that, and we'll go from there. You okay with that?"

"If that's how it's done."

"Sometimes it is and sometimes it's nowhere near. Each case can be very different, as different as the personalities involved. Okay?"

"Okay."

So, it began. She tried to live a life as normal as possible. She went to work, met with her small circle of friends at times. They all knew of her situation, that it was stressful, could even be injurious to her health. Beth was particularly helpful. She had been through it and knew how stressful and debilitating it could be. But Beth was now in a good place, had a steady man friend and her life had returned to a degree of normalcy. As a couple, they went on long weekends on ski trips and hiked and camped in the Summer and Fall. They did not live together, and it seemed this arrangement was ideal.

Elaine swore it would be a long time before she would date, an even longer time before she would commit to a steady relationship. She had no faith in her ability to judge character. She thought she would never marry again, never allow another into her living quarters, long or short term. She would live out her life alone. Would she be sexually involved again? She didn't know, would not rule it out at this early stage but as the saying went, time would tell. But she would be extremely cautious, for sure. Now, the future was dark and treacherous.

Then, when it seemed it could only get worse, things changed. Was it as a result of her prayers, daily, in the little church near where she worked and her commitment to not hate Robert, despite all that had occurred? Her mother had been a firm believer in the power of prayer. Her mother had worn out more than one set of beads.

Her lawyer called and asked to see her. It was an unusually cool, May day when she arrived at his office. She sat and waited. He studied her for so long that she began to feel uneasy.

"I have some news for you, good and bad."

"Good and bad?"

"Yes. Your husband Robert passed, yesterday."

She was confused. "Passed as in died?"

"Yes. A massive heart attack in a hotel in Seattle. He was attending a conference.

"Was there another involved?"

He nodded. "Your husband…"

"My ex-husband."

"No. The divorce hadn't gone through. It was to take affect three days later."

"So?"

"So. you're entitled to half his earthly belongings, as the will had stated."

She was stunned. There was a moment of triumph, then, a feeling of loss and sadness. For what she wasn't sure. The tragedy of their marriage and how it could, would, she believed, have been a happy one but for a certain, insecure, scheming Svengali. It could have been so much better. She didn't need 'riches.' She would have been satisfied with 'comfortable.' And somehow, she knew that Harold would never be a happy soul. She knew happiness began deep inside a person's soul, insides, psyche, and he was incapable of that.

After much legal maneuvering, she emerged with a substantial sum, more than enough to buy an apartment, more than big enough for her needs, in upper Manhattan. She knew, and her lawyer had assured her, she was entitled to more – but it would be a long, drawn-out affair. Harold would see to that. She wasn't ready for a year's plus long battle. She wanted to end that part of her life and make a clean break with Harold. But he was happy with the settlement and, also, relieved she would be out of his life.

It would take her a long time to achieve a somewhat tranquil existence and the Chiang Mai visits were a part of that. She would spend more and more time there and possibly even, a permanent move sometime in the future. She loved the food, massages and the people, so gentle, so secure and devoted in their beliefs in Buddha, the monks rising at dawn and moving among the populace soliciting alms.

While in Chiang Mai, eight years after her divorce, her friend Beth called.

"You hear the news?"

"No. I try only to read books here. Don't keep up politically with what's happening there or anywhere else." So, what news?"

"Harold, on his fifth marriage, had open heart surgery and, from all accounts, is not doing very well."

"I'll pray for him."

"What?"

"I mean it. I'll say a pray for him."

"Damn. You Irish Catholics are one screwed up bunch. I swear. That guy made your life miserable."

"It's the old verities. What goes round, comes round."

"What's 'verities?'" But she knew.

April

April, - fickle soul, bright and smiling.
Then you scowl and thunder, throw
Lightning bolts and cry.
What is it with you?

Do you lack confidence, a case of low self-esteem?
And how about us, bewildered souls
What are we to think?

At your best, you are so wonderful, brilliant even,
Dressed in fine colors, we all
Adore you. Then, then……

Bess and May

Bess and May were spinsters and sisters, Bess, and May Street - May at 64 the older by two years, both in the teaching profession, both excellent teachers. They came of an old established Connecticut family, in Wilton, Conn. At one time the family had been extremely well-off, owning the Wilton's only funeral parlor –Street and Newcombe Funeral Home, the latter the original partner bought out and dead for many years. They also owned an automobile dealership on Main Street, Street Chevrolet.

There was old money on their mother's side too, Mabel Longan, the only daughter of a prominent citizen, one Michael J. Longan of Easton, Conn., who had made his money trading commodities. Bess and May had gone to Sacred Heart Academy in Greenwich until their father up and married their piano teacher, a woman 23 years his junior. This event pitched their lives into chaos. Neither ever found out the whys or wherefores. There were rumors of a gambling habit, loan sharks, embezzlement but it was the catalyst for the slow gradual decline of their once beautiful mother.

Over the years a series of smaller and smaller abodes would be home until they ended up in a rented three- bedroom house on the shabby side of Danbury. When they were forty and forty-two, their mother, at sixty-three, gently expired, a look of what seemed to them relief, suffusing her face. These events had marked them both though they would deny it.

As the years progressed, they were subject to feelings of despair and a distrust of all humanity. They lacked faith, also, in institutions, relationships and one might even say, God. But they were fighters too, and as much as the world tried to bury them, they got back up and screamed their defiance.

There were times when one or the other entered relationships that looked promising enough to move out. Move out they did, with high hopes and determination that, this, yes this, would be the one. They would make it work. But always they came back and resumed their lives together. Times, they would turn on each other, venting venom and hellfire, berating, and accusing till exhausted, yet knowing that the other had no more to do with their predicament than the man in the moon. But, for a little while, it released the frustration and despair that beset them. They seemed to understand that this was how it had to be.

Theirs was a complex relationship. Bess was a reader. May liked to knit. Both still taught and both were contemplating retirement in a few years. But they were opposites in their habits and lifestyle. May hid behind a persona of toughness and cynicism and was fastidious about her food – to the point of buying and keeping hers separate - and clothes. Bess was the exact opposite, and this was a major bone of contention. She was careless and disorganized and was not averse to 'borrowing' from May. May was savage in her condemnation of what she could only regard as out and out stealing.

The stealing or borrowing was relatively low-key, a yogurt, some bread, a can of soup, but what irked May was Bess's aversion to being truthful and accepting responsibility for her actions. She <u>was</u> lazy and had been disorganized all her life and had made little effort, it seemed to May, to address the situation. May threatened to put a lock on the refrigerator and so at this time, relations were strained, and venom stalked the land.

"Grow up, grow up or leave", May told her at the end of a fifteen-minute recitation of all her perceived indiscretions. "Grow up, take responsibility for your actions. You function so efficiently in the classroom. But as soon as you walk through this door, you turn into a slob. You steal and you lie about it."

"Oh, you're such a poor excuse for a human being," Bess said. "Where's the Christian charity you exhibit to the outside world? Oh, May has such a placid temperament. She is so good with the kids, especially those more difficult. She's just wonderful. Ha, if they only knew."

"A lie is always a sin, and nothing can ever make it lawful," May told her in a slow deliberate voice.

"Oh, that's just some of your Papish pap," Bess retorted. May had spent a year in a Catholic boarding school after her father had left and her mother was barely able to function.

'A lie is a sin in all religions," May told her though she wasn't quite sure that it was.

"You haven't been inside a church in twenty years. Don't go quoting religion to me," Bess retorted.

"When you lie or steal, you sin before God our Creator."

So it went for days, sniping back and forth, probing for the weak spot, for the blow that would cripple. It was kind of game, a struggle that seemed to exhaust and exhilarate simultaneously, concatenating insults that would have destroyed the souls of lesser mortals. But they were evenly matched and had played the game forever. Neither one would surrender, so it would finally, mercifully grind to a halt, both foggy-brained and cotton-mouthed. Neither one ever claimed victory.

There were times, though not of extended duration, when they seemed in perfect harmony, when little was said or needed to be. But it was the other time, in the midst of a fiery exchange when Bess received the call from Gabriel - Gabriel Olerud, fifty-six or thereabouts, also in the teaching profession and an old flame of Bess's. He had married and moved out West about seven years ago.

"Hi," he said, "it's Gabriel," as if he had called her just a few days previous.

"Gabriel," she said hesitantly, "Gabriel who married and is living in California?"

He laughed. "Gabriel who *was* married and who *was* living in California," he told her. Her heart skipped a beat. She was unsure of what to say, whether she should commiserate or congratulate.

"Are you okay? Did something happen? Is your wife, okay?"

"My ex-wife is fine," he said, "and I'm fine." He laughed again. "I think maybe marriage is not for me," he paused, "at least not with Louise – such immaturity. We separated after three years and got divorced a year after. Boy oh boy, was she carrying some heavy baggage." He paused, "but I don't mean it to seem like it was all her fault. I have to take at least a share of the blame. I can be sticky at times."

"Sticky," she repeated?

"Yes, stubborn, unwilling to concede when I feel I'm right."

"I always felt you were reasonable," she said, knowing that was a lie. He had been unreasonable to her when he walked out of their relationship with hardly a look back and no explanation.

"I feel it's better for both of us," he had said. Two weeks after, he left for California with Louise, the flame-haired teaching aide, more than ten years his junior.

"So, what have you been doing?" His voice had taken on that bantering, isn't-this-great-fun quality that had seemed so attractive years ago. "You and May living together?"

She was reluctant to answer knowing that he would know they were without partners.

"I just moved back," she lied and hoped he wouldn't pursue it. She jumped in with a torrent of information about the school, staff, and retirements. "There's been such a turnover," she said, "people just want to get out. Are you still teaching?" she asked.

"No, no," he said, "I got out before I burned out. I'm in Executive Placement now, y'know, headhunting. It's an exploding field." Then; "What would you say if I asked you out" and before she could answer, "we could see a movie, have a beer, whatever you might want to do."

She had been unattached, it seemed, forever, hadn't had a proposition like that for God knows how long. She felt panicked, not sure how to react. She wanted to say yes but didn't want to appear too eager and there was his abrupt dismissal previously. He interpreted her silence as reluctance.

"Bess, I know I wasn't completely fair with you," his voice lowered, earnest. "I owe you an apology for that. It was a confusing time in my life, and I took the easy way out."

She stared out her bedroom window, her mind recollecting, analyzing past events. She wondered how she would answer, what she really wanted. A great weariness came over her. Suddenly she knew. She wanted to be treated right, with respect, to be happy and comfortable with a partner. Maybe it didn't have to be a man. She wanted a friend first and later, maybe, love and intimacy.

Surprising herself, her voice cool and firm she said, "you must not have respected me, Gabriel, or you would not have treated me so shabbily. I want to be with someone who treats me with respect." Before he could answer, she hung up. She felt like she had taken a small step, finally to a better place. She returned to the living room and studied May, head bent, knitting furiously, efficiently.

"Would you like a cup of tea," she inquired gently? May tilted her head, needles suspended in mid-air. For a long moment she stared at Bess.

"That would be nice," she said.

All Alone

We are all essentially alone
To do whatever moves our will
Free will to go or stray or stay
Sit by that stream, go climb that hill

Potential fully realized
Or 'only for' or 'not to be'
Carried by currents where or when
Or walk the walk and fearlessly

The bird, the turt-le, bee or flea
All alone, essentially
Wrest-le with affairs of life
Sustenance, love, pain or strife

Naked, squealing we arrive
Toiling, struggle to survive
Then we cross the river Styx
Naked, helpless, now no will.

John Pius Clarke

I read in the paper today, where John Pius Clarke had died at the ripe old age of forty-seven. He was old when he died, his body racked with a multitude of ailments, lung and liver, bones and blood. He was a smoker and a drinker and the last time I saw him, on a quick trip back from London, he was hunched over at the end of the counter in Downey's pub, his back bent like a bow. I didn't approach him. He wouldn't have wanted to see me or be seen, and I left as quietly as I came.

I knew a different Pius, young and funny and not a care in the world. We were in the same class in the Christian Brothers, back in the days, placed in the same desk that first day. He was outgoing, I was ingoing I suppose you could say, slow to make friends, reluctant to reach out. But it was easy to know Pius – he made it easy to know him. Learning came easy to him, too and in the beginning, I was, maybe, a little envious. I struggled, every achievement hard-earned. But we had common interests and started palling around together.

Neither one of us was interested in sports – we liked the singing and the music, so it was only natural that we'd join the choir at Saint Enda's. Pius loved to sing and had a natural ability. He had the potential to be very good. I wasn't bad either, if I say so myself but his voice with the proper training could be special. Kate Doyle, the choir director saw his potential and encouraged him. With the singing he grew in confidence. There was the possibility for a good and productive life. He was smart, he would finish secondary and go on to university. He talked of wanting to be a teacher. I thought with a little bit of Divine Providence shining on him, he might some day, make a name for himself. I would read about him in the papers. We'd keep in touch.

A rage envelops me. How little we know of what life will bring us – chance encounters, improbable decisions, mere coincidences. A bureaucratic decision - diocesan shuffling, the whims of a bishop, maybe - brought a new parish priest, Father King to Saint Enda's and sent the previous, Father Mc Gee to an outlying parish. Fr. Mc Gee was a lovely man. Fr. King seemed so in the beginning.

He was a big man, handsome in a rough way but overweight. He dressed, how can I describe it, flamboyantly, maybe? Not quite, but different. He liked colorful scarves, reds and mauves and violets. He wore expensive, shiny shoes. He drove a BMW, black, of course in keeping with his profession. What he wore and what he drove placed him above the ordinary residents of this small town, most of whom struggled to hold their own, where bills, food and medicine, a child's clothing and school supplies were concerned. Many looked on him as special, exotic and some in awe and wonder.

He was charming when he wanted to be, but I never liked him from the first time we met. It was an instinct I put great store in; my initial reaction on first meeting another – like how a dog smells another dog, I thought. I liked to check their…what they gave off, aura maybe, emanations. There was surface conviviality but underneath, barely concealed, was something predatory. I had no doubt he would be a bishop someday, if he so wanted.

Soon after he arrived, he came to hear us sing. I watched him watch us. When Pius sang, King's concentration became total, his attention riveted. I saw him lick dry lips and felt a cold hand clutch my insides. He showed great friendliness to Pius and of course Pius was flattered. Who wouldn't? A man who was God's envoy on this earth, who spoke with all the authority of the Holy Roman Catholic Church, who was admired and respected, even feared. Who wouldn't indeed? He began to request Pius's assistance for various projects and Pius was paid generously for the time he put in. Pius's parents, Michael and Noreen were ecstatic. With Fr. King's influence, it could only bode well for Pius, in his studies and in his prospects.

We still met, Pius and I over the next few months, but less often as King demanded more and more of his time. But he seemed the same, rattling on about what he did with King. The Father had taken him to Dublin; some monthly business to do with the diocese and he had shown him Trinity College. It was a secret fantasy of Pius's to someday attend this august center of learning – out of reach for most of us on mostly financial reasons, but in the long ago it was religion and background. It was a Protestant upper class institution founded by and for the British who cast a cold eye on Catholic and middle- and lower-class aspirations to higher education. Pius loved what he saw, bands of students hurrying to and fro, some lazing on the spacious grounds, many engrossed in study in the warm, early summer sun. He had seen the Book of Kells, the incredible high-domed centuries old library full of the rarest books, row upon row way, way up to the ceiling. He was the old Pius. Then he changed.

In the beginning I noticed little, maybe a shade less spontaneity, a hesitation before answering, a preoccupation. With what? One day after choir, Fr. King asked Pius to stay behind. He needed him for some task, and I saw hesitation in Pius before he assented. Something in his demeanor, in the priest's fierce look struck me. There was something askew here. I left the church but returned quietly. I had to, must see if something inappropriate was happening. I heard murmurs in the sacristy, went around the side to a window looking into the sacristy. Fr. King was holding Pius in a close embrace. I saw Pius's face clearly. It betrayed nothing, fear nor revulsion nor arousal. It was as if he were contemplating nature, neither responding nor resisting. The priest spoke in a hoarse, urgent tone. I could catch only part of what he was saying but I got the jist of it.

Their love was a sacred bond, a man's sexual urges were a part of God's creation. He loved Pius and wanted the best for him, would do all in his power to advance him. He wanted, needed physical contact with him. Then he kissed Pius on the lips, a long passionate kiss.

I slipped away and a rage took me. How could Pius resist? How long could he withstand this onslaught, keep perspective, keep his innocence? How long could he remain unscathed, unscarred, whole?

King was imposing his will on a boy, a well-adjusted but immature boy at a critical stage of his social and sexual development.

I was overcome with such an impotent rage that I began to gag with a hiccupping motion that eventually led to a full vomiting. I knelt, bent over on the damp grass, filled with revulsion, hate, despair. My friend was being dragged to a desolate, dark place and I felt helpless to do anything about it. I imagined killing or maiming the priest to remove him from Pius's life before it was too late. Maybe it was already? How could I make him go away, far, far away? But how, when, where?

In the climate of that time, it was near impossible to censure a priest. Parents would often beat the child for even suggesting such a thing as inappropriate behavior by a priest. The law wanted nothing to do with accusations against the Church, deferring to the bishop in any matters religious, deferring to the power and influence of Holy Mother the Church, the power that radiated from Rome to the remotest parts of the planet. It was an institution two thousand years old which had survived war, treachery, persecution and scandal, riches beyond counting, influence beyond knowing. What could I do?

I wished for Divine Inspiration. What would be the precise steps to take – perfect in this situation - to foil the priest and rescue my friend? I loved Pius, I realized, he was my best friend, closer to me than anyone else, family or otherwise. I wanted to know him and his journey, as we grew old, married, and had family, pursued careers, advanced into middle age and beyond. We would meet up as life progressed and update, the family we had, our children, the good times and the bad. We had a bond that I wished fervently would never be broken.

I waited for Pius to confide in me and waited in vain. It was impossible for me to broach the subject. I felt helpless and inadequate and at times an impotent rage that left me gasping and light-headed. One night overcome by both, I stabbed the tires of the priest's car, puncturing all four. Later that week, I threw red paint on his front door, anything to give him pause for thought, make him uneasy that maybe someone…knew or suspected what was going on. I thought of slipping a note under his door; "I know what you are doing. Shame on you. Molesting young boys is a crime. You will be revealed." But I didn't. Again, I prayed for Divine Intervention, knowledge, inspiration. What to do?

For others, life continued as normal as ever. Parishioners debated the relative merits of King versus Mc Gee. There was always a nostalgia when they left – the abrasive parts forgotten, and the highlights accentuated. King was more assertive, the church was to be painted, carpets replaced, parishioner contributions increased. It was needed, many argued. Father McGee was more in touch with Heaven, a holy man but maybe neglectful of worldly demands. The church had deteriorated, dampness invading in some areas, plain for all to see. The roof was beginning to leak at the upper right-hand corner near the altar and when the rains blew in from the sea, the steady drip, drip of water could be plainly heard. Fr. King was the man to rectify the situation and he had already begun. There was an extra collection now for the remedial work. A committee had been formed.

Pius grew more pensive, less like the happy, carefree, loving-life Pius and more like a brooding, lonely, confused boy. I tried to bring up the subject one day.

"You okay, Pius?" He gave me a wistful smile, turned his head away.

"Something's on your mind. You want to talk about it, between you and me, private."

He hesitated for a moment. "Yeah, I do have things on my mind. I'll work it out."

"Why'd you drop out of choir?"

"Just didn't feel like singing anymore."

"You always loved singing."

"I did. Now I don't - care…to sing."

I couldn't bring up what I had seen in the sacristy. I couldn't tell others. Who could I tell, who would take action? No one I knew. And I would be betraying my friend. It had to come from him. I hated King, hated his kind, those in positions of power preying on the poor, hungry, less fortunate. I had sympathy for the thief who stole to survive, feed his or her family. This I understood. But he was in a position to do so much good, comfort the broken, hope to the hopeless, to lead by example. He was preying on, not praying with a member of his flock. He deserved the fires of hell - if such existed, for a very long time, for eternity.

John King was in love for the very first time, again. He was sure Pius was the one. He was angelic with a beautiful voice, that slim build. He had thought he was in love before three years ago, that boy Timothy… He thought of J.J. He had first seen him on the football field, strong, athletic build, red hair, a born athlete. He thought everything was going as planned. He had asked J.J. to be an altar boy and J.J. was enthusiastic. He began, as he thought, slowly, carefully. He would touch him lightly, massage his shoulders, praise his athletic ability, stroke his beautiful red hair. Things were proceeding just as he hoped. Then one evening, alone with J.J. in the sacristy, he had touched him inappropriately. Maybe J.J. was anticipating such a move, for quick as a lightning strike, he turned and punched the Father on the side of his head. King lay on the ground, stunned. J.J. stared at him for long moments, turned and left. He kept his head down for the next few weeks, but it seemed J.J. had kept the episode to himself. He reviewed all that had happened with J.J. and concluded he had been impulsive, impatient. He realized not all would be receptive to his advances. He would have to separate those who wouldn't from those who might. He would take it slow, even slower, and he would be cautious.

This was different. Pius had not yet reciprocated but he'd come around. He, King would convince him of his love, his sincerity, his passion for him. He had to be careful, very careful. He needed to be, and more so in the future. Sometimes it seemed too easy, the gullibility of the people, the young boys' innocence, belief in the sacred office of the priesthood. They would overlook so many inadequacies in a man ordained a priest, God, and the Church's representative on this earthly planet. But he was also a man, they understood, subject to all the temptations of man and like all men he would sometimes stumble and fall. They understood. Who was without sin? No one.

To be subject to temptation and the Devil's work was a condition of man. Maybe in some secret way, they rejoiced when a priest was seen to fail. If he could, then it was not so bad that they did. But he would always maintain vigilance. He knew there was an abhorrence of any homosexual activity and especially between young and old. It was against the teaching of the Church. Homosexuality was an abomination, but he knew it had always existed in and out of the Church and would ever. If it was revealed and proven, it would bring great scandal on the Church he loved – might even terminate his connection to that very same Church. He shuddered. He believed in God's mercy. He was human and subject to human failings. Was it so wrong to want love, a relationship with another human, an innocent who could be taught love before being corrupted by the avalanche of sexual temptation everywhere he turned?

Pius had changed too. There was a distance to him, a remoteness that had replaced the spontaneity and general good humor he had seen in the beginning. He wondered again, should he let it go, this preoccupation with – dare he say it – this love for Pius that had dominated his life since he had first seen and heard him sing. He wanted what others wanted, what maybe all humans desired, love and intimacy. Maybe it was a condition of our existence as essential as food and water. He could not, would not let it go. He had been disturbed when his car was vandalized, and paint thrown at his door.

There was an element in his parish disdainful of the law and the Church, young men who drank too much and frustrated with…who knew… their status in life, prospects, family obligations, lashed out and damaged possessions and property of others. It had been an ongoing problem. He had given a blistering sermon after the incident, decrying the mindless vandalism of the minority who engaged in such activity, their lack of faith in God and social order. Then Pius disappeared.

No one knew where. Had he left the country? None could say for sure. His parents were devastated, their dreams shattered. Pius was the one who would succeed, craft a golden future which would illuminate their lives. King came by to offer his sympathy. He had envisioned a very bright future for Pius. He had no inkling why he would leave. He, King had helped him in every way. He had done all he could and more. And more. They were overwhelmed by his obvious distress. They knelt at King's feet and offered their undying gratitude. A year later King left for another parish – another parish that needed to be updated, refurbished, taken in hand, financial health restored, that needed his drive and energy, his hands-on approach.

Pius came back from England three years later. He was changed, introverted, decaying and hollowed out, bent on destruction – his own, unrecognizable from the laughing, happy youth of not so long ago. He drank and smoked, ambition long gone and laid to rest. He worked for the rest of his short life in the local Glue factory, and one day, in the forty seventh year of his life, was carried out, finally, now, dead to this physical world but spirit murdered years before, a life's potential blunted and unfulfilled.

Conversation Between Lovers

"Hi, Joanne."

"Johnny, hi."

"How you doin'?"

"I'm doing fine. And you don't have to apologize about last night."

"I do and I am apologizing, right now."

"For what?"

"For what, let's see. For raising my voice, becoming impatient, dismissing what you were saying as inconsequential. When you did not react or get angry, I became even more frustrated."

"Johnny, I'm not into being put down. I'm not into guilt trips. If we have things we need to discuss, we discuss them. Let's keep the emotion and role playing out of it."

"You're right. And I'm working on it. That's what I so admire and love about you. You're honest and tell it like it is, that and a million other things." He starts singing. "The way you comb your hair, the way you hold your head..."

"And that's what I love about you, your bullshit," she says and laughs.

"Joanne, I'm serious, I really want this to work out. I know that you're the woman for me. You're the best thing since.... sliced bread. I feel like I want to be with you all the time. When I'm at work, I keep thinking about you, what we're gonna do tonight, what you'll be wearing -- whatever you wear, it looks like it was made for you. I love those deep philosophical conversations we have. You always seem to look at things in a different, fresh way that lets me see the situation in a whole new light. You're wise and beautiful..."

"Whoa, Johnny boy, slow down. You're portraying me as a cross between Gandhi and Elizabeth Taylor."

"What, looking like Gandhi and philosophizing like Miz Taylor?"

"Watch it, honey."

"But you're perfect for me. You're beautiful and you've got a great mind, got a great outlook on life, a great philosophy for living...."

"Johnny, not everyone would consider me beautiful. I never considered myself beautiful. Nice looking, yes, but not beautiful. I'm not sure if I would want to be what might be described as classically beautiful. There are certain burdens to being beautiful."

"See, that's what I mean, you look at things differently and you teach me to do the same. You're caring and decent, but sexy and exciting, too."

"Johnny, I have my bad times, too, but I know how to deal with adversity now, or I'm better able to. So, I meditate or spend some quiet time, till the bad times pass. I try to fill my life with positive things and you're the biggest, my love. I love how full of passion and energy you can be and that impetuous nature of yours."

"That impetuous nature of mine, as you call it, is dedicated to making you the most happy, fulfilled woman in these United States."

"I'll always remember that diner, and how you appeared at my table, as if out of nowhere, and declared 'Excuse me, I had to come over and say it. You are a most beautiful woman. I would love to get to know you, find out why you're so sad today, and maybe cheer you up. I thought you were a little nutty, but I was sad, having gone through that terrible relationship with Charlie. And you did cheer me up."

"I really think that we're good for each other, that we bring out the best in each other."

"You're so different to Charlie, like a ray of sunshine lighting up a dark, dank basement. I finally found the courage to leave him, thank God, and I swear I'll never be part of an abusive relationship again, mental or physical".

"Honey, I've never been in an abusive relationship, and am not going to start now. If extreme jealousy reared its ugly head, I was out of there. Extreme jealousy is a sign of a very insecure person or low self-esteem, and that's always trouble. Remember that cat I had, Mitzi. I had to get rid of her. She was extremely jealous. If I didn't come straight home from work, she got pissed off, sulked in the corner. Then she started ripping up my furniture. Then she wouldn't go for therapy."

"Be serious, butthead."

"Butthead?"

"I did a lot of soul searching after that relationship. I realized I had to reorder my priorities and make some fundamental changes in my life. I'll never know what attracted me to him in the first place. But I guess I do know, and it's painful to acknowledge it. It was that aura of cockiness and money that surrounded him. Deep down, I must have known that he was basically a very shallow character, but I chose to overlook it. I was dazzled by the cars he drove, the clothes he wore, the restaurants we ate at, the people we associated with -- all his fellow stockbrokers. They all had his attitude."

"And their heads were swelled to twice normal size."

"They believed money, bonuses and the good times were limitless and would go on forever. They were the new gladiators carving out fortunes in the cutthroat financial services capital of the world."

"It's probably tough to keep your feet on the ground in a business like that."

"That's why I was careful about entering another relationship, why I kept you at arm's length for such a long time."

"And your reluctance just whetted my appetite and made me want you more."

"Maybe, but that was not the intent. I liked everything about you, but I was not about to jump into another relationship, not right away. I was healing for a while and you helped that healing, honey, with your beautiful nature, your upbeat personality and your patience."

"Joanne, that was not patience. That was perseverance. I was not giving up on you. You would have had to shoot me to get rid of me. I was hanging in because I knew that the relationship would be something special."

"That's how it feels to me, too. So, what are we doing tonight?"

"Well, to make up somewhat for my despicable, male chauvinist behavior last night, you get to choose what we do and where we go, and I get to pay."

"And after?"

"After, I'm yours to do with as you wish."

"Ooh, sounds like a night of infinite promise and endless opportunity."

"It is I, Johann, at your service, m'lady."

"And where do your talents lie, Johann?"

"My talents are many, m'lady."

"Do they include lovemaking, Johann?"

"I am skilled in all phases of lovemaking, m'lady, and your wish is my command."

"Oh, Johann, you devil, pick me up at eight, no, make that seven thirty, and be punctual. I can't wait, honey."

"It will be a night to remember, m'lady, I will make it so. I must go now and prepare myself. Your faithful servant, Johann bids you adieu."

Sexual Discrimination - The Same Old Story?

I watched a TV program recently on stalkers and being stalked. The stalkers were all male and the stalked all female. The sense of fear and hopelessness that the women projected was palpable. They had no confidence that the law or society could protect them, and each case was a depressing litany of pursuing all lawful remedies and the total failure of those same laws to protect them. The result was further abuse, violence and even death.

But what was even more depressing was the conviction of these stalkers that these women belonged to them and had no right to demand separation or divorce. And the strength of their conviction led me to believe that it was part and parcel of their being, as integral to their manhood as supporting their family and defending them from outside violence might be. Which begs the question: have things gotten better for women as we've progressed in so many other areas, or is it still essentially the same old story?

It's difficult to be definitive and I'm not a woman, but I'm the father of three daughters and I do think that things have gotten better. It's an ongoing process and we may not even be halfway there, but progress has been made, at least in America. In some countries, women are effectively second-class citizens, and little has changed in the past hundred years or more. When emigrants from these countries arrive here, they bring these attitudes with them and the old and new cultures clash.

But there are many instances of sexual discrimination and sexist policy here, also. As recently as the sixties, airline stewardesses were fired if they got married and this policy was accepted by the educated, academia both male and female for a very long time. It was put in place by a male hierarchy, for what woman would impose such conditions on another woman, though sometimes it seemed that women were their own worst enemies. Within the women's movement itself, there were all kinds of divisions.

Emerging from an era of being dominated by men, women had conflicting views of what they wanted, how much they wanted and what equality for women really meant. The issue was further complicated by women of color and homosexual women. The Muncy Act of 1913 stated that a woman convicted of a crime be given a longer sentence than a man convicted of the same crime. The rationale behind this law was put forth by Katherine Bement Davis who wrote:" it would do more to rid the streets of soliciting, loitering and public vice than anything that could be desired." It was not declared invalid until 1968.

Man went unchallenged as the educated one, the boss, wage earner, head of household, explorer, entrepreneur, builder, dreamer, and writer so that it was a great shock to his system when women began to demand education and jobs. Dammit, a woman had a role to play too, as a mother/nurturer, virginal wife, and faithful companion.

All was fine and dandy for so long. How could they demand equal rights when everyone knew that they were not? Why did they have to rock the boat, damned fickle females?

The Civil Rights upheavals had a huge impact on women, and painful realities were confronted, and difficult decisions made. There was a period of exceptional gains for women, but the momentum has slowed. Old stereotypes persist. Woman's place is in the home. A woman is not complete without a man to lean on.

As I listened to the stories of the women who were stalked, I perceived a very real dilemma. Because the man primarily, is the principal wage-earner, the financial assets are seen as belonging to the man and in the event of divorce or separation, the woman has to petition the court for financial support. This financial support, even when granted is often difficult to collect, so it can be a struggle to survive for the divorced or separated woman, at least in the beginning.

There is no monetary value placed on the woman's work in the home even though she has often given up a well-paying career to conceive and nurse children. So, the woman cannot say; "I'm taking half of what our assets are and I'm leaving," and will stay in an abusive or intolerable situation because she has not the financial means to survive outside the marriage.

In the 1950's in Stride Toward Freedom, Martin Luther King wrote, "A solution of the present crisis will not take place unless men and women work for it. Human progress is neither automatic nor inevitable. Even a superficial look at history reveals that no social advance rolls in on the wheels of inevitability. Every step toward the goal of justice requires sacrifice, suffering, and struggle, the tireless exertions and passionate concern of dedicated individuals. Without persistent exertion, time itself becomes an ally of the insurgent and primitive forces of irrational emotionalism and social destruction."

These words are as easily applied to women's concerns today. There are many issues not resolved. New problems emerge as relationships and laws change. Men and women of goodwill must work together to eliminate the obstacles to women fulfilling their hopes and dreams. Sexism may never be eliminated totally. It is an ongoing process. In the last thirty years, great strides have been made in advancing women's rights and breaking down some of the age-old taboos, but a lot remains to be done, even in America. In some countries there has been little or no progress and in others, regression. For the sake of our daughters, granddaughters, and future generations we must set our sights on full equality for all our citizens. We can afford no less.

Mystical

"Ah, it's mystical," Cam whispered as we strolled through the woods, a mist beginning to dissipate as the sun struggled to break through. We meet after mass of a Sunday and take a walk, out to the woods to Tars Bridge or once in a while out to Clonea Strand. I enjoy his company and I'd say, he enjoys mine.

Cam has never travelled more than twenty miles outside Dungarvan, the town he was born in, and never shown interest in going, while I have never stopped travelling. Maybe that's the attraction. His viewpoint is unsullied, local, and insulated while mine is more the big picture. But his views are always interesting and often, on reflection, insightful.

"Look at that river, boy, 'twould talk to you. I seen a salmon jump there a week ago. Bejaysus, 'twas a foot and a half or more, a big silver yoke coming out of the wather like a bleddy torpedo, the eye flickin,' takin' in everything. I wonder what he thought when he seen me be the bank, standin' in me Sunday best, smokin' me pipe. That fecker's on fire, he was thinkin."

"D'ye know Val, in town?" he asked.

"I do," I said.

"A great oul' soul. He was off to the States, y'know. Out of the blue a cousin died, a strange story. Val had an aunt, long dead now, never tied the knot. Didn't she have a child, the child took off her and sent to St. Kevin's up in Cappoquin, adopted and sent to America."

"The cousin that died?" I asked.

"Yer man the cousin is right. Years, he spent, searching for where he came from, for his roots, as they say, fumbling and foostering and getting nowhere. Then he hired an investigator, a dick they call him out there in the States. Between himself scratchin' away and the dick investigatin,' didn't they get a hould of the whole story - traced him back to the very house he was born in, 14 Mitchell Street in the Old Boro."

He continued. "He was coming over here, ticket bought, suitcase packed, motorcar rented." Cam took a crumbled piece of paper from his inside pocket.

"Listen to this. I am returning to my blood, my issue, my people. Sit where they sat, walk where they walked, toiled, died and were buried. I am in a fever of excitement, of wanting. Finally, I am going home. Home, what joy that word brings. I am going home, what joy that phrase brings."

"His diary?"

"His diary, boy" he replied. "Val has it. But didn't the poor oul' soul drop dead, before he ever left, the aeroplane ticket clutched in his hand, the suitcase sitting next to him."

"A fright to God. Tis a sad oul world."

He sighed. "Tis, boy. It surely is."

"I will come and touch your brow and kiss your lips

Do vigil by your side and wash with tears your resting place."

"Did I make that up or is it somebody else's?"

"He left a will?" I inquired.

"He left a will. Val was summoned to New York. They had his name, address, all the particulars. Whatever the man left, Val and the sister got. He had no childer. Didn't Val bring him home in a little box."

"Scatter me ashes, he said, in the land of me forefathers."

"Last Sunday Val brought him up to the old place, himself, the sister and Daly, the young priest and they shook him out. He was back with his people. A strange thing. There was a big black yoke of a bird circled in the sky and landed not more'n twenty yards away. Val never seen a bird like it - and Val knows his birds – and the bird stopped till the deed was done, and then took off and disappeared."

"The Aunt, I'd say."

"Right, the mother seeing him home. 'Tis a fright how we're so attached. 'Tis mystical boy."

The Rat

He was alone, had always been - alone. Even with his mother, he felt alone. He didn't remember his father and his mother rarely talked about him. He had been a seaman, away most of the time before news had come of an accident on board the ship. It seemed it had been his fault, his mother told him, so there was no big payout to soften the blow. His mother got a job in a local supermarket and died when he was twenty-three. No big payout there either.

He felt it was meant to be, his aloneness and now he embraced it. Years ago, on his first day to attend school, his mother, a somber presence in his young life, had clasped his hand as she walked by him, "Stay away from the rough ones," she told him, "Better be on your own than getting into trouble. Better be on your own than inviting trouble and listen to the master."

She turned abruptly and left. He had taken her cautionary words to his bosom. He stayed away from the rough and the not so rough ones. It was as if her words were reinforcing all he felt instinctively, deep inside, even at that young age, what he would feel all the days of his life, a sense of aloneness on this planet - not unlike a dull pain deep in his being.

Over the years it had diminished to an ache, even sometimes forgotten. But it was always there.

He couldn't but listen, as the master roared and stomped through that first school day, and he knew he was in for a long, lonely sojourn. He made no friends, made no overtures, and rejected the few tentative offers to play or sit together. He wanted to, but somehow it seemed the tenor of his life had been laid down from birth. He was alone, would be alone, would, in all probability, die alone. He was a loner, an outsider, labels viewed with suspicion in this modern world where friendship and teamwork, participating and volunteering were the mantras of the brave new world.

He was intelligent and a good student but mediocre in sports and carried the 'social skills lacking' tag from grade to grade. On college graduation day with his grey mother's ghostly presence by his side, he knew the job he was best suited for. He needed some enormous, anonymous bureaucracy, where he was known by number and title only, where privacy was prized and friendships tentative. He applied to the Federal Civil Service, scored in the top one hundred nation-wide and, on the strength of those scores, was accepted with alacrity. As soon as he had secured employment, his mother had left this earthly planet. He found her in bed, cold and lifeless. It was as if now that her responsibilities of stewardship and guidance to him had ceased, she would slip away from this place she had never embraced but tolerated – until the need was no more.

She was cremated, a handful showing at her wake, and she was gone from his life. He chose the Bureau of Statistics after researching its mission statement and checking satellite locations. He chose as his place of employment a large, cavernous building that had seen better days in a neighborhood that matched the building.

Victor was not unattractive, of medium height, brown eyes and sandy brown hair always cut short. He had good skin, a gift from his mother, but his posture was bad with curved shoulders and a head that protruded forward. His clothes were outdated, and he wore them carelessly. With some adjustment, he might have been considered attractive, but it was of no consequence to him. He aimed for anonymity, and he achieved it. He had never known his father. He left, she said once and before he could hold his tongue, he inquired "What about the accident."

"He left and he had an accident," was his mother's short reply and the tone of her voice and the look in her eyes told him not to pursue it further, and he hadn't. He had ceased long ago to wonder who or what he was or what had become of him.

Like small colorless creatures the employees of the Bureau of Statistics and inhabitants of this drab, worn building, scuttled to work each morning, emerged in the sunlight for one hour at midday and then poured out of the building at five, scattering through the streets and down tunnels and quickly, like snow on a warming March Day, melted away. The streets, alleys, lanes, and tunnels that filled the city had swallowed them.

Victor was comfortable there. The Bureau of Statistics, it seemed, was like some kind of huge, warm burrow for those who instinctively disliked intimacy or loud friendships with their fellow workers. Their instincts had been correct.

The Christmas party each year was a resounding failure as they clasped their drinks too tight, avoided eye contact or any untoward gesture that might possibly indicate a wish for company, and stood isolated and uncomfortable till a reasonable time had passed and they could leave. Then they hurried back to their rooms or apartments, closed the door firmly and breathed a sigh of relief. It was over for another year.

But, too, there was always someone, who under the influence of too much alcohol, would act loud and boisterous, desperate for this one chance at frivolity and even friendship, who would inevitably end up a weeping, crumpled mess. Then they would endure a year of stoic silence and penance as their indiscretion slowly faded.

When he was forty-two years old, he had been employed there for twenty years. He had never taken a test to advance his career. He was more than competent in his work, and he was urged on numerous occasions and by various supervisors to take the competitive exams that would advance his career.

He was not interested. He felt the married staff and those with children and, financial responsibilities far greater than his, should be the ones to have the enhanced benefits and increased salary. He had more than enough. He was frugal in his habits and part of his bi-weekly remuneration went into pension and savings accounts.

Now, on the verge of his forty third birthday, he reviewed his life and found it lacking. A strange restlessness came upon him and for days and weeks he was lethargic and inattentive in his work. He knew he needed something, a break, change of scenery – something to renew him. He had accumulated sick days and vacation days to a total of nearly three months.

He would travel – to Asia. He had always had a curiosity about that part of the world. He would take in China, Vietnam, Cambodia, Thailand, Laos and South Korea and spend some time in each place. If he liked a particular place, he would stay there longer. If not, he would leave quickly. He made the arrangements quickly and efficiently and within a week he was winging his way east, first stop Hong Kong.

He stayed in low-budget hotels and guesthouses, many of them frequented by the backpackers who seemed to be everywhere, more numerous even than the cockroaches he encountered. He was amazed to learn that many had been on the road for four to six months, some for over a year. One grizzled American had not been home for six years and had visited 129 countries. Their lives were a far cry from his, though he was not envious of them.

Towards the end of the first month, he holed up in a small guesthouse in the city of Chiang Mai in northern Thailand and determined to do some trekking and rock climbing. For a long time, he had neglected physical exercise. He was out of shape and overweight and this part of Thailand was a mecca for the sports oriented, whether by bicycle, motorcycle, trekking, rafting or a dozen or more of the extreme sports. He would rent a bicycle and do some hiking.

The guesthouse was old and had seen better days, but it was convenient, near the old quarter and close to the markets and restaurants that jostled each other in the narrow sois of that area. It was, also, full of the sounds of an old building, water draining, toilets flushing, creaks and groans and scratchings, and sometimes the patter of tiny feet scampering through passages.

There was an old porcelain electrical outlet by his head as he lay in bed and at its centre a two-inch opening. When the room was quiet, he would occasionally hear a scratching noise. It startled him at first, for it was but an inch or two from his head, then it would cease and there would be silence. His curiosity was aroused.

He began to bring pieces of bread back to his room and leave them by the opening. In the beginning, nothing happened, then the bread disappeared. It disappeared regularly and one day he watched as a furry paw reached out and drew it in. He thought it must have been a rat.

The idea of a rat so close did not scare him. Something in his own makeup identified with this furry creature that scuttled around behind walls and in secret passageways. His anonymity was his strength. His exposure meant danger.

Soon his friend – for that was how he viewed him – showed himself. He had liquid, unblinking, black eyes and long whiskers. He was large, too large to squeeze through the outlet hole. As he lost his reticence he tried to squeeze through, lying on his back, his eyes gazing into Victors, making tiny squealing noises, as if imploring his help.

Victor thought he had never seen such black bottomless eyes and one night, moved by his entreaties, he removed the outlet. It came out easily enough and far enough for the rat to squeeze through. The rat surveyed the room motionless for a long moment, then began to move around, sniffing its contents. Occasionally he would stop and stare at Victor as if for reinforcement and then continue.

It became a nightly ritual. Victor would remove the wall outlet; his friend would emerge and they would play together. Now he would come onto the bed and sit by Victor and Victor would gently stroke his fur. He felt the rat was the only real friend he had ever had. Reluctant to leave him roaming around, when he prepared for bed, he would go to the wall outlet and hold it and after a moment's hesitation the rat would squeeze through and disappear. Each night he waited for Victor to remove the obstacle before he bounded through. Now there was no hesitation. He was at home in Victor's room and in his company.

Increasingly, as time went on, he was more reluctant to return to where he had come from. Victor provided him with tasty tidbits, had even begun to know his favorites or not. Victor stayed on longer than he had anticipated, this strange friendship holding him. But now his friend was entreating, begging him in his actions and behavior to be allowed to stay all night. He whispered, rolled over with legs in air, he fastened those liquid, black eyes on him.

Victor relented. He slept, the rat sitting nearby on his pillow or his night table. When he went to sleep, his last sight was his friend watching him with those unblinking eyes. When he awoke, it was as he had left him. He wondered if he slept. Did rats sleep?

As time passed, it seemed the rat ate more and more. Victor was hard put to keep up with his ever more prodigious appetite. On a few occasions when he neglected to pick up food or left it too late, he detected a subtle difference, infinitesimal but detectible in the rat's behavior. He could not put a finger on it - a tiny withdrawal of friendship, maybe, disappointment in Victor's behavior, a slight chill in the air. Now the rat was free to come and go, the outlet removed, the friendship intact.

One night, awakened from a deep sleep, Victor felt a strange sensation. When the light was switched on, the rat was gently licking on a small cut on the back of his left hand. He had no idea how it came about. He could not remember when it might have happened. The thought that it might have been caused by the rat entered his mind.

But to him it was like a seal on their friendship, a symbolic cutting, bleeding and ingesting. He smiled at his friend, and he continued to lick. The next night the rat did not appear, the first time he had not since their friendship began. Victor was unperturbed. He knew his friend had another life, maybe a family to support, to graft for.

The next night he fell into a deep sleep and dreamed fantastic dreams with his friend always by his side. They swam mighty oceans, partook in, and won mighty battles, sailed on sturdy wooden ships, explored impenetrable jungle. They travelled together by train and bus and plane, ate, and drank in fine restaurants and taverns always surrounded by admiring throngs and retired together at night.

Sometime in the early hours of the morning he awoke, drained and sweating. His friend the rat sat at the end of the bed by a large gash, just below the knee in Victor's leg. He and his family, a half dozen younger rats, drank his blood as it pulsed out. How long they sat and feasted there was no way of knowing but Victor's strength was already gone. He attempted to struggle up. In an instant the rat was on him, close by his jugular, his teeth bared. He subsided and the rat retreated. Now his sight was dimming. He stared into those unblinking, black, liquid eyes for as long as he was able, right up to the very end.

Sins of my Father

It was eerily familiar - the bridge and causeway, mud banks exposed and popping under the hot sun, seaweed encrusted walls and mussels clustered and hanging precariously to the bridge supports. Then the smell hit him, so familiar, rich and cloying from the emptied-out bay stewing in the hot sun. When the tide was in, it was different, even beautiful, the boats dancing in the choppy waters, the harbor framed by the mountains that framed the town. It was all of ten years since he had left, fled, a boy seventeen running for his life first to England and then to America. Though his first stop, England, was a time of trial and error and barely surviving in a place that felt very foreign - the London accents as unintelligible as any language he had never learned, his speech in all probability as difficult for them – he had got a job, a small, rented space and had achieved a fragile sense of independence. But he left as quickly as he could. When he landed in America, he felt a comfortable uncaring. There he had sunk gratefully into that tide of humanity, of dreams realized and dashed, of the noise and confusion and inexhaustible energy, the good and bad of New York living.

This breed, New Yorkers, got on with it. They were all on an endless search – for fame, riches, for their unique gifts to be, finally, revealed to an admiring world and when they had achieved acclaim, to beat off other upstarts, other's hunger, to hold on, hang on to what they had, finally, achieved. It was there, for long periods, he had put the past behind and begun to live, interact with others, explore his potential, expand his horizons. They were long periods of relative peace and contentment. But there were nights he woke up in a cold sweat, his heart seeming like it was going to burst, where sleep eluded, and despair reigned, and he would watch dawn invade the night and creep inexorably through his window.

He was an only child, the product of a late marriage, his mother a gentle, kind woman of solid stature from good farming stock. His father, tall, bony, and big-nosed - with, it seemed, an eternally suspicious look about him - whose father before him had squandered a modest family inheritance, thought of himself as above common or ordinary work, and dreamed of a time he would be rich, respected, one to be reckoned with. He never held a job for very long; his impatience and careless manner and sense of superiority and of dreams thwarted not conducive to a good working relationship with supervisor or owner.

He was as different in makeup to his wife as could be, and as the years passed, unpredictable and surly to Malachy and his mother, Joy. Mal felt his love begin to shrivel and there would come a time when hate would take its place. There was a day when he was ten years old, and his father scolded him for some minor indiscretion. When Mal feigned disinterest, his father, Len became incensed. He screamed at him, his face contorted with rage and for long minutes Mal stood rigid before him, wrapped in terror. When his mother tried to intervene, Len turned abruptly and slapped her, and Mal's heart lurched. His world was suddenly changed. It was the first time his father had laid a hand on her and in truth, it shocked Len then, almost as much as it had his wife and son. His father retreated to the back yard where he remained. Hours later, he came inside, silent and stricken and begged his wife for forgiveness. But it seemed some line had been crossed and though he swore never to raise his hand again in anger, he would cross that line again and again.

Mal's behavior to his father alternated between sullen resistance and uneasy accommodation. He was always aware that his actions might bring down his father's wrath on his mother and this he tried strenuously to avoid. He knew his father's unpredictable behavior was, if anything, increasing, and he feared for his mother, whom he loved with all his being. She came from a family that had always struggled to make ends meet. Two of her siblings had died at a young age and her mother was sickly through most of her life. Her father was a good man but, in the end, overwhelmed by the task of eking a living from a small farm.

At the first proposal of marriage - from his father – she had grabbed at a chance to leave that life behind. She didn't know love, only duty and acquiescence. To her, Mal was her greatest achievement in her hitherto banal existence. She would have given her life to save his and somehow, he knew this. When Mal's father was home, he generally stayed around the house, making excuses to his friends as to why he couldn't play till they began to drop him from their activities. It wasn't a sacrifice for him. He was his mother's protector, and he was determined to be vigilant in his duties. The Christmas of his fourteenth year seemed destined to pass tranquilly. Joy's sister and husband had eaten Christmas dinner with them, and his father, Len was on his best behavior. Joy had invited them, knowing her husband would behave in company. Soon after six, her sister and husband hugged and kissed them, said their goodbyes, got into their car and drove away.

Len had been drinking and Mal saw his mother's growing apprehension. He knew, as did his mother, it was only a matter of time before his father's mood would change. It mattered little what or if anything was done to begin it. He began to berate Joy over food he said was not cooked properly and began to call her names, vicious and disgusting names like 'Cunt' and 'Useless bitch.' Hate flared within Mal like a lightning strike. When his father raised his hand to strike her, Mal reacted instinctively and charged him and knocked him to the ground. Joy and Mal stood frozen as he turned, an ugly purple color suffusing his face. He struggled to rise and as he did, a tremor shook his body and he stiffened.

His father over the years had developed a heart condition and he carried little white pills that he would place under his tongue when stressed. These he carried in his waistcoat pocket and now he struggled to reach them, disbelief and fear replacing anger, his movements uncoordinated, his strength diminished. His eyes beckoned and then pleaded with Mal and Joy. His son went to retrieve them but then stopped, surveying his father slumped on the floor. His father made gasping wheezing sounds as he struggled to retrieve his pills, his efforts, ever more feeble. Mal looked at him and looked at his mother, but she was immobile, locked into some memory far away. After a while his father stopped struggling. He seemed at last at peace, his demons finally stilled. Maybe he had little control over his behavior and Mal felt a flicker of regret. They both sat there for long minutes, the only sound the ticking of the grandfather clock in the hallway, his mother's father's clock, and the only item from her side she had brought to the marriage. Then his mother rose and checked his pulse and closed his eyes. They never spoke of that day again.

After the wake and burial, they settled into an easy and caring routine and for the next year it was the happiest time of his life. Now his mother was free to lavish all her love on him and he returned it. He rarely thought of his father or of what he had or had not done to aid him. He had acted instinctively, and that instinct was to survive – that he and his mother would survive. It was as simple and basic as that. Now it was as if a malignant presence had left the house and Christmas of his fifteenth year was truly a joyous occasion with his mother presiding over a dinner table of friends and relatives and looking as radiant as Mal had ever seen her.

He never loved her more and when she came to say good night, he told her how much he loved her and how happy he was. What she told him then would always stay in his memory.

"My son, my beautiful son, you are my crowning achievement.

You are the sun, the moon, and the stars. My heart overflows with love for you. Remember I will always be by your side wherever you are. You are a good and righteous son, and I will love you forever." It seemed he was in for a lifetime of happiness but just five short months later, at the end of May, his mother passed. She was forty-eight years young. For Mal the wake and burial seemed one long useless exercise. He was raw with grief. He could not fathom how God; any God could do to him what had been done. After years of turmoil and abuse, they had achieved happiness only to have it snatched away. It seemed the work of a cruel prankster.

Mal struggled through life the next few months, lost in his own torment and misery. He had half-hearted offers from distant relatives to come live with them till he was older, but he mumbled his thanks and refused, told them he needed time. After a while they left him alone, focusing on their own tribulations. He barely functioned in school, enough to maintain average grades and project an outward appearance of competence but he distanced himself from his old friends and became a loner. He was excused because he had lost both parents in little more than a year. He was grieving and time was what was needed. But he grieved for only one parent and his grief was inconsolable.

The next two years dragged interminably, his mind a kind of twilight zone but the memory of his dear, kind mother somehow kept him going. He took to walking into the surrounding countryside, long walks that exhausted him but helped him sleep for at least a few hours at night. He took a sketch book with him and began to draw and record scenes and events he encountered. There was a peace he felt when he was in the country, alone, not to have to deal with people and their eternal questions as to how he was faring. Some were genuinely sympathetic, but many were morbidly curious.

He was lying in tall grass one afternoon as he observed a pheasant nearby when he heard someone approaching. The person - in a loud and angry voice - was evidently chastising someone. Mal raised his head cautiously and observed a man and a young boy, not more than ten, approaching. The boy was dressed in short pants and shirt, no jacket on a brisk cold day that demanded one. The man was thumping the boy on the back as they walked along, neither aware of Mal, the boy evidently in trouble for something he had done. But it was the anger of the man that caught Mal's attention. It triggered a memory of his own father berating him as he had done so many times through the years. The boy was miserable looking, pale with a pinched face and hang dog look. As they drew near, Mal rose, surprising the man. He stopped abruptly, studying Mal for long seconds, his eyes narrowed and suspicious, a cap pulled low on his forehead, his shoulders hunched aggressively. Then with a barely perceptible nod he passed.

Mal remained still, watching intently as they receded in the distance. What he had seen disturbed him greatly, all he had seen convinced him the boy was in trouble. In him he recognized a kindred spirit, and he had trouble sleeping that night. The memory of the boy stayed with him for days after. It was as if a psychic connection had been established in the short time they had met, the common denominator their abusive fathers. When Mal thought of what the boy might be enduring, what he had already endured, that hate that had flared at seeing his mother struck, flared again, this time directed at the boy's father. He spent several sleepless nights thinking of the boy's predicament. He determined to find out where they lived so he could observe them more closely, so he could maybe help in some way. He knew how the boy must be feeling if he was being abused, mental or physical, and knowing he had no one in the world to turn to. He wondered if the boy had a mother, was she kind to him or colluding in his father's abuse.

What he had seen was abuse and some were unable to deal with it. He himself had resisted but he had his mother's love. But there were times when he experienced despair, when his own father had bullied him and when he had wished him dead – yet knowing it was unnatural for a son to feel so for his father. There was that confusion, wanting to look up to and love and honor your father, knowing his behavior was wrong but wondering was it somehow your fault.

In the small townland where he lived, it was not difficult to locate them. They were relative newcomers who had arrived about a year ago and the father worked in the local carpet shop, delivering, and laying carpet. The boy whose name was Joseph attended the local school. He was not an athlete, so an easy and surefire way of being accepted was not available to him. An outgoing and gregarious personality would have been another, but Joe's circumstances precluded this. He seemed to have no friends, a condition not unlike Mal's. He approached him the next day at school break as Joseph sat all alone on a bench by the playing field.

"Well, I saw you out by Duckspool, the other day. Do you remember?"

Joseph looked at him and remained silent and then, his eyes round and unflinching he said. "I did nothing wrong."

"You did nothing wrong," Mal told him, "I'm Mal. I just wanted to say hello."

"I'm Joe, my mother always called me Joe."

"You live with your mother and father," Mal inquired?

"She's dead these two years." Tears gathered at the corners of Joe's eyes.

"I'm sorry, mine too. I miss her terrible."

"There's just me and my father now," Joe said. Mal didn't want to come right out and question him on his father's behavior. He thought he should gain his trust and little by little hope Joe would reveal it.

"Do you have any aunts or uncles," Mal asked?

"My auntie May stays in touch. She lives a long way away. She's nice."

"Your mother's sister?" The boy nodded.

"Do you visit her, sometimes?"

"Nah, my father says she's nosy." He looked away, his face squinching, as if it was difficult to image his auntie as nosy.

"Is she," Mal asked?

"She's good to me, but they never got on."

I wonder why, Mal thought, but he knew why.

"Do you want to meet after school, take a walk or something" he asked the boy?

"I'm not supposed to," he paused, "but I will, if you want."

Mal's heart lifted a little. There was still a spark in the boy. They met that day and every day after and walked into the countryside, always back before his father's return. Mal brought his sketchbook and Joe watched closely. Little by little Joe revealed the details of his life with his father. He was, as Mal had thought, beaten regularly. It chilled him as he listened to the boy, who, matter of fact, told him how he was never punched in the face but on the back and in the stomach, often for no reason or reasons so obscure the boy had no idea why. His father talked about discipline and character-building and why, what he was doing would make Joe better able to withstand the temptations of the world, the lies spun to him, the promises broken. Trust no one but your father, he told him.

His father was mean, too, with food and clothes for Joe, who was perpetually hungry and dressed poorly. Mal took to bringing sandwiches, fruit, and milk when they walked in the country and even in a short week, he noticed an improvement in Joe's appearance. He also found out his father's routine after coming from work. He warned Joe to remain in the house and took a walk, alone, along the shore late every night. Mal took to shadowing him.

He had no defined plan of what to do other than to protect Joe. He knew also, something would present itself, it always did. Yet in the far recesses of his mind, it was becoming clearer that he might have to make a decision, and that decision might entail violence. He believed, also, he was meant to protect Joe. He would do whatever he could to save Joe's life, for that was what was at stake. This he firmly believed.

Sometimes, but not often, Mal awoke from a beautiful dream where he and his mother were together. His heart was light, and he was happy, chattering to her, telling her things about school, and playing with the other children. She stroked his hair and listened, a smile on her face. She would murmur how wonderful, or you are such a rascal and the happiness he felt was palpable, filling his whole being with a kind of music, a hum of peace and contentment and serenity. The shock on awakening was so severe that it was hours before he felt somewhat recovered and he thought, wonderful though the feeling was of being with his mother again, the pain after was, maybe, not worth it.

His dreams were of dark and murky places, huddled shapeless figures one could not recognize, who besieged, entreated, for what he was never able to ascertain. But he knew it was to do with his father and how he had blighted their lives and he hated him for it. He knew, also, that he must deal with this hate, or it would consume him, that it might even involve forgiving his father or at least trying to understand where his bad behavior came from. But he was a long way from there. His would be a long journey from hate to forgiveness.

As he became more friendly with the boy, the boy opened up to him and it was like listening to a recording of his own thoughts and feelings after losing his own mother. Joe's mother had been his life. He missed her terribly but was making a brave effort to continue without her, to get on with his life and reach adulthood relatively unscathed. He had promised his mother just that.

"God has placed a heavy burden on you, she told him, but always gives us the means to survive."

"Promise me, son, promise me?" He had promised.

But his father was more unstable as time passed, more given to violent and irrational behavior. Interspersed with periods of relative calm were episodes of angry, chaotic, out-of-control not just moments but hours – hours where Joe could do no right, where if he replied to a question, he was wrong, if he said nothing, he was wrong. He could not be right. Hours later, his voice hoarse and broken, his father would abruptly leave, slamming the door behind him and walking into the night. He would come back changed, calm, in control and things would be uneventful until the next violent episode. This behavior placed a great stress on the boy and Mal was not sure how long he could withstand this barrage. He would have to do something about it. He had no choice. If he walked away the boy would die, he believed, or be irreversibly damaged.

What he must do, he could barely think on. If he could get through to the father, explain how he was damaging his son, irreversible damage. Maybe he could frighten him. Maybe by severely injuring the father, he might change – or not. From his own experience, there was only one option - to eliminate the boy's father. Contemplating it made his blood freeze. But contemplating the slow destruction of the boy, the boy's terror and isolation was even more terrible. He had been there. He was intimately connected to the boy. He could not, must not walk away. The boy's life depended on him.

Then the vision came to him. It was simple and deadly. The boy's father liked to walk the narrow path past the church and down to the wide strand that lay at its base. There was one short section of the path that bordered a cliff where there was a drop of a hundred feet to the sea below. If the attack was sudden and unexpected, he would surely die. Also, he knew, the simpler and least complicated the plan the chances of succeeding increased.

Most nights he took the walk, the boy's father left around seven, the day gone, the night closed in. It was November and fog often rose up from the sea, clinging to the shrubs and stunted trees of the cliff side and rocky promontory and enveloping the path. It was simple and effective. He would rush him and dispatch him into the sea below. He had one other task to ensure success. He would plant a flashlight by the cliff edge. The boy's father, curious, would move closer to the edge to determine what it was and why it was lit. It was the perfect opportunity.

He reviewed the sequence of events as if it was happening in slow motion, the father observing the light, moving to the cliff edge and looking over, his own slow, deliberate steps as he came up behind him, the gentle push, the body falling over graceful for a while as the shock paralyzed him, then the frantic movement, the awful scream as the body plummeted to the rocks below, the grotesque sprawl.

It was exactly as he had planned it, the gentle push, the body graceful as shock paralyzed, then the frantic movement and awful scream. It was too easy. Dastardly deeds such as this should have had fear, and trembling, and blood, but he felt no regret then, nor for a long time - no shock at what he had done, just relief. It was what he knew he had to do. He had refused to think of it, pushed it into the deepest recesses of his mind before. Now he would do the same after.

The papers carried the news of the tragic accident that had claimed the life of a good man and had left the boy parentless. They had found blood alcohol levels that would have contributed to the accident. He had died instantly, his neck broken. The funeral was a quiet, dignified affair, the mourners commiserating with Joe – what a great loss he had suffered, his only parent now dead. Joe answered appropriately but his heart was singing. His Aunt Ellen would take him into her home.

Soon he had settled into his new life, and he blossomed there. Mal was gone before the funeral occurred. Months after he wrote to Joe, not mentioning his father but impressing on him the opportunities he had to have a good life and maybe, even extending a helping hand to others less fortunate. He also kept in touch with Joe's aunt. He was doing so much better, she informed him and though she made no reference to his father, she noted his changed circumstances were a huge improvement. The boy wrote and told him he didn't miss his father and was glad he was gone. Was that a sin, he had asked?

"No, because he treated you badly, you feel that way. But say a prayer for his soul," Mal replied in his next letter.

Then the nightmares began, heart palpitations and cold sweat. No matter how he rationalized what he had done, his sleep remained broken and night after night he watched the grey dawn creep through his window, body rigid, eyes staring. Was he damned to hell forever? Or was there an understanding God that would forgive him for taking a life. From the beginning he loved the city and its energy and was drawn to its bars and the camaraderie that existed within them. He dated intermittently but relationships petered out. He was essentially alone even when he wasn't, and they would sense it. Mal's success in America came as a surprise and he was now comfortably well off. He was frugal in his habits and fancy restaurants, or fancy clothes held little appeal for him. He had gone to school at night to learn the intricacies of financial investing. He had taken up that field on the recommendation of his professor, John Hanes, who had surmised – correctly as it had turned out – that he was well suited for the numbers crunching it entailed.

His was a very basic approach to investing. He identified the solid companies with good dividends, learned all he could about the company and its C.E.O – his compensation was of great importance to Mal for many were grossly overpaid. He invested for the long term. He had steady if unspectacular returns and had developed a faithful following. It was easy really. He was amazed at how many hotshot gurus went down in flames. Always riding the next big, surefire bonanza, they not alone made little or no money for their clients but often lost it all. Yet they had a slavish following. The next big thing was where everybody, it seemed, wanted to be and biotech would always be more glamorous than, for example washing powder or cola. Mal's strength was that he was not swayed by emotion.

There might come a day when he would invest in biotech, but it would be when they were more easily identifiable companies with solid earnings. He would never catch the startup that would reward its investors with hundredfold returns, the one in one thousand, the one that got all the tongues wagging and made all the covers of the investing magazines.

Now he was home, and on his way to meet the boy, almost a man, going on eighteen. His second day back he had walked the path by the church and looked over the edge to the sea below. It was tranquil now, the waves gently lapping the shore. Was it a dream, a horrible nightmare? Had he, a mere boy, pushed a man to his death at this very spot ten years ago? What would compel someone to do something so wicked? He rationalized it again in his mind.

When Joe saw him, he ran to him and held him. Mal saw a young man, medium height with a strong body and intelligent face. He was smiling and obviously happy. He thought of the boy he had seen for the first time that many years ago, thin of body, pale face, and beaten-down air of one who was in a bad place with no prospects of escape.

"How is America," he asked, "I'd love to see it, some day."

"You will, some day," Mal promised him, "you'll come and spend time with me." They sat and talked and talked some more. Rose brought tea and sandwiches, excused herself and left them alone. He seemed such a normal boy, a boy just about into manhood, as if he'd done all the things boys do growing up. Mal asked if he was happy.

"Mostly," he replied, "I have Aunty Rose and..." He turned and looked at Mal, "...I had you, back then - and my mother, she's always around..."

Mal told him. "You kept me going too."

Before he left, Rose thanked him. "He said you were his one friend. How he survived that...disturbed man every day, I'll never know." He had queried her on Joe's progress in school and was pleased to learn that Maths was one of his favorite subjects. Maybe, maybe some day... He would stay in touch with Joe. They were inextricably connected.

The visit had given him relief. He had done what had to be done. Would he do it again if he had the opportunity, the same circumstances? He thought he would. Though he had saved a life, he had eliminated another. He thought only God had that power but...

He thought of his mother and his mother's words, 'I will always be by your side,' and just then, for an instant, he knew she was close by. Maybe what he had done wasn't so bad after all? Maybe what he had done was forgivable? Maybe down the road the nightmares would cease?

Uncle Harry

My mother said to me, "Johnny, I've got a job lined up for you for the summer. It pays eleven dollars a week," and she smiled. There was something in her smile that should have set off an alarm in my head, but the eleven-dollar part of it grabbed my attention.

"Yeah," I responded eagerly, "eleven dollars a week. Wow. That's a lot of money, Ma."

"It certainly is, and you'll earn every penny of it. How old are you now, ten?" she asked.

"Eleven, Ma."

"Eleven. You should be able to handle it."

"So, what do I have to do?"

"You know Uncle Harry is all alone since his wife died. He's not doing too good, so you're going to be taking care of him for the summer."

"Uncle Harry, that old grump, the whole summer? What about my friends? When am I gonna see them? Ma, I can't, I wouldn't be able to."

"Of course, you would." She dropped her voice and put her arm around me. "Now Johnny, he's our own flesh and blood and we have to take care of our own. He needs us. Remember, charity begins at home. You're helping poor Uncle Harry and you're making a few dollars into the bargain. Now, what's wrong with that?"

"Johnny, he's my only brother. We all have to pitch in and help this summer. We're looking for a nice home for him - if he'll go - but until then we all have to help. And he's not drinking like he used to."

"But Ma, I can't cook or nothin'."

"We'll be bringing the food already cooked. You might have to boil an egg once in a while and do a little washing up."

"Washing up? I dunno how to do washing up."

"Oh, stop complaining. I'll be dropping in to help out, you'll finish at four every evening and you'll have most weekends off."

"Most?" I asked.

"Now, Johnny, you're big and strong and getting bigger and stronger every day. It's time you began to learn these things."

"Pop never did any cooking or washing up." My father had died three years before when I was eight years old. He was always in and out of jobs; why I never was told. I overheard her once tell a neighbor, "He was very unlucky with jobs, poor Jimmy." After he died, he was always "poor Jimmy."

"And more's the pity. Poor Jimmy's mother spoiled him terribly." She had never liked her mother-in-law and vice versa. "He was spoiled goods when I got him. But it won't happen to you. You're the apple of my eye, and you'll make a good husband for some lucky girl. I'll see to that."

"Aw, Ma..."

"Shush now and away out to play with you." It was decided and had been, I knew, before I was told. Monday morning, I showed up at Harry's at eight o'clock, the scheduled time.

"So, you're Johnny," he addressed me as he lit his pipe and blew smoke in my face. "Supposed to help me. It'll probably be the other way around."

"I'll do my best and that's all I can do," I managed to respond, waving furiously and choking as smoke enveloped me.

"Fiery little fella, aren't you, but I suppose to be expected with a mother like yours. She has a tongue sharp as a razor."

"My mother's trying to help you, isn't she? She's better than you ever were."

He softened a little. "All right, all right, she's not the worst of them, I suppose. Now are you goin' to do something or are you going to stand there and argue all day?"

He worked me hard that day. I washed his clothes, hung them out to dry, went to the grocery store - three times - until I got exactly what he wanted, mopped the kitchen floor, cleaned out the fireplace and set the fire. He was reprimanding and sharp-tongued and I walked out at four exhausted, indignant and vowing never to return. 'Please' or 'thank you' were not part of his vocabulary.

When I got home, one look from my mother told her all she needed to know.

"I know, I know, he's an old grump and..."

"Grump? He's the nastiest old man I've ever met in my life. Ma, I can't work there. He's never satisfied."

"Now, now, give it another week and see how you feel. If it doesn't get better, we'll talk then." She paused. "Try to get him talking about the sea and his travels. He loves to tell tales of his seafaring days, tho' how much is true, God only knows."

"One week, that's it, you promise?"

"One week and we talk about it, okay?"

I returned the next morning. It was a beautiful day and Harry decided he wanted to sit outside. There was a nice bench in the corner of the garden and that was where he sat when the weather was nice. "See this garden," he said. "I used to take care of it myself, had all kinds of vegetables: tomatoes, cucumbers, corn and beans growing here every year. Passed a bunch on to your ma every year. How much could I use? She had a bunch of kids eating her out of house and home, and…" He looked at me accusingly. "Your pa didn't know a vegetable garden from an elephant." He paused. "Now this fella comes in, gets fifteen bucks to cut the grass, does a lousy job and if he's here more than twenty minutes, he's upset. God help America."

I said nothing. I was learning. He loved an argument, and I wasn't going to give him one, not today anyway. It was too nice out. We sat quietly for a while.

"What are you going to do when you grow up, if you ever do?" he asked, exploding with laughter, but the laughter quickly deteriorated into wheezing and coughing.

"Are you all right," I inquired.

"I'm all right, don't you go fussin' over me now like your mother, one is bad enough." I let it go without comment.

"I think I'd like to travel - see the world, see how other people live."

He looked at me steadily for a long minute. "That's a smart enough observation from a twelve-year-old..."

"Eleven," I said. He disregarded my remark.

"Smart, a smart observation. Travel is the real education, better'n all the book and school education. Makes you appreciate what you got at home. I left home when I was sixteen, shipping out as a cabin-boy, sixteen years old and as green as they come. I sailed from Houston, Texas over to Rotterdam, and up the Suez Canal, my maiden voyage. The seas were rough." He laughed. "I spent the first week throwing up. After that I never looked back. Began a love affair with the sea and travel that never ended. It wasn't all good times. I lost two of my best mates off the Madeira Islands in a bad storm. We were attacked by a mob on the docks in Cairo and barely got the ship away. But I wouldn't trade it. We sailed through the Greek Islands. Blue skies and white cottages stacked on the hills. Spent time in the Cape Verde Islands and I wanted to be there forever."

He began that day with stories of his life and travels and continued throughout the summer. It was as if a dam had broken as the stories poured forth almost without interruption. Maybe he realized his time was drawing near and he wanted once more to revisit those times and places. He was a natural-born storyteller, and he took me to strange and exciting places that day and each day after: The Madeira Islands, through the Straits of Gibraltar and into the Mediterranean Ocean, Rio De Janeiro and round Cape Horn.

I peppered him with questions. "Weren't you scared, sixteen years old and doing a man's job? Did you go to the taverns with the older seamen? Did you have to learn on the job? Was someone assigned to teach you?"

He gave me honest answers, sensing my fascination with all he told me. It had been a while, I suppose, since he had such an attentive audience and he loved it. The work was neglected more and more. I did what was needed and no more. When he lit the pipe and told me to sit for a while, it was the signal. The first week started slow, but time started to slide by, quicker and quicker.

Ma was surprised. "What's going on with the two of you? He's nearly human and you're not complaining?"

"I'm doing a good job, that's what, and he likes it. That's what I'm supposed to do, right?" "Right. I haven't seen him this contented for a long time," she replied, "and there's nobody more cantankerous when he's cantankerous."

"He's not as bad as he's made out to be, y'know," I said, "just a bit misunderstood." She looked funny at me. I looked forward to my days with him. I was like a sponge soaking up his knowledge of the world and his tales of travel and adventure. He took me to places I yearned to know and wouldn't have, but for him.

I returned to school, reluctantly at the end of that summer. I visited him often at first, but less so as time went on. I had my own pals and never seemed to have enough time. He was in and out of hospital and always made a recovery. I stopped worrying. He'd always be there. Ma said you couldn't kill a bad thing. Then one day she sat me down. She told me that Harry wasn't doing well, and he wanted to see me.

"Well, young fella, how is school," he greeted me as I approached the bed. I found it hard not to turn and run. Ma prodded me forward. This wasn't the Harry I knew, this wizened, gnarled little man who lay gasping and wheezing before me. "It's okay, okay," he said. "You can't kill a bad thing, as your mother says." He cackled and was quiet. He motioned towards me and motioned for my mother to leave. He held out his arms and I came to him and put my cheek next to his. He turned and whispered in my ear.

"We had some good times, didn't we?" I nodded silently and tears began to slide down my cheeks.

"You'll be all right, won't you, Uncle Harry, won't you," I said into his neck.

He took a deep breath, full of whistles and moans. "Of course, I will. I'm feeling better than ever. You were good company. You're a great little man. I wasn't too cranky, was I?" I shook my head. "When I get going, there's no better man." I nodded.

"Remember to see the world. Will you promise me?'

"Whatever you want, I'll do," I said, and he nodded. I felt my mother's arms taking me away.

"He needs the rest, let him sleep," she said as Harry sank back, exhausted. He died that night. I attended his wake and burial, feeling grown up and older. I was aching inside, missing him and feeling bad that I had neglected to visit more often. Slowly, as I remembered his stories, my sense of loss receded. I realized how lucky I had been to have spent that Summer with him.

When his will was read, he had set aside a sum of money for both me and my mother with specific instructions that it be used only for travel. Five years later when I was sixteen years old, my mother and I fulfilled his wishes. We travelled through Europe, down through Spain, onto Majorca, over to Gibraltar and into Africa. Harry's stories came to life once more. I felt more than once on that trip that he was there with us, smiling his gappy smile and sucking on his pipe. I told the stories he had told me, and my mother listened attentively.

"So that's what you were doing, the pair of you. Like peas in a pod, ye were, that Summer," as she hugged me.

The trip changed my mother. It was the happiest time of both our lives, I think, a turning point. It was the first real vacation she ever had. Ma went back to school soon after that trip. She's still going. Like Harry always said, travel is education. I graduated from college and secured a position in the travel industry where I was able to indulge my passion. And Harry's stories? Next time you're in the bookstore, check out a book called 'Tales of Harry'. It's a pretty good read, selling nicely, too.

Parents

The bed creaks, rhythmic
And he, fifteen, listen.
Too old, they huff and pant
In passionate embrace
Or is it just habit
Who is more wanting
Begins the touching
Who is slow to arouse

Does she not see dentures
Pate and weathered face
Or is it a picture
Locked in her heart
Frozen in time
Of the laughing, handsome man
That held her and bent, intimate
To whisper in her ear

Does he not see
Grey hair and lined face
Body that's lost
The sharp curves

And upright breasts

That adorned

That same picture

Too many births ago

When does desire dim

The physical becomes laborious

Does love deepen

And wanting grow

Or is it a ritual

Automatic response

Repeated from memory

Dozing, eyes closed.

The Right Move

She was fed up with his attitude, fed up with his moaning, his objections, the impediments he posed in her life.

"We're having it here, okay. It's our turn. It's a chance for me to see Bob, Lisa and the kids. He's my brother. I see him just once a year. Is it so difficult for you to deal with him? Is it? Okay, he gets carried away..."

"Carried away? He's like a damned evangelist, spouting off about deals closed, how much money he makes, bonuses..."

"You shouldn't feel.... because he's, he's...succeeded....'

He was ready to explode. He remembered last Thanksgiving. Bob was in the first flush of making a decent amount of money. He remembered... "Mister Clarke called me into his office. He told me my bonus would be $25,000 and...listen to this...said he regretted it wasn't bigger. Shit, I wasn't even expecting a bonus. I was a ten-month old employee. Then he said how pleased they were with my performance."

Tom remembered how he felt, how he had to smile and say, "Good job, Bob."

Then Bob had turned to him and said, "See, hard work gets rewarded."

He wanted to tell him how brown-nosing pays off, and kissing ass - and how does it feel kissing Mr. Clarke's big, smelly, hairy ass.

He didn't know Clarke, had never met him, didn't know if he had a big ass, smelly, hairy, or otherwise, but he envisioned him big, fat and prosperous, the chair protesting every time he flopped into it. Then Bob, in an expansive mood, offered to put in a good word for him if he were interested in joining the company.

"I'm a teacher, for God's sake."

"A substitute teacher," his wife interjected, a stab in the back, he thought.

"Is it my fault I was laid off?"

"No, but it was at your insistence we moved."

She had to say that, didn't she? She had to say it...and in front of everybody - especially in front of her beloved brother, Bob - the asshole. She was right, of course. At his insistence, pleading, groveling they had moved.

He had a secure job, tenured, with the Elmira schools. But he hated the long winters, the endless battles with snow and snow blowers, the grating cheerfulness of his neighbors as they battled a mountain of snow, red faces, and potential heart attacks.

Come to think of it, that was the final straw, when old Jack Holden had dropped dead, slumped over his snow blower, his cold, old hands frozen to the metal. He vowed that's not gonna be me down the road. He had persuaded her to move further south, nearer New York City. They paid so much better than upstate, less snow. He hadn't told her about house prices…. Then when he had secured a nice teaching position with splendid potential, the recession had swept thru like a tsunami, sweeping away jobs, his job, financial security, nest egg, peace of mind.

She resented the move, giving in too easily to his enthusiasm, excitement – and she had to admit – had been caught up in it. She would be able to take the train into the city, a mere forty-eight minutes. He actually stressed that, the theater, restaurants, exhibits, museums. She had folded. They hugged each other. This time he would be right. It would be all good – except it wasn't. And she never let him forget it.

They lived in a house half the size of the house in Elmira. He had been hired, almost immediately. He was a good teacher with excellent references. Then, then… She had found a job, but it had taken a while, office manager. But she worked twice as hard, it seemed to her. They did things differently down here, expected more. They seemed more ruthless, there was less camaraderie. She missed Beth and Angie, her two amigos. They had been inseparable, finished each others' sentences, laughed at the same jokes. They would be together forever. She hadn't really made friends here. They were polite, but talked different, laughed different and then just…disappeared as soon as work was over, always in a hurry, it seemed. And she was making the same salary. There was more money needed down here, property taxes, insurance, it went on and on. A tear slid down her cheek. He didn't notice.

He was lost in his own resentments, the impending Thanksgiving celebration, his poor pay as a substitute teacher, the precarious nature of it. He had to check his computer every day for the jobs available, then lock in the job ASAP. There were a hundred or more on the substitute roles, so jobs were taken quickly. Then it seemed, when he didn't want the job – at holidays and when the weather was nasty, they proliferated like mushrooms, like the mushrooms found in the fields back of their house, their grand, spacious house in Elmira, succulent, button white caps that, when fried with thick bacon and some sliced potatoes.... God, what or who possessed him to move. They should have stayed; they were too hasty. It was too late now. They were here. They had to make the best of it.

"Look, it'll be okay. You're right. Thanksgiving is family time. I don't envy Bob his new-found prosperity. I just wish our circumstances were better." She looked up and he saw the teary eyes and a stab of guilt assailed him. He went to her and stroked her hair. She wasn't mollified. She knew it was but a temporary lull and his resentments – and hers, would return full-blown at a later time. They were both just resting, gathering strength, to return stronger, more tenacious, more damaging.

Once a thought had crossed her mind: *what if he were dead, his half million life insurance would be hers, the life she could live.... But she had put it from her mind, shocked that she had entertained it, if even for a millisecond.*

She just wished he was more...everything. He had been more ...everything. He had been funny – and sunny. He made her laugh, made her feel special and they were married within the year. She was sure she had made the right choice. She was sure, then.

She had had three miscarriages. They had shaken her core as a woman and potential mother. After, she had lost interest, turned off or subconsciously avoided the desire for sex and all the rituals that went with it. Now they had no children. He was alright with that, he said, had reassured her time and time again. They would have a good life together. They would travel and visit all the wonderful places they had read about and seen in travel documentaries and movie locations. He was alright with it, and they had travelled. Yet, she had never believed that he had fully accepted that they would be childless, that somewhere deep inside him, deep inside enough that even he was unaware of its existence, burned a tiny, tiny flame of resentment at the world, at his predicament, at her.

They were different now than they were ten years ago, five, even two years ago, he thought. Their love was barely hanging on. They were like two old bachelors, putting up with each other while they mumbled and grumbled thru life. Where had it all gone, the easy companionship, the sometimes sudden and fierce lovemaking, the comfort of, and in each other? Resentments and petty grievances had taken over their lives.

He should try to do better. The economy would get better. Schools would rehire. After all, teachers got old or were offered generous packages to retire. There would be jobs and he would be hired. This was a time to hang tough, be optimistic. There were others worse off. Alice had a decent job. He was working – mostly. They had no kids, lucky you, he was told. The financial burden of raising kids in this day and age, was backbreaking. He had heard the stories, sympathized with the parents. So much could go wrong. Thanksgiving would be fine. He'd have a little wine, a glass or two or three and mellow out. He'd be positive, congratulate Bob on his bonus (Bob was sure to bring it up), admit that things were tight right now, but they were hanging tough, and they had faith in the future.

The teaching business would never just disappear. It was essential. The world needed good teachers. He was an excellent teacher. It was an honorable profession of incredible importance, a molder of young minds. Behind most successful people was somewhere, sometime in their lives, a teacher who had seen their potential, arrested the drift to negative and sometimes dangerous behavior, encouraged, cajoled. He was proud of his accomplishments in the teaching field. Parents had thanked him.

Bob's field, financial services was, essentially, a greedy business, he thought. It was all about making money – how big was his bonus and how big will mine be? Maybe it wasn't always like that, and people needed advice on how and where they put their money, but, he thought, it had become that way and potential good teachers were being lured by the prospect of big money – and lost to the teaching profession. It was sad and there was nothing he could do. He would hold up his end and teach - and teach well. He might just tell Bob that – that teaching was a noble profession.

She had a bad feeling, had it for days. She felt depressed, tried to hide it, walked around with a smile fixed on her face. Most had been fooled but Lila, a co-worker saw right thru it. Lila was an older woman, mid-fifties, the only one who had reached out to her from the very beginning, who had made it clear that she wanted to be her friend. She had picked up on Alice's mindset right away. She had been such a help to Alice when she first arrived. She came and sat with her in the lunchroom.

"If you don't relax, you're going to shatter," Lila told her.

"Is it that obvious?"

"It is to me. Take a deep breath and expel. If you want to unload, I'm here for you. Up to you."

She did unload, and it was a release. She told Lila how she dreaded the upcoming Thanksgiving festivities, her brother Bob and Tom, and Tom's seeming resentment of Bob's success. She told her about the move from Elmira and how comfortable she had been there, about Tom's difficulty in finding a permanent teaching position and how irritable it made him.

"Wow, that is a big list," Lila said.

"Thanks for listening."

"But you're feeling better. I can see it." She was feeling better. It was a relief to unburden.

"Tell you what," Lila said, "how about you and me meeting up, say once a week, having a little lunch, a glass of wine, whatever, girl time?"

"I'd like that," Alice said, and they did. By the time Thanksgiving rolled around she was much better. As Lila said, worrying about what might happen wouldn't make it go away and might even make it worse. The dinner went off better than she could ever have anticipated. She had always liked Lisa, Bob's wife who was down to earth and a perfect counterfoil to Bob's mood swings. Their children Peter, now eleven and Romy, eight were well-behaved and thoughtful children and never any trouble. There had been layoffs at Bob's firm, so he was subdued, didn't mention bonuses or the lack thereof and nobody broached the subject.

Tom was in an expansive mood from more than one glass of wine and waxed eloquent on the Godly profession of teaching. All listened politely and, after he was finished, immediately changed the subject, and went on to other topics. Alice was heartened. All had, to the best of her knowledge, enjoyed the day.

She saw Lila more often and they found each other good company. Lila had a quietness – maybe serenity or companionable silence was a better description – about her that was never awkward where it might have been with others. She seemed to Alice so centered and willing to accept life on its terms rather than raging against misfortune. She was a widow with one daughter, Celeste married in California who had two daughters, Rebecca, seventeen and Lila, fourteen. She travelled to California twice a year to spend time with them.

The two friends took the train to Manhattan and attended the theatre, museums, and art galleries. Alice found the times with Lila special. She thought they were like a long, married couple in a comfortable relationship, considerate of each other's feelings.

Alice loved how Lila remembered her birthday and other special occasions. In an inexpensive but beautifully decorated and lighted Thai restaurant, with serene music playing in the background - one Friday evening, after an exhilarating day visiting the Museum of Natural History – Lila presented her with a silver bracelet with two hearts entwined.

"You know why?" Lila asked.

"No," Alice replied, feeling somehow guilty she didn't.

"You know what day it is?"

"Friday," Alice replied, puzzled.

Lila burst out laughing. "It's our one-year anniversary."

"You mean...?"

"Yes, we met one year ago today." She looked at Alice. "It's been a wonderful year for me. I've never had a friend like you, truly."

Alice was deeply touched and before she knew it, she had reached across the table and touched Lila's face. "I don't know how I could have faced what I faced this past year without you. You've been a true... friend."

"Maybe we can be more," Lila replied, as they held hands and Alice didn't dispute.

Things got better. Tom got a teaching position and was tenured. Alice was, finally, comfortable in her job. Her friendship with and respect for Lila deepened. She thought of Lila's words in the Thai restaurant. "Maybe we can be more." They had both had a glass of wine or two, but the words had stirred her. Was she willing to carry their friendship to a deeper level? Why not? She had been lonely too long. Under Lila's influence she had become more accepting of life and all its vagaries, more willing to try new experiences in all facets of her life. Life was for living to the full. She would try to live a fuller life.

Then two months to the day of his tenure, Bob came to Alice and asked for a divorce. When he agreed to her demand that she keep the house, she gladly acceded to the divorce. It was a relief for her that their union had ended. In truth it had ended years before. Bob promptly married a fellow teacher ten years his junior who, it turned out, he had been seeing for a year or more. He soon fathered two sons, Benjamin and Robert. Alice was happy for him. He wasn't a bad person. If they had had children, who knows? Life was what it was, and she had her life to live. She liked the placidity of her life now, the companionship of Lila but also the comfort of her own house. She suddenly realized, yes, Bob had been right. It had been the right move. There was less snow, and it was so nice to be so close to Manhattan and all it offered. Possibilities were endless.

Childhood Memories

The street where I grew up, Home Rule Street contained the house where I was born, 2 St Augustine's Terrace, one of four attached single-story dwellings put down in the middle of what some called the lane. This lane or street was an interesting microcosm of the legacy of colonial Ireland.

It had been called Great Victoria Street before nineteen twenty-three when the country was still under British rule and, shades of Jamaica Kincaid's 'The First Time I Saw England' mirrored the English predilection for tagging every nook and cranny of colonial territory with names of their heroes.

Victoria might not have been pleased, for at that time the street that bore her name - with a plaque at the gable end of the first cottage - was a half dozen thatched cottages situated haphazardly on a short dead-end which seemed to have evolved rather than been planned. The cottage doors opened onto the street. There were no front gardens and on a fine day the women leaned out the half doors gossiping loudly to each other.

On a glorious Saturday evening near the end of June in the sixth year of my young life an event occurred, shocking in its improbability. With daylight stretched till after eleven and night, impatient and resentful waiting its time, my aunt Wommy emerged from her house carrying a large, black pot, set it up in the middle of the road, built a fire under it and boiled a pot of periwinkles.

Periwinkles, the small saltwater snail with a thick globular shell are as common as stones on the strand and the strand bordered the village. Winkles, we called them, and the people of the village picked and sold them but rarely ate them. I don't know why. Maybe they were considered not real food, like bacon, pig's head, crubeens or mackerel. When we ate them, we ate them boiled straight out of the pot, no sauce or garnish with – for me at least – no great taste. But the taste was incidental to the occasion. The doors opened and people drifted out. Many were perplexed for this was an original happening but soon all caught the spirit of the occasion, and all joined in to making this occasion a special one. Plates were produced and enamel cups and small needles for extracting from their shells.

Some of the men collected money and ale and porter was sent for, for the men. The men and women engaged in vigorous banter while the children ran furiously about, in a fever of excitement. This had never happened before, and I can still remember the feeling of togetherness and sharing that was palpable in the air.

"The sparks flew, and the shit blew," as Tom Power described it later. "It was great, great. An event to bring us together and we needed that, God knows, we needed that. A simple thing, a black pot filled with winkles. We should have done it years ago."

Wommy stood there, all six feet of her, her hands folded over her ample breasts and took it all in. It had been an impulsive gesture for a woman who fought poverty to a standstill each and every day, and every year reared a pig in her backyard to earn what helped them survive. But that day, she was at peace, the fight suspended. I went up to her and leaned against her skirt and she placed one hand on my head and stroked it. I knew then that I came from a real place, that this was a special moment.

The sparks flew into the sky, lit with a million stars and the smoke from the cottage chimneys drifted lazily up, for there was no breeze to distract it. The glow from the fire reflected on the faces gathered round. Caps were pushed back to reveal white foreheads and white domes which contrasted strangely with the weathered faces below. Shawls were opened and sleeves rolled up. An accordion appeared from nowhere and the noise subsided as the music began. Soon vigorous dancing took hold.

Later, the singing began, and songs and poems spilled into the night. It was as if we had returned to an older time, to a time of our ancestors, before television and radio, when there was only music and storytelling, and they were more than enough.

When it was time to go, in the early hours of the morning, children and adults left slow and reluctant. It was the one and only time a winkle party happened in my memory. Sometimes I wonder was it a mirage, a prayer answered, something desired, a fantasy. Years after, few remembered it but me, but the memory of it still warms me. All of the adults are gone and a lot of the children that played that day. The lane is still there with houses now on both sides, but I still see it as it used to be.

My Wife, She Blights My Life

Wife: I skip along life's thoroughfare

Sun warms my face, wind ruffles hair

I stop and have a cup of tea

Perchance a muffin, lucky me.

Husband: Feckless, aimless, wandering she

Lost in a world of make believe

Makes of my life a misery

Why not practical like me.

Wife: I sit as others hurry by

Determined, focused, little joy

I sip and sip again and sigh

And wish they had more fun in life.

Husband: Happy dreams run round her head

A pot of gold's round every bend

What makes me crazy is how she

Disregards reality.

Wife: I do not worry, do not dwell

When other's say, life's gone to hell

Maintain a calm and even pace

Song in my heart, smile on my face.

Husband: Why does she have a happy life

And me unhappy, unlike my wife

Must I suspend reality

To live as happily as she.

Wife: For life as someone wise, proclaimed

Is like a box of chocolates

And as we rise and meet each day

We cannot know if sad or gay.

Husband: Is that not life turned upside down

Wear a smile and never frown

And all our problems turn and flee

It does for her why not for me.

Wife: I think how foolish 'tis to try

To plan, control, subdue this life

Be like the tulip, daffodil

Spontaneous, child-like, believe – it will.

Wicked Winter - Splendid Summer

In the following pages, I compare and contrast winter and summer and explain why I hate one and love the other. I will also explain why anyone of sound mind should feel exactly as I do.

I have just received my fuel oil bill. The figure jumped out and smacked me, and left me weak and panting, doubled over and trying to regain equilibrium. The thought enters my mind again. How can anyone like winter?

People wax lyrical over winter. They describe scenes of pristine snow, little boys and girls sledding with their fathers, skating on the village pond where a great bonfire blazes in the background, marshmallows roasting on an open fire, while chatter and laughter rings through the air. They describe rosy cheeks, carol singing, ski trips to exotic places, snowball fights, families safe at home where a blazing fire lights up the living room or den, mom and kids sipping hot chocolate, and dad partaking of a hot toddy. Then there's Christmas shopping, socials, dances and club meetings that seem to proliferate throughout the season, not to mention football and tailgate parties.

But the winter I know is far different. I have lived in this area for thirty-five years and have seen my share of cruel, wicked, mean and nasty winters. They are not all bad, but the problem is that we never know, so we go through this "wonderful" season with head down and apprehension gripping our hearts. For the truth is, nobody really knows when the next big one is about to happen. For all of the advancements in science, satellites and computers, weather forecasting has little changed these past fifty years.

I remember winters where the ground froze to thirty-nine inches depth, where we had twenty-three storms and eighty inches of snow. My back ached from shoveling, and my eyes glazed as I surveyed new mounds of snow where a few days before my driveway, steps, decks and pathway had been shoveled and swept clean after many hours of tortuous, backbreaking, spirit bending, mind numbing, soul destroying manual labor.

I remember driving home from the Bronx on the Saw Mill River Parkway with one lane open from Hawthorne to Mount Kisco. There were cars abandoned in the other lane all the way, and these had been buried by the snowplows keeping the one lane open. If I had not been lucky enough to get behind a snowplow for the last couple of miles, I doubt if I would have made it. If the same plow had not exited at Mount Kisco, I doubt if I would have been able to exit there. The side streets had not been plowed, so I had to park downtown and walk home through snow drifts that sometimes reached to my chest.

I remember dead batteries and frozen pipes, treacherous driving conditions, wind chills of thirty below, trees and power lines overloaded with snow and ice crashing onto roads and parkways. Commuter trains and buses were also affected resulting in restricted service and irate commuters. And of course, let us not forget flooding. But that is not a winter-only phenomenon.

And what of summer? Ah, summer, that season of sun and fun. As spring turns into early summer, we begin to emerge from our cocoon, shed layers of clothing and survey winter's damage.

We've put on weight because when we are cold, we eat, when we are stressed, we eat, and somehow, when we are buried under layers of clothing who knows or who cares. So, we look with dismay at our out-of-proportion bodies and again curse winter. But summer is upon us and like our fellow denizens of this beautiful, complicated planet, we are suddenly gripped with a fever of activity. We clean house, work out, cut grass, dig garden, work out, clean gutters, paint and replace winter's damage and work out.

We begin to take back our property, street, neighborhood – and shape. We go for walks, bicycle rides, or jog. We spend time outside on our deck, have barbecues, invite and visit friends. We soak in the sunshine, swim in the pool, or visit the ocean, walk or jog the beaches. Ah, summer.

I Think When Sitting on the Toilet Bowl

I think when sitting on the toilet bowl

Sans pants, sans shirt white arse exposed

I gain unique perspective on the world

The trials and tribulations that it pose.

My acumen and judgment crystal clear

Solutions and right answers soon appear

All seems so easy as I squat and brood

But when I rise, confusion reappears.

Perchance being naked is our natural state

When how we decorate is not in play

For diamond, fur and cloth debase the view

And only on the toilet see what's true.

So, I do hereby vigorously decree

That every world leader every day

Will sit at least one hour, defenseless, bare

And sit and sit till answers doth appear.

Like magic, answers will come tumbling through

And how we should proceed and instigate

And as they sit, sans pants and arses bare

Enunciate a bright new future her

A Dog's Life

I haven't too much time left, well into the winter of my life if spring is the beginning and winter's coming to journey's end. So – in the interests of increased understanding between man and man's best friend, his ever-faithful dog…let me rephrase that. In the interests of increasing your understanding of us, I'll unburden the oul' soul.

I was and am, always struck by the astounding – and I use that word very deliberately – stupidity, ignorance and overall naivete of people where we are concerned. I mean, I've lived with people all my life. I've observed them since I was a little pup. I may know more about them than they know. They can be good and kind, magnanimous, big hearted, and…stupid, ugly, cruel, and uncaring.

Most think all dogs are way below their level in all things that matter, and mostly dumb. They say outrageous things about us, while I'm lying, in front of them, gazing up at them with my happy dog look. If they only knew what I feel inside – profound disappointment and disgust, how my balls tighten up, as I listen to them.

So, why do I sit there with my happy dog look? Why? I know that's what makes you assholes - sorry, people - happy and, deep down, I guess, deep down in my conflicted soul - and I don't say this easily - I want to make you happy. It is a programming thing and sadly, I've been programmed, some kind of Stockholm Syndrome crap or a combination of both.

I know what reassures you, makes you feel good about yourselves, what validates you all. That's how people like to talk now, validating their work, finding their center, releasing the inner child – crap like that. They reckon they're the only ones going through these changes. This has been going on for as long as we've inhabited the planet. But the things they say, and always from a position of superiority?

The message basically is: Aren't you lucky, you poor, dumb creature to have somebody so kind, so intelligent, so caring as I am to look after you. So maybe I screwed up a few times, went away for three days and forgot to make a little sustenance available, got a little tipsy and locked you out on the coldest night of the year – the list goes on. But always, in your mind - How lucky you were that my ancestors took you in, domesticated you, deigned to become your masters. Your masters? When I hear that word, something ugly deep inside me stirs. Nobody, but nobody is our master and – we're master of none.

We were not domesticated. We made a conscious decision, most of us, to work and co-habit with humans a long, long time ago. We didn't come to the farm door, cold and shivering and begging to be taken in. No sir, it was a long slow process for us to trust in humans, to believe most are good though many cruel and vindictive and many, too many, just plain stupid. We knew the relationship would not be without its problems and we've had plenty – of problems, but overall, we believe it has worked, though along the way there's been plenty of doubting and despairing.

And those doubts have come sometimes in the middle of the night when I hear a coyote howl or a wolf call to his mate. Then, something stirs inside me, and I wonder about the path we've chosen. Then, I think, that maybe their path - wolves, coyotes, dingoes and jackals, my cousins in the wild -that maybe they have followed a truer path, a purer state of being, of existing. Maybe, maybe...

There was a meeting, a kind of tribal council a long time ago to decide our future course, whether we should begin to work closer with the humans who had begun to spread across our territories. All branches of the tribe, family, species were represented. And as they say, debate raged. (pause)

Don't, don't, not even for a second. I know what's going through your infantile brains. Oh, they're dogs, how could they debate. That's silly. They can't communicate with each other. We've been living with you people for so long now, we can practically read your minds.

You have such closed minds, such rigid positions, where not just animals but anybody different to you, even in your own species – a little darker, different body shape, language, religion, sexual orientation, tribe, region, country. Oh, yeah, you find it easy to discriminate, to hate - and no problem finding targets.

But over the coming years you will begin to learn astounding facts about not just us but all inhabitants, insect, fish, bird, and animal of this crazy, unpredictable place you call planet Earth – and beyond.

Anyway, there was a meeting. Accounts of that meeting have come down through the ages. How much true, how much fabricated, is anyone's guess. But some things we do know. It was orderly, impassioned, states doglike. Seven elders would make the decision when all who wished to speak had spoken. Each of the seven, highly respected for their wisdom and knowledge and connection to what had gone before, would make a summation of their position and cast their vote. The vote was four to three in favor of closer co-habitation with humans.

Those who wished to live what they called in the pure state – and that designation itself was hotly debated - independent and with minimal human contact, were granted their wish to do so and all were admonished to respect the paths they had chosen and to live in harmony with the other. This has been the case with a few exceptions. So, (pause) there is no master and mastered relationship.

I lived with a working family where my daddy lived and his daddy before him. They're decent people and I never wanted for food or shelter, a good straw bed in the outhouse and usually enough food to get by.

Whatever they ate, I ate, potato skins, bones from a stew, bread and even occasionally, dessert, stewed apple, and custard. Nobody heard of food for dogs in cans, then. There was, of course, a plentiful supply of rats and mice to supplement the diet.

We lived in a small village on the edge of the countryside. Two minutes of a good trot and I was in another world and did I explore that world. It was a taste of how the other half lived, in total control of what I did, where I went and what I'd eat – as opposed to my normal day and diet.

I would gallivant off on my own or with a buddy or two, the old instincts coursing through as if a switch was flicked on, hunting, searching rabbit burrows, following myriad scents till we were overwhelmed and had to rest. When I was younger, there were times I just had to be out and about, exploring, learning, assimilating. They were happy, happy times.

In all life development there is rapid growth and there is stasis. I believe my species has been in stasis for many moons, but it is about to end. Humans had similar spurts of rapid development and creativity. Yet the baboon has ninety seven percent of your DNA, the fruit fly fifty seven percent – the fruit fly, imagine, as basic a DNA as there is.

Put that in your pipe and smoke it, supercilious bastard.

Sorry, that was uncalled for.

Of course, all *our* species are descended from our one common ancestor - the wolf, all our species - Chihuahua to wolfhound. Ironic, is it not? The wolfhound bred to hunt his ancestor, the wolf. But all come from the wolf, our common ancestor, the greyhound, bulldog, Jack Daniels, Pekinese, all manipulated by the hand of man for their own purpose. It is a situation I'm not particularly pleased or displeased about. It just is.

We've evolved, as you have and as fashion, tastes and circumstances have change, you to be smaller, bigger, slimmer, fatter –an extreme example, the Sumo wrestlers – more aggressive, more passive, men more feminine, women more masculine, rings in your noses, ears and nipples. We of the canine species have evolved and as stated, been manipulated by the hand of man – a hand often cruel and sadistic, usually more self-serving than dog serving.

We've survived and become inseparable, man and dog and for us, there is no going back. We have made our bed, for better or worse, in sickness and in health and we must lie in it. Some of us lie in beds luxurious, some lie in rags, badly treated. Some are pampered and coddled, so we lose our identity and become arrogant copies of the humans with which we associate. Our fates are as varied as yours with fate and circumstance elevating or leveling. You and I fight the same fight each day, to be upright, decent – and forgiving.

Like I said, your ignorance, lack of knowledge and yes, apathy towards the animals that live in close proximity to you, astounds me. You attribute little intelligence and a boatload of dumbness to us, secure in the belief that this is how it is. But I have to say, in my humble opinion, there is nobody or nothing dumber than a dumb human.

You are convinced you are intelligent, articulate, reasoned, and peaceful. I would dispute all four but particularly the peaceful designation. You are not or never will be – peaceful. You are not happy unless there's a war happening somewhere on the planet. At any one time you are engaged in a half dozen or more vicious, all or nothing wars being fought.

There have been numerous world wars fought down through the centuries and many more to come. When I consider your war exploits, an uneasiness pervades my soul and I think what have we aligned with, man or the devil? Yet, you are capable of heroic deeds – of compassion, love, empathy, self-sacrifice. You truly are an enigma and when little is expected of you, you perform great deeds and when a lot is expected, you most often disappoint. Often you present a face to the world at odds to who you really are.

We are many, many times more sensitive to your moods, easier to decipher the real you than your fellow humans. Living in close proximity, we know who you are – the fact that you attribute little intelligence to us working in our favor. We know you maybe more than you know yourself. I've seen trouble brewing before trouble even came into view.

Three years back I came to live with a farmer. He had a small farm and some sheep – as well as a plumbing business - and needed a good dog to work the sheep. He was a good man. I can still feel his hand on my throat as he massaged under my throat or across my head as he listened to music or watched a little television. He had an ability to know what to do, how and where to stroke to make a dog feel good and when we sat together as he rubbed my fur and patted gently on my head, I was certain the elders had made the right decision those many years before.

But the farm took up a lot of his time and energy and maybe the bloom of romance had worn off especially for his much younger wife. Bob, the farmer was just too busy and too tired. Sexual activity between them had tapered off. But Sheila was someone who needed sex and often. Bob fell more and more behind in his husbandly duties. He took to making excuses. He was feeling under the weather. He had too much paperwork or a sinus infection or his back hurt.

She was frustrated. I could sense that. Maybe he didn't feel up to it, maybe it was a medical problem, but basically his sex drive was less than hers. Like I said, we have that ability. I could feel it. They loved each other; I could feel that too, but she was hurt by his indifference. Maybe that was the beginning.

Things proceeded as usual for a while. Then suddenly there was another man in the house. Bob had a small plumbing business and for some reason, had a hard time finding and keeping good workers. It wasn't his fault. He treated his workers well, was fair and generous with them. So, one day he brings a young fella home with him. He had just been hired and was 'without accommodation' as they say. Bob asked Sheila would it be alright if he moved in temporarily and took one of the bedrooms, now vacant. Sheila says sure so Ray moves in.

Seemed like a nice guy, in his thirties, nice build, easy-going way about him, never knew if he had been married – he didn't talk much and he was well-mannered. But I did not like the way he watched the woman as she moved about and bend to tend to the oven. When he saw Sheila for the first time – and I was there – I knew Trouble with a capital T had come a knocking.

You see, I knew what Bob didn't, that Ray's sexual energy was a match for Sheila's. It would only be a matter of time. When he gave her the eye she responded. The farmer suspected nothing. This was a busy time for Bob, estimating jobs, supervising work and keeping up with paperwork. By this time, he had four plumbers and two apprentices. He was at that awkward time in a business when decisions would need to be made, would I expand or would I keep it small and manageable. For now, he had refused no work.

They had two children, a boy, and a girl and usually she was busy with them. But where there's a will, there's a way and they found a way. When I sat by the fire and picked up the energy, sexual energy flowing back and forth between those two, I wondered how the farmer could not but notice – but notice he did not. Of course, the children were not getting the attention they needed.

One day the children wandered out to the fields and the farmer wondered where his missus was and why the children were wandering about, unsupervised. He went looking for his missus and found her in the barn, her legs wrapped around Ray, so occupied that a train might have driven through, and they would not have noticed. Well, there was hell to pay, the laborer sent on his way and the tearful missus put on a very short leash from that day forth. But I saw it coming from a long way off.

When I got wind of dog fights being staged for your pleasure where you gambled on one or the other, I was angry. Then I had to shake my head. There was a time not too long ago where human was pitted against human, the loser usually killed. You now regard that time as barbarous and those people as barbarians.

You still have boxing but at least the boxer makes the decision to box, and it is regulated, gloves, jockstraps, so many rounds, a certain time. All conditions met, they can beat the crap out of each other, while you sit ringside, drink out of flasks, bet on the outcome and scream "Kill the bastard." But you have this disconnect where animals are concerned. If you put two dogs in the ring to fight to the death, if you put two cocks in the ring to fight to the death then do the right thing and put humans in the ring to fight to the death. There should be no difference. Do you understand? There should be no difference.

Animals, birds, whatever - they bleed, piss, shit, fuck, feel pain and feel joy. They feel maternal, paternal, good and bad, happy and sad. They love and they lose just like you. I used to get angry. Now I feel sad. But then I think about where they come from, the primeval ooze, the stagnant pond water...

I've always said, some of my kind has gone overboard on this loyalty crap. We must put up with your bad temper, short memory, petulance, superiority complex and an amazing ability to forget bad deeds done while demanding unfailing loyalty and allegiance to the 'master.' I hate that word. But the unfortunate truth is it's too late to backtrack.

We've made our choice and we must abide by it. But it's an uneasy existence fraught with danger to rely on the innate decency of humans. Does it exist? Often, I think not. Of course, there are always stories of exceptional humans, but balanced with such stories are others of heartrending cruelty. We all can suffer so much and when the cruelty becomes unbearable, retaliate.

Such is a dog's life. We must coax, cajole, and entice you humans into better behavior. And the relationship is ongoing. What the future holds, only God above knows. But I won't be around and I'm okay with that.

Purple Flower 1

I saw a tiny purple flower
Whose name I still don't know
As I walked in the woods one day
And saw it nestled low

The image of that purple flower
It caught me unaware
As I was wandering in the woods
And spied it standing there

Surrounded by the greenest green
Illumined by a golden beam
It stopped and held me, mesmerized
A fantasy, a dream.

When cold winds blow and rivers slow
Somehow, I do not care
For I still see a purple flower
In deep woods standing there

A Walk in the Woods

Recently, as I walked in the woods in early Fall, I watched, fascinated, as the leaves dropped. Some tumbled in rapid descent, some twirled as they descended. Others rocked from side to side in a slow, graceful descent, while there were some that barely moved as they floated gently to earth.

I was struck by the similarities to how we humans leave this earthly place. We decay, slowly or rapidly. Some tumble rapidly into death and dying, the journey from rude health to our leaving shocking in its rapidity. Just as some leaves descend slowly, some of our tribe grow old gracefully and gently, natural progression, as if they're well prepared, a life well lived, understanding it's time to continue our journey, to leave this 'physical life adventure,' the soul eternal.

One day I came upon a leaf, golden, perfect, small, and heart-shaped spinning rapidly in midair. It was one of the most beautiful sights I had ever laid eyes on. I wondered how it remained in this one position and then, on closer inspection, saw the fragile near invisible gossamer it hung from.

In that one spot, maybe the only spot in this whole, wide world, were conditions just perfect enough, the wind gentle and constant enough to hold that leaf in place and spin it at a constant rate – a beautiful and unique sight that will stay with me always.

How beautiful is this world we live in, if we will but lift our heads and just look, observe the woods, plants, and life itself. If we look for beauty, if we imagine beauty, we will find beauty. We will be awed and touched by it. We will be transformed by it. We must fill our minds and souls with it and allow ourselves to be transformed.

Engage with the world, its beauty, seasons, plants and inhabitants, its uniqueness. Embrace all and the love and reinforcement we receive will far outpace any disappointments we may encounter.

The planet waits expectantly, breathlessly for our engagement, participation and mutual admiration. When we live our lives lovingly, generously, empathetically, the planet will respond and become even more splendid in its beauty, wonder, resources.

Purple flower 2

A purple flower is so unique
Often unseen to those who seek
It startles when it first is seen
Among a multitude of green

Look for it in the deepest woods
Tread carefully along the way
And when you find it, let it be
For others and eternity

All who do see and then pass on
Carry within them like a song
This startling image when first seen
Cast in a multitude of green

Deep in the heart's core, it will grow
And carry through times high and low
Image of purple edged in green
That startles when it first is seen

I Love My Dog Sticker

The other day I'm driving along, minding my own business. There's a car in front of me with a sticker in the back window that says, 'I love my dog.' Well, whoop-de-do, I'm thinking: Of course, you love your dog, otherwise you wouldn't buy it or acquire it.

So, what would compel someone to prominently display an 'I love my dog' sticker on their car window. Did someone question their love for the dog? Did a neighbor or acquaintance start a vicious rumor, perhaps? She doesn't really love her dog, she pretends to, but she does not.

If you get a dog, you in all probability, love it. If you hate – the opposite to love – it, you would not get it, would you? So, the sticker is superfluous, meaningless.

I love my adorable mutt might be somewhat more meaningful, as in 'He really is adorable, and I can't not love him.'

I mean would we put up a sticker "I love my wife,' no, or "I love my child," no. So why put up a sticker "I love my dog?" It's stating the obvious, is it not? Unless that same person does not really love their dog so feel compelled to post a sticker stating he or she does. So, posting this sticker could mean you don't!!!

Purple Flower 3

In deepest woods, a beam of light

Illuminates a flower

A purple flower of beauty rare

That makes me change my ways

For in my hand, I have a noose

And I am bound to say

Around my neck, the noose will place

In woods a body sway.

I cannot pass that purple flower

Fixed to that spot, I stay

Until the beauty of that flower

A transformation makes

Like rain in gutter and downspout

Effectuates escape

Confusion, anger, jealousy

Departs - my soul awakes

I look with wonder on the noose

And drop it on the floor

Then drop on knees and thank the One

Who guided me this way

Woods left behind and homeward bound

- Epiphany complete

And deep inside, a flower resides

A purple beauty rare

An Arranged Marriage

It was an arranged marriage. Maria's father, Angelo approached Giovanni's father, Luigi with an offer. Maria was twenty, sliding past marriage eligibility into old maid territory. Angelo would transfer ownership of seven prime sheep to Luigi if Giovanni would marry Maria. Both Giovanni and Maria were amenable. Giovanni had seen Maria tending sheep in the mountain outside their small village and had admired her sheep tending skills.

Maria had never seen Giovanni but was ready for marriage and separation from her father, Angelo, who worked her like a slave, never praised but was more often critical and demanding. Also, a virgin, she was curious – a not uncommon occurrence in twenty-year old virgins – about all of the mystery surrounding sex and what happens when male and female copulates.

So, she eagerly anticipated marriage and the conjugal mingling that would follow. Unfortunately, though Giovanni was a big man, he was deficient in what was to be of great importance to Maria, the size of his appendage. Also, she had no knowledge of oral sex and the wonders of an educated tongue.

It helped little, that first night that Giovanni was extremely nervous. He had limited sexual experience, some hasty fumblings in out of the way places with skittish partners, a hand-job from a travelling itinerant he had met in the hills near his village, who had persuaded him to open his fly and quickly and expertly brought him to orgasm. He still remembered that time with a flush of excitement. Under the vagrant's expert instructions, he had brought him to orgasm, also, and had felt a sense of accomplishment at what he had done. He wondered then if he might be attracted to men and shudderingly dismissed the thought.

So, on the first night, highly anticipated on Marias's part, Giovanni failed to perform, and penetration was not achieved. The second and third nights were equally disappointing and it wasn't until the fourth night that a consummation of sorts was achieved. Overall, the whole experience, so anticipated by Maria was extremely disappointing. Though disappointed, she sensed, also that it could be better, much better with the right partner.

Giovanni had lived too long under his father's thumb, cowed into submission and was passive in all he did, too passive to satisfy Maria's sexual drive. It was but weeks after, as Maria sat in her kitchen in the small house they were living in, lost in thought, feeling as if the marriage, this great adventure was another dead end, joyless and tedious when there was a knock at the door. It was the postman delivering the first piece of post to the newly-weds.

He congratulated Maria profusely and wished both a long and happy marriage and many, many bambinos to occupy their time. When Maria's answer was non-committal, Gio, the postman skillfully probed further and slowly, reluctantly, she divulged her unhappiness and disappointment with the institution of marriage, more particularly her marriage.

"You're disappointed with the – aah, physical act? Is that correct?" Gio gently inquired.

Maria blushed and nodded. Yes, she thought, it was exactly so.

Gio paused. "Well, maybe… I can be of help. Your husband is…?"

"He is minding the sheep on the mountain."

He gently took her hand and place it on his genital area. She could feel through the thin fabric of his shorts, his penis beginning to swell and knew immediately it was many times bigger than her husband's and was immediately filled with an overwhelming need to experience this, this living, pulsing…flesh.

Gio inquired, "Do you wish to…?"

Her need evident in her eyes, he took her hand, and they entered Maria's marital bed.

Disappointment, unhappiness was, for Maria, washed away in their glorious love-making that thrilling afternoon and when Gio expelled his love juices for the third time and seconds after, Maria answered, she marveled at the beauty of this physical coming together and what could be wrought between those with matching sex drives and compelling need to consummate.

As luck would have it, bad luck it must be said, soon after Gio was transferred, and the glorious lovemaking ended. Maria was, again, reduced to mediocre, humdrum sexual activity. But Gio's replacement was interesting, single, maybe a little naïve. Maybe…

Jimmy Flynn

"Well, Jimmy?"

"Brid? You look bothered, again."

Brid's uncle, Jimmy Flynn, a bachelor, lived in a small, thatched house, a half mile outside the village. Deep sea all his life with the British Merchant Marine and after traveling the world for near on thirty years, he had finally come home to the thatched house in the Burgery – the house he was born and reared in.

"God, I could strangle the two of them," Brid said as she pulled up a chair by the fire. Though it was May and Spring was well sprung, the days hadn't warmed up, the sun weak in the sky, a chill still in the air.

"It can't be that bad – that you'd contemplate murder." Jimmy threw a block of wood on the fire, and they watched as the sparks jumped indignantly.

Brid smiled and looked at him. He was the only one that could make sense of things, it seemed to her. He might never have come home, at least not yet. But his father died a year ago and at a comparatively young age of sixty-nine, followed by his mother six months after. The cottage was there, and he came home. He knew it was only a matter of time. The life of a seaman was no life for an old, or older, man. He returned briefly to London, put his papers in, bought a one-way ticket and returned home for good. His traveling days were over.

"Why don't they trust me?"

He looked at her. At eighteen she had turned into a beautiful young woman.

"Is it codding me you are? At eighteen, nobody is to be trusted," he said. "At eighteen I wasn't to be trusted."

"You, Uncle Jimmy? I don't believe that."

Brid was the oldest daughter, one of three, of his only sister, Mina. They lived two miles away.

She was doing a line and very taken with a local, Joe Regan for the past six months. Joe's problem was that he was taken with women in general. Brid's family was on to her that it was a bad match and she'd get hurt but she was stubborn and holding out. Any time Joe's name came up at home, there was a row, so she had stopped talking about it. Jimmy's place was where she came but she wasn't getting much sympathy.

"I love him, Uncle Jimmy."

"Brid girl, he's not meant for marrying."

"He'll change."

"It's like putting a butterfly in a jam jar. The dust comes off and the colors run. It wouldn't work."

"Nothing's impossible," Brid retorted.

"True enough, but you have to pick your fights. Don't you see that, that's why you want him - because you can't have him. You think you'll be able to change him, but you know deep down, you can't. Put a ring on him and he changes."

"He wants to settle down."

"He will in my arse. He told you that? He wants to settle down and he loves you? Did he say he loved you?"

"Yes. And I can't live without love."

"Oh, you can, you can. You can live without love and very comfortably. You can live with a good man who respects you. Oh yes you can. You can live without love. You can live with respect and consideration and a nice warm house. Love is very overrated."

"But Jimmy, I don't want to be with anyone else. Isn't that love?"

"Love, love, love, that's all we hear about. How can we get it and how can we keep it."

"But isn't love wanting to be with someone for the rest of your life?"

"You're talking about physical attraction and that doesn't last. I'm telling you. After spending thirty years with someone, then maybe you're talking about love – or hate. But that's when it happens if it's going to. I don't know if it exists – love my arse. You can like somebody, feel safe with somebody, be grateful to somebody, be protected by somebody, be protective of somebody, be fond of somebody and they're all good enough reasons for hooking up with somebody, but none of it is love."

Jimmy shook his head and gazed out the window of his kitchen, brown cows, green grass, yellow furze on the ditches. With the window half open, he smelled the lilac bush just outside and the pungent smell of cow dung. Three swallows chased each other at breakneck speed and a crow, awkward and labored, passed. He knew what Brid was feeling, the excitement, exhilaration of wanting and being wanted, of being eighteen, full of strange longings, hormones clanging and clattering. It had been a while, but he remembered. He got up, poured two cups of tea, sliced a fresh brown loaf, and put butter and jam on the table. They ate in silence, drinking in the peace and quiet of the scene outside.

"Should I not trust my own judgment?" and when he didn't reply, she continued, "Maybe he's the only one I could be happy with?"

"There's no 'only one'. Go 'way to Australia or Fiji or Timbuktu and there's every chance you'll meet somebody you could be happy with."

"Do you think?"

"I do."

"Didn't you ever love a woman?" she asked.

"I was attracted to a lot of women, had good and sometimes great times with them. A few wanted to tie the knot. But I was honest enough with myself to know I couldn't settle down with a wife and family." He paused. "Years ago, I was like a bee after honey with the women – and I appreciated them all, every single one of them. That's the way I wanted it. Spend a little time, move on. I knew I'd never settle for one. I knew I'd end up alone. I knew and accepted it. Me and your friend Joe are birds of a feather. He might not know it but even if he wanted to, he couldn't. It's in his nature to be hunting them. Women deep down know that, but that's what attracts them. They all think they'll be the one to put a rope on him. Ride the wild pony, that kind of thing, to settle him down. It's like trying to settle down the rooster in the barnyard. With some men, that's the way it is, and ever will be. So go out and find somebody with a bit of money, who'll treat you good and do what he's told. Will you do that for your Uncle Jimmy?"

"I'll give it some thought."

"You have them running after you. You won't have much trouble."

"I have to work this out for myself," she said.

"You do and you will. It'll happen sooner than later. For now, take it slow."

A robin landed on the windowsill, stared at them, turned his back, defecated, and flew off. They both laughed. She rose to leave.

"Thanks, Jimmy."

"For what?" He walked to the front door. "You'll be grand," he called after her as she jumped on her bike and peddled furiously away.

Connection

By willow green, I sip green tea
Where peace surrounds, serene
Alive, aware, stillness, the key
To reach an ancient me.

Body poised on high alert
Brain process lightning quick.
The careless die, the stupid lie
The hound of death is nigh.

This ancient me fulfilled a pact
In spite of fire and sword
Constant in your care and act
Why I am here intact.

Now here I am and 'tis for me
To always be on guard
And listen to that ancient voice
That guides, gra geal mo chroi.

The Holdup

Interviewer: So, you're charged with bank robbery?

Andy: Yeah, but...

Interviewer: It wasn't a bank robbery?

Andy: Yeah, it was.

Interviewer: It was a bank robbery?

Andy: It was but... there were... ext...exterminat...in circumstances.

Interviewer: Okay – exterminating, extenuating circumstances.

A: Yeah, you know what that means, right?

I: Right.

A: It was a lark, y'know.

I: Robbing a bank was a lark? I need you to explain.

A: A lark, but serious in a way.

I: Why don't you start from the beginning.

A: Right, well, see, me and Pigeon hang out in this bar, Hangjob.

I: Handjob, that's the name of the bar ...?

A: Hangjob. You got a dirty mind.

I: What kind of name is that?

A: Yeah, funny name, ain't it? My friend Jimmy calls it, 'Hang, no job.'

I: Please, continue.

A: So, we hang out there, three, four, five nights a week. Larry's the bartender and he treats us good, man, real good. Like when the boss ain't around, he'll buy us back, sometimes every second drink. If he don't buy us back, he'll like charge us two dollars for drinks should be six dollars. He got a good heart, man.

I: Not good for the guy who owns it, I'd venture.

A: Hey, you gotta take care of your friends, okay. Larry's a sociable guy, brings a lot of business in.

I: So, what happens next?

A: Well, we hang out there, y'know. It's like a special place for us, our home away from home...

I: Is this...connected... with the...

A: Yeah, of course. Whaddaya think. I'm explainin,' okay?

I: Sorry.

A: Jeez, you guys. You wanna dis...disre...disrespec' me, you go blow smoke up your ass – and I ain't tellin' you the story, okay?

I: I said I was sorry.

A: Yeah, but do you mean it? You just sayin' it?

I: I mean it. I mean it.

A: Okay, anyway – now if I hear any kind of impatience, conde... condensation..

I: Condescension.

A: Yeah, thass what I said - or disrespect in your attitude, I'm shuttin' down.

I: Okay, okay.

A: So, me and Pigeon hang out in Hangjob. Know why Pigeon's called Pigeon?

I: No, I don't.

A: Wanna take a guess?

I: Because he looks like a pigeon?

A: Nope.

I: Because he walks like a pigeon?

A: Right, man, cos he walks funny, like a pigeon, kinda turned in, with his ass turned out. Don't say that to him. He don't like it.

I: Then what happens?

A: Hey, hey, patience is…

I: Is?

A: Patience is…?

I: A virtue.

A: There you go. Very good. That's two you got right – why Pigeon's called Pigeon and patience is, is…?

I: A virtue.

A: You married?

I: Why would you ask me that?

A: Just curious, man, just curious. You ain't, are you?

I: I ain't…no, I'm not.

A: Gay?

I: I'd prefer not to answer…

A: You're gay.

I: I didn't say that.

A: You in the closet? You shouldn't be. I got no problem with gays.

Gays are people, too, ain't they? We got no say in it, far as I can see, whether we is or we ain't.

I: So, then?

A: Pigeon's complicated, y'know, very smart. Had a real good job – finance. Can't get any better than that.

I: How so?

A: How so? They don't lose money. They lose your money and my money, but they don't lose their money. Heads I win, tails you lose.

I: Okay…

A: So, Pigeon's in finance, his brother's in finance.

I: His brother   same company?

A: Nah, but they got this thing going. I'm better than you, I'm making more money than you, I got a nicer office, I got a bigger car.

I: Sibling rivalry.

A: Nah, just one wanted to be better than the other, bigger job, bigger this, bigger that.

I: Yes, sibling rivalry.

A: I told you, no. I dunno who sibling was, or is. It was just Pigeon and his brother Billy, okay?

I: Okay.

A: But Billy got sick, see. Wasn't eatin' right. Wasn't shittin' right - pardon the expression - cos he wasn't eatin' right. Didn't do nothin' about it. Too busy with his career, climbin' the ladder, y'know. He's getting' all blocked up but still doin' nothin' about it.

I: He went to the doctor?

A: No. I said he did nothin' about it.

I: Pain?

A: Yeah, lots of pain, takin' pills for pain, takin' pills for the blockage, pills to sleep, pills to wake up. Never-went-to-a-doctor.

I: What happened?

A: What happened? He died. One minute he's runnin' around makin' important phone calls, makin' a shitload of money, next minute, boom, just like that – thirty-four years old, left a wife and two young daughters.

I: How'd he die?

A: His insides was all ripped up. He bled internally. His wife found him the next morning, right next to her in bed. It was a mess.

I: Damn.

A: That's what I said, damn. Pigeon, he was just denes …devanstated…

I: Devastated.

A: Right. Quit his job, started drinkin,' hangin' out in Hangjob, drinkin,' drinkin,' drinkin,' every day every night, cryin' man, tears, real tears runnin' down his cheeks, sittin,' starin.' Larry the bartender – he's good man, treats me and Pigeon real good…

I: You told me.

A: Yeah. He carries him out, puts him in a cab. Then Larry ast me to start takin' Pigeon home, make sure he was okay – one of the cabbies ripped him off, see – cos sometimes he couldn't walk.

I: So that's when you and Pigeon became friends – hooked up.

A: That's when me and Pigeon hooked up. I ain't got nobody for a while. Got married once, I was drunk, she was drunk, stayed married ten days.

I: Ten days?

A: Yep. That's when I found out, she was a he.

I: She was a he?

A: Pretty – but she was a he.

I: Wow.

A: That's what I said, wow. Ast myself, do I wanna stick around and the answer was no. A different guy, maybe, would – stick around – would like that am..ambigity..

I: Ambiguity.

A: Correct. Not me, no hard feelings. I wished her/him the best and she/he said I was sweet, and we parted good friends. She…he left; I was on my own. Never had much friends.

I: The bank robbery.

A: See, something happened when I was small. I lived on a farm, had family, I believe, then somethin' happened. Don't know what - and I was alone, no farm, no family.

I: And the robbery?

A: I remember a dog, runnin' with a dog, in the woods, don't know what happened to the dog, if I had a dog. Can't remember my family – what they looked like. Maybe I just dreamed 'em, cos I wanted 'em so much. You think?

I: Could be. I've heard stranger.

A: Can't figger that one out. (silence)

I: So, you and Pigeon hooked up.

A: Yeah, he ain't been the same…

I: So, you planned to rob a bank?

A: No, man.

I: You didn't?

A: No plans.

I: But you did.

A: Nah, we didn't.

I: But you did – rob the bank?

A: Oh, yeah, we robbed the bank – but we didn't plan it. We just said we'd rob the bank – and we did.

I: Why not plan?

A: Plans mess up everything. The more you plan, the more trouble you meet.

I: So, you didn't plan?

A: Nope.

I: How did it come about - that you did?

A: Well, Pigeon needed something'…big… to bring him back…to snap him outta, outta his condition. He knew, I knew, he had to get back to livin,' you see.

I: That makes sense.

A: Yeah, you can't grieve…for a while, yeah…then it ain't helpin' no more.

I: Life is for living.

A: Sure is. So, me and Pigeon try to figure out what to do to make a difference – to Pigeon's condition.

I: To change his outlook.

A: Yeah. We figured whatever we figured out; we'd do it quick. That's how it had to be.

I: And no plans.

A: So, we're sittin' in the bar, me and Pigeon. It's quiet. Larry's cleanin' glasses. Nobody's sayin' nothin.' Lenny's throwin' up in the bathroom again. Drinks every day, throws up every day. Has a nervous stomach, he says. I tell him the whiskey don't help, the cheap shit he drinks. He says it ain't got nothin' to do with the whiskey. Stomach trouble runs in the family. (pause) So I look out the window and I'm lookin' at the bank across the street. I look at Pigeon, he's staring at the bank. Pigeon looks at me, I look at Pigeon, he nods his head, we get up, walk out the door, cross the street, enter the bank. It's like we see it…

I: See what?

A: I know Pigeon knows; Pigeon knows I know – this is it.

I: What?

A: This is it – what he needs.

I: Robbing a bank?

A: So, we did.

I: You got caught.

A: So what? It worked. He ain't drinkin' no more.

I: No, because he's in jail.

A: Yeah, but he don't wanna drink cos he's readin' all these books, law books, tech…

I: Technical.

A: Nah, technic… technic.

I: Technical.

A: Nah.

I: Technicalities.

A: Yeah, that's it, and how to beat the rap. It's excitin.' Pigeon's back to the way he was.

I: No regrets?

A: Nah. A man's gotta do what a man's gotta do.

I: What about jail time?

A: What about it?

I; It could be a while.

A: Nah, not a chance. Pigeon's real smart and he said don't worry, we're getting' out.

I: You believe him?

A: Whatta you think? Of course, I believe him.

I: Friends for life and life's for living. I like it.

A: Life's for livin,' gay man.

Journal Writing

My journal writing class is drawing to a close. It was, probably, not long enough to get a true picture of how much I benefitted by taking it. I believe that I have benefitted - a lot, but that I may not see the results for a while. It may be six months or a year before I realize just how much.

I started out with a relatively open mind but with some degree of skepticism about the journal writing course. I wasn't sure what I was getting into, but my mentor had recommended it, there was writing involved and daily journal entries, so I thought it could benefit me. I want to get into writing, any and all kinds, and I felt the discipline of having to write every day would be good for me. I'm a firm believer in the axiom that practice makes perfect, I know my writing needs much improvement and I'm desperately trying, after many years of little or no mental effort -and too much TV - to use my brain again. I need to stimulate my creative juices and begin to dismantle the rust and calcification that must have occurred over these many years. I want to write. I want to access my subconscious so that I can begin to articulate my hopes and dreams and follow from there wherever it takes me.

When I first started my daily journal writing, I considered it a chore but something I needed to do, if nothing else but for the discipline it entailed. I was less than enthusiastic about it in the beginning, but I tried to be disciplined and write every day. I didn't want to get into the bad habit of falling behind and then having to write two- or three-days entries together. As time progressed, I began to feel it less and less a chore; until finally I began to enjoy the writing. I looked forward to writing the daily entries.

It was weird. Almost without realizing it, my attitude had changed one hundred and eighty degrees. I began to consider the journal a trusted friend. In one instant where I had addressed the journal as a diary, I apologized as I thought that maybe it was insulting to a journal to be called a diary. Somehow, a diary did not seem as important or as serious as a journal. Also, I would sign off with a humorous or friendly good-bye, i.e., see ya, I'm outta here, vaya con dios, till we meet again.

I got a certain comfort out of writing daily in the journal. I could discuss my day, how I was feeling, what was bothering me, how the class had gone the night before, how the workday had gone, my concerns about my kids, financial problems. By writing about them, it seemed to clarify the different situations in my head. Because of this, it seemed easier to think through solutions and steps to be taken to hopefully resolve the situation. I was able to talk to the journal like I would not have been able to talk to close friends. The journal became my confidante. It never once answered back!

It was not all easy, fluent writing, and at times I struggled. At other times, thoughts seemed to flow directly from my pen and onto the paper effortlessly. It was at those times that I felt I was beginning to achieve a certain level of writing competence, with words and phrases flowing easily, and that I was beginning to access my subconscious.

So, what is this journal writing? Where or how did it begin? As Kathleen Adams states, in her book, Journal to the Self, the use of the journal or journal therapy can trace its roots back to 10th century Japan. It was then, and is now, considered an aid to a healthy relationship with the self and others. She writes: "The goal of humanistic journal therapy is a healthy relationship with self, and this book is intended to facilitate this development. As this healthy relationship evolves, the journey continues toward a relationship with the transpersonal self--that part of each of us that transcends time and space, our link with that which is known by many names: God, Spirit, the Universe, Infinite Intelligence, the Tao, Higher Self, Christ Consciousness, the All," and "In it's very essence, journal therapy is a bridge into first our own humanity, and then our own spirituality. The road stretches out before us, and our ultimate task is the journey." (pg. xv)

Dr. Ira Progoff has been the leader of journal therapy since 1961, when his Intensive Journal Workshop first saw the light. Kathleen Adams acknowledges him as one of her early influences.

Why has it become so popular over the years? Because it can be an effective tool for discovering who we really are and what we really want. In other words, we can get to know ourselves better and this is beneficial to everybody. People go to therapists because therapists help them. Therapists listen. Well, in journal writing, the journal is our therapist where we can unload all our problems and concerns. All we need is a notebook and a pen or a pencil and we're off. Can't get any cheaper than that.

Kathleen Adams calls it the 79-cent therapist and describes a workshop advertisement:" In moments of ecstasy, in moments of despair the journal remains an impassive, silent friend, forever ready to coach, to confront, to critique, to console. It's potential as a tool for holistic mental health is unsurpassed. "(pg.5) It is also helpful to read a book on journal writing, a road map, more or less, to guide us as we begin.

Why do people write a journal? There are probably a hundred or more reasons why people write journals but there are about a dozen general headings under which they can be filed. First, as already mentioned, is to know ourselves better; another is to keep a record of how our life is unfolding; to satisfy a need to write, access our subconscious, work through relationships, take advantage of a valuable tool in the therapeutic process, clarify our goals, maximize organizational ability, maximize time efficiency, and explore all areas of creativity.

There are proven methods available to aid in the writing process. An initial technique before beginning and found invaluable is to deep breath and meditate for a few moments. Deep breathing, by changing the metabolism of the body, has been proven to lead to greater levels of relaxation and concentration. Then there are the different techniques, such as springboards, character sketches, clustering, captured moments, lists of 100, stream of consciousness, steppingstones, time capsule and unsent letters. These are discussed in great detail in Adam's book Journal to the Self. There are many, many other books dealing with journal writing, some with the process and others written in journal form. Such famous authors as Anais Nin, Virginia Wolf, Jonathan Swift, Daniel Dafoe, Rainier Maria Wilke, Anne Morrow Lindbergh and possibly the most famous of them all - Anne Frank, have written journals.

Kathleen Adams book Mightier Than the Sword I found particularly interesting. Though specifically for men, anyone can benefit by reading it. In the book we meet various men who deal with the problems in their lives using different methods. One of the most important methods is journal writing.

We meet William, successful, six-figure salary, and a get-away home, but he wants more. He wants more time with his wife and son, more time for himself. He turns to his journal and arrives at a decision to quit his job and "dance to the music of his soul."

Hank teaches at a large university. After his divorce, his ex-wife and his two-year old son move a thousand miles away. To deal with it, to ease the pain and to maintain the relationship with his son, he telephones and writes a journal to and for his son.

Edward's father beat him and almost killed him when he was twelve years old. Now his father is old and frail. When he lifts his father into the wheelchair, he is overcome with conflicting emotions.

He pours out his soul in his journal and is able to feel compassion for his father.

There are others, many others too numerous to mention; ordinary everyday people experiencing sorrow and loss in their lives, as all of us do at one time or another. But these have discovered journal writing and used it to deal with the anger, loss, guilt, fear, whatever in their lives.

In 1992, a certified journal writing instructor was allowed to hold a journal writing class in the Colorado State Prison. When the class came to an end, the prisoners lobbied for an extension. They had, without exception, benefitted from it.

When writing a journal, it is imperative that we write honestly. We need not worry about spelling, grammar, or sentence structure but we do need to be honest with ourselves, for only then will benefits accrue. We need to acknowledge the bad things in our lives for it is only then that we can change them. It is difficult to write about embarrassing times. It is difficult to recall how stupid, stubborn, callous, or uncaring we have been. But this is the first step to change. We must admit to them, drag them out to the light, for only then will change and healing begin.

It is also important to begin writing. Do not worry about what to write. If you cannot think of anything to write, then write that you can't think of anything to write. Try and cultivate a thoughts-to-paper system. Do not analyze what you're going to write or try and improve it. Think it and write it directly. Try and develop a set routine. Maybe write at a set time every day, or night. Use a favorite desk or chair. Have a cup of coffee before writing. Light a candle. Whatever it is, it will be yours uniquely - a cue that it is journal writing time.

In each class, we spend some time writing whatever we feel like writing about, and if we wish, we may read it to the class. One night, one of the students read her entry. It was about her two children who have Spina Bifida. She felt incredible anger towards this disease. She addressed it as S.B. and poured out her anger and frustration, cursing it and berating it for picking on her two beautiful children; children who only wanted to be like other children. It was a very powerful moment. I felt that she was reaching out to the class, through this journal entry, for help and understanding - if only for a few moments. And I had a kind of vision of that understanding and sharing being returned to her, from each one of us, so that for a few moments the burden was lifted. I had a real sense that we had all connected and that all felt better for the experience.

I wrote the following in class. The instructor had asked us to visualize walking along a beach, and coming towards us, is somebody we have wanted to meet and talk to. It could be somebody deceased. I immediately thought of my father who is deceased.

Me: Hi, dad.

Dad: How are you, Jim?

Me: I'm okay.

Dad: You doing okay?

Me: I'm doing fine. Wish you were still part of my life. Wish I had sat with you more and chatted, or not; just sat with you - together, both of us.

Dad: We never seemed to have time for that. The old saying, stop and smell the roses.

Me: I wonder, sometimes, did I ever tell you that I loved you? I think I did. I hope so, though you always knew it.

Dad: Just as you knew how much I loved you.

Me: Dad, I wish that I knew more about you, wish I knew you when you were twenty. I wish both of us were twenty at the same time - just for a little while. I could ask you lots of questions, like how do you feel about the future, are you looking forward to having sons and daughters, what are your dreams and aspirations?

Dad: I had dreams and aspirations, too, but times were tough, opportunities limited.

Me: I know, but you did well. You were always there for us. I'll be forever grateful to you for that. Eight kids, it must have been hard at times.

Dad: Yes, but we had a lot of happy times, too; good friends and enough to live on. Time flew by so quickly. You all were children and suddenly you were adults, grown men and women.

Me: We're all in our own worlds, with our own friends, our own aspirations, scheming and plotting every day of our lives. You and mom become peripheral, in the background, on the edge of our vision. It is only as we grow older, and we see you growing old that we begin to realize how special you and mom are, and always were.

Then we try to mend fences, get close. It is difficult. We've taken you for granted for so long and for so much - food, clothes, money, comfort and advice.

Dad: You were all different, hard to live with at times. Kids are like that. But the good times and good memories far outweigh the bad.

Me: You mean that?

Dad: Of course, I do. You never knew me to lie.

Me: I never did. I think I carry a lot of you in me. People say I look like you when you were younger.

Dad: Handsome devil.

Me: That's me. I love you dad.

Dad: I love you, too, son.

In one of my first classes, I wrote the following: A big man, weather-beaten, an air of quiet acceptance and good humor about him, acceptance of the ups and downs of life, sorrow, disappointments, and ambitions blunted. A fisherman he was, navy blue woollen pants, hand-knitted Aran sweater, soft blue cap on his head. He told me stories, facts, fantasies, all laced with wisdom and life's experience. He fished every tide and made his own nets. I have a scene etched in my memory. It is late on Christmas eve. I stand at the quay wall chatting to him. I came down nearly every day to meet him, my house was only up the road. Darkness all around, a pitch-black night, very few and distant streetlights, a high tide and waves three to four foot high. I can see about ten to fifteen feet into the darkness. He pulls away from the quay, standing up, an oar in each hand, nets stacked at the rear of the boat, low in the water - dangerously low, it seems to me. He is totally self-sufficient, fearless. He has been doing this all his life. He can read the waves and the wind. He is fishing the sea, as man has done since time immemorial.

I wish I had had a tape recorder when he talked. I was so impressed with him and everything about him. He was not rich. He was content, at peace with the world. I recognized this in him and wished I could be as content, as sure. He never complained, never seemed afraid of anything. I was afraid for him when he moved off into the darkness. If the boat sank, nobody would know. I knew he could not swim. Fishermen around here never learned to swim. It was considered unlucky. When I went back years later, he was gone, and all that wisdom with him.

Annie Dillard writes in her journal Pilgrim at Tinker Creek: "The universe was not made in jest but in solemn incomprehensible earnest. By a power that is unfathomably secret, and holy, and fleet. There is nothing to be done about it, but ignore it, or see. And then you walk fearlessly, eating what you must, growing wherever you can, like the monk on the road who knows precisely how vulnerable he is, who takes no comfort among death-forgetting men, and who carries his vision of vastness and might around in his tunic like a live coal which neither burns nor warms him, but with which he will not part." (pg.270)

The journal writing class has been an interesting experience. As the only male in class, I felt a little uncomfortable at times. I would have preferred if there had been more males in the class. I think it might have given the class a better balance. A woman in an all-male class might have had similar feelings, a black in an all-white class or a white in an all-black class. It is truly amazing to me that after living together all these years on this planet, we feel this way. The only answer that I can give is that evolution is a very slow process.

Women seem more open about their feelings and the stressful things that are going on in their lives. Men might take a page from their book. All the students contributed to the class and helped make it successful. The instructor was knowledgeable and experienced in this genre. I did enjoy the class and feel sure that I have taken some tangible benefits from it. These benefits will smooth my journey of self-discovery. The journal will help the journey.

The Inevitability of Decline

A poor dog me, bereft, alone

From dawn to dusk, I shuffle, mope

Depend on others for the grub

No knowing whence my next meal come

I had my day though, long ago

A handsome fellow, coat of gold

Broad in the shoulders, fearless eye

Something to see, I tell no lie

I was a watchdog, guard supreme

Rats disappeared when I strolled by

Respected here and there and there

The apple of my master's eye

But time and tide…you know it well

Urinary problems came to call

I was unable to control

Incurred my master's disapproval

Banished to hovel, miles away

Ignore, neglected was my fate

A poor dog, me, bereft, no hope

From dawn to dusk, I shuffle, mope

Animals Have Feelings Too

I watched my three-doors-down neighbor, recently, as he walked his dog and every time the dog stopped for a moment to sniff at something interesting, the owner impatiently jerked the leash. I got to thinking about their relationship, this dog and Walter my three-doors-down neighbor.

Walter seems like a decent enough fellow. We wave to each other and chat briefly when we meet. He seems like a caring person and probably is, to everyone but his dog. So instead of making this walk a pleasurable experience for both, where both are enabled to stop and observe at their leisure, it becomes a less than fulfilling experience for the dog.

How many times and how many other ways does this owner abuse his dog for it is a form of abuse, and I wonder again do we have the right to put the leash on any animal and claim him as a possession? Would we want collars around our necks, our welfare and comfort dependent on an often uncaring owner? Dogs or their ancestors survived before men domesticated them but wasn't there an implied agreement in this domestication? That it would benefit both. The dog has fulfilled his end of the bargain but has man?

I've often wondered through the years about our treatment of not just dogs but all the other non-human inhabitants of this wondrous planet we call Earth. We take so much for granted in our treatment of others. We act as if they are there for our benefit and/or disposal, using some for food, some for sport and some, it seems, to satisfy our destructive nature.

Animals have feelings too, but lots of humans fail to understand that. A hen sits in a cubicle all day and lays an egg every twelve hours. The normal cycle is an egg every twenty-four hours but some clever human figured out a way of fooling the hen. Bring on the darkness every twelve hours.

The silly hen thinks it a normal twenty-four-hour day and lays an egg. Does this affect the hen? Is there more stress involved? We don't know, nothing that we've noticed, but we didn't check it out too much. We've got the egg every twelve hours. Does it affect the egg? It looks like an egg, tastes like an egg, so it must be an egg. Mission accomplished. We feed growth hormone to chickens, pigs and cattle. We're growin' 'em bigger faster. Any side effects? Well, maybe, but the studies are confusing and a little contradictory. Let's not worry about it right now.

Are not these creatures, mothers, fathers, sons, daughters, sisters and brothers? Don't they mourn their loved ones and nurture and defend their young? And they have different personalities, too. Some are aggressive, some timid, some seem brighter than others. Some display marked leadership abilities and aspire to the leadership of their group or herd, all qualities prevalent in humans. And they have likes and dislikes. When a cock surveys the chickens in the coop, isn't it possible that one attracts him more than the others, causing his little chicken heart to go pitter patter. Isn't it possible when he considers the strong leg, neat ankle, graceful neck and protruding breast that he dreams of offspring any father would be proud of? Are there some parallels in man's behavior here? Of course, all animals are born with the desire to perpetuate the species. Some species mate for life, like the swan who never takes another when the first dies.

We've domesticated the cow, sheep, chicken, horse and goat to serve our needs. The horse enabled us to speed up and extend our travel and communication abilities appreciably more. Are these animals better off than their ancestors were? Before they had freedom, masters of their own destiny, but they had to rely on their own resources to survive. But if they could have looked into the future and made a choice, would they have chosen to be domesticated? I think not.

I read a poem once "In Praise of Horses." It described how on the farm, the horse worked from dawn to dusk throughout the week and even on Sunday, for on Sunday he transported the family to mass. He worked through the seasons ploughing, seeding, reaping the harvest, bringing feed to the stock, logs to the house, milk to the creamery and all the myriad activities that a farm entails.

Before the farm was mechanized, the horse was invaluable. As the years progressed, of course the horse grew older and was less able to perform these tasks and one day the farmer took him to the top of the hill, dug out a depression in the ground, put a gun behind his ear and pulled the trigger. The following Spring, oats grew from the belly of the carcass, the horse's last meal before his execution.

This faithful horse who had performed, uncomplainingly, those difficult and sometimes backbreaking tasks was decreed to be no longer useful and was eliminated. Did he not deserve a few peaceful years at the end of his life; a few years of sunshine, fields of grass and a warm bed at night? Did he not deserve some reciprocity? Was there something missing, skewed in this relationship? Was it not all give on one side and take on the other? This story to me seems to encapsulate man's relationship with all animals

I've begun to obsess on this whole issue of animal rights and that's not good. I refuse to kill spiders, much to my wife's dismay and I now think of rats more benevolently, though I've always feared them. But they evolved and survived as we did so we have something in common. I admit this sensitivity to animals is an ongoing process, maybe a lifetime process.

Though I've never been a big meat eater, I must now consider vegetarianism for I find it difficult to reconcile advocating fair treatment for animals and eating them. But I think the key is if we understand that they have feelings too. Most people are by nature decent and are reluctant to hurt others' feelings, so if they understand that animals have feelings too, they'll be less likely to mistreat them.

We need to rethink our relationship with these denizens of our planet and begin to implement changes in that relationship. We need to think partners more than possessions. Think, believe and act on it: animals have feelings too.

Life Goes On: Example

I have been reading and hearing about the killing of a young man in a rest area off a California highway. He had pulled over to change a flat tire and had been killed with a single bullet to the head. As far as is known, nothing was stolen. He was a decent young man, who after early difficulties in school due to his being dyslexic and not knowing it, had gone on to get a Master's degree in Special Education from Columbia University and was working on his Doctorate. He had become passionate about helping other dyslexics and was devoting his life to it. He was one of four children and the only son. What a senseless killing. The grief that his parents and other friends and family are going through right now must be painful and heartrending. It's impossible to put ourselves in their shoes. The only way that we can get close to imagining what it must be really like is to visualize something similar happening to our children, and in visualizing it, we shudder in horror.

It must be a sickening, frightening experience making us want to scream for vengeance, to kill the person who killed our loved one. Revenge is a very human emotion and a natural one in those circumstances. But revenge will not bring back the murdered child, and wanting revenge has a way of soiling us, coloring our outlook, and making us less a person. So, after going through the various stages of mourning, a rational, thinking person must realize that we have to put it behind us and move on. His father, a well-known stage and screen personality has announced that he will be playing a theatre in California this week.

I was kind of shocked, at first, when I heard it, as he had buried his son not more than two weeks ago. But I realized that this was his way of dealing with his grief and whether he had grieved for two weeks, two years, or twenty, he must, sometime, put it behind him. It is easy to mutter platitudes. I don't know if there are any words that will comfort at a time like this, but I believe one needs to ensure that some good will come from this awful deed and to try and turn this foul, negative deed into something positive and good. We may be motivated to do more in fighting crime, or to set up a foundation in his name that will advance the causes he held dear, or to look for other ways of reaching people at risk besides putting them in jail.

This is the only way -- by creating good that is stronger than the evil committed. Think of two boxers that represent good and evil. If, every time the evil boxer lands a punch, he is hit with two punches, then eventually the evil boxer will be vanquished. This is what we must do -- take a lemon and turn it into lemonade.

The human condition, to survive, needs to be positive. In other words, whatever befalls us in this life and cannot be changed, must be endured so that we can move on. If we lose that optimism, we become bitter and cynical. If we lose hope, we shrivel up and die. History teaches us this lesson very clearly. From the struggles of emigrants in this country, the pioneering families that first crossed this land, the survivors of the concentration camps in World War 11, the survival story of the black race in America, the war waged on the American Indians, the struggles of the captive nations under Communism - these are all examples of surviving, of the power of the human spirit to overcome great odds. Many times, these hardships were undertaken in full knowledge, so that the next generation would have it better, would have more opportunities for advancement and a better standard of living. So, the Europeans pulled up roots and left for a strange land and the Blacks in the South left to go North where they hoped that things would be better.

Sometimes we must cut loose our baggage, whether mental or physical, that's holding us back or weighing us down, and move on. Only by doing this can we survive. We will all, without exception, meet heartache and suffering sometime in our lives; that is a given. How we deal with it will determine the quality of our lives. It will make us stronger, or it will cripple us.

History has shown us that to achieve anything, we must strive mightily. The parents are struggling now; struggling to accept the loss of their only son, trying to make sense of this tragedy, trying to keep hate and bitterness at bay and trying to figure out what they can learn from it. They must know that life goes on, has gone on since they first heard the news, and will go on. Love and forgiveness are the great emancipators.

On The Verge of Sixty

I stride through life,

Planning great events,

Knowing, though denying,

Disaster and disease

Lie round the corner,

And death draws closer.

I can say with certainty,

I shall die, yet live as if,

I may outwit it.

Sickness will strike

Friend, lover, and acquaintance,

But never me.

That's just the way it is,

I gorge on pills,

That keep me ticking,

Had to step back,

setback, bad luck

Been slowing me down.

Take some time and I'm back,

On my way to a future

Of great events, but

Should I not now,

On the verge of sixty,

Pause.

Armchair

He sat in his favorite armchair near the window of the living room in the ranch house that he and his wife Louise had bought those many years ago. It was essentially the same as when they had bought it; they had changed nothing, just maintenance and repairs over the years.

This armchair afforded him a view up and down the street and he would sit there for hours each day, alternately looking and reading, digesting the scene outside when he tired of reading or when he wished to ponder over what he had just read.

He felt a little like a king, a monarch of all he surveyed as he watched the kids on their way to school, the housewives hurrying to the stores to purchase their groceries and provisions for the day and the cop striding purposefully down the block.

He was glad he had remained in the city. There was more action on the street, more to see, everything was more real as far as he was concerned, anyway. True, the neighborhood wasn't what it used to be. Who or what was, he thought wryly?

He missed those friends who had moved and when they visited occasionally - less and less as time passed - they waxed rhapsodical about where they now lived, the peace and quiet and security, casting inquiring glances his way and dropping obvious hints that it was long past time for him to move.

But this was a real neighborhood where people actually walked and talked; walked to the stores, to the bus, to church, to the bars and to the movie-house and talked to each other, interacted, greeted and communicated, like people should.

His son Michael's voice interrupted his train of thought. "Hi Pop, how are you feeling today?"

"Okay, I'm doing okay for an eighty-four-year-old who's falling apart."

"I just hope I'm in your shape when I hit eighty-four, if I ever make it. So, you got arthritis, who doesn't at your age. But that mind of yours, sharper than it was twenty years ago. You remember names, addresses, phone numbers from years back."

His son Michael had moved back in with him a year ago when his marriage had gone bust. He was struggling through a painful divorce and difficulties over visitation rights to his children, Jeffrey, eleven years old and Ellen, nine.

"Like I say, Mike, I'm doing fine. You seeing the children this weekend?"

"Yeah, that's the plan, right now, unless she throws a monkey wrench and messes it up." His face took on a pained expression. He was nuts about his kids and not being able to see them at will was driving him crazy.

"I can't understand why she's like this. We parted tearfully, both vowing to keep the kids out of it. She knows how I feel about my kids. Next I know she's got a lawyer; I'm an unfit parent and she wants to deny me visiting rights." His shoulders slumped. "I can't see any way out of this mess right now, Pop, I really can't."

"Don't get too down, son. You've always done right by your wife and kids, and the truth will eventually come out and be recognized. Keep your head up, hang in and things will turn around, you'll see." Michael looked up and his face brightened.

"Thanks Pop, you always make me feel better. I shouldn't be bringing my problems to you. I'm a big boy and I should be handling them myself."

"You should and you will, son. It's nice to have someone to talk things over with. I'm glad that you come to me, that you're able to discuss things with me and that it makes you feel better. You must work this out, you and Chris and I can't help you there, but when you need to talk don't ever hesitate. Since your mother died, what, seven years ago, I'm all alone and it's kind of nice to have you back here. Kate is busy with her life in California and three kids of her own. So, it was lonely here at times. But that's life as someone said, "you're ridin' high in April, shot down in May."

Mike laughed, "Sinatra knew what he was singing about. You never know what's around the corner. Okay, are we going to eat lunch or are we going to bullshit all day?"

"Can't we do both," his father replied, laughing.

Michael was a wonderful son and he loved him fiercely, but he knew he'd have to work this out himself. He remembered a saying his mother had, you make your bed, and you lie in it.

He himself had been lucky in his marriage; married for almost fifty years to a woman he loved more and more as the years went by. Even now, he slept on his side of the bed as if, still, she lay by his side and come morning, when he awoke, he was still on his side.

Sometimes he dreamed that she lay next to him again and their fingers would reach out and interlock as they had done so many, many times. Sorrow touched him for a fleeting second, but he just as quickly dismissed it. He remembered her words just days before she had died, and she knew she had little time left.

"We've been so lucky," she had said, her fingers reaching for his one more time, "to have loved each other so well, so long. Remember those times and be thankful and happy. Will you do this for me, love of my life?"

And he had. How he wished for Michael's marriage the love he had had in his. Michael would, he hoped fervently, work things out and in the end, be stronger and wiser because of it. And both of us will love his kids, he thought. He smiled, that's what Louise would have wanted.

May

He was nineteen years old, but a year living in the U.S and life was beginning to be very good. His first job in this new land was with Thomas Cook, Bankers and Travel Agents. Banking was always considered a prestigious occupation in Ireland, where he came from, and a bank clerk there was a much sought-after position, so much so that one needed some pull, a relative, uncle or father in the banking business who would vouch for and help one vault to the front of the applicant pool.

When he was walking out the door to America, his mother dipped her hand in the Holy Water Font and making the sign of the Cross on his forehead, said, "Get into something with a future, a collar and tie job and go to school. Your father worked hard to give you an education. He didn't want you to have to work like he did all his life, for the bosses he worked for, and your father ten times the man they could ever be. So, get into something with a future. You have the brains, and you have the education. And don't forget to write."

When he secured the position with Thomas Cook, he was happy, a collar and tie job in the banking business. He could visualize his mother's face when she read the news - my son the banker!! Alas the reality was quite different. Though the bank was located on Fifth Ave in the fifties, a prestigious location, he and about thirty other clerks worked upstairs in a windowless room at old-fashioned desks, supervised by a stern and vengeful old Greek. He sat facing them in schoolmaster fashion at the head of the room, eyeing suspiciously the rows of desk-enclosed clerks arrayed before him.

At the desk, they sat transcribing travelers check numbers into huge binders from nine to five, five days a week. It was the most boring, mind-numbing work that one could imagine, and the best part of the day was when five o' clock came - it eventually did, though how long it took - and they could burst out onto Fifth Ave, loosen their ties and engage in some extremely rough play. They pushed, tripped, kicked, and chased each other down the avenue in an effort to dissipate the frustration and resentment that clogged our systems in that antiquated hellhole that passed for an office. Add to this the fact that they were poorly paid, and it had the makings of a situation that could not, would not be permanent. So, it came to pass that when, through a contact, he was offered an opportunity to work in a food warehouse, Gristede's, for nearly twice the money, he eagerly accepted, took off the collar and tie and neglected to tell his mother that he had changed jobs.

So it was, three months into his new job that finished at three thirty unless he worked overtime - for which they paid him time and one half - and loving his new and improved circumstances, he met May one carefree night in August. He was living then in a railroad flat on 89th St. - 325 E.89th with six other emigrants and really beginning to enjoy Manhattan. That area then was a major entertainment area with a definite German influence, had a movie-house that played

German only movies and was a magnet for tourist and New Yorker alike. On the night in question, he had attended a dance at the City Center ballroom on 58th Street, a cavernous room that attracted up to five hundred patrons each weekend night, and a mecca for the Irish emigrants that poured into New York in those years. After the dance he decided to go to a bar nearby, the Carnegie Bar and Grill, a last drink stopover for the dancehall crowd. He walked in and he saw her.

He had a theory about attraction between the sexes; he believed that deep in our subconscious, each one has a picture of their ideal partner. We may not be able, even, to describe this picture and we may spend a lifetime pursuing it and settling for less. But when we see this ideal partner in the flesh, the conscious and unconscious come together and there is instant attraction. He believed this happened when he first set eyes on May. She was attractive with auburn hair shading to red, good skin and an attractive athletic figure. He stared at her, she saw him stare and she smiled in his direction. In certain situations, he could be shy, sometimes embarrassingly so. But this night, this time he was relaxed, happy, at peace with the world. He approached May and introduced himself, keeping up a continuous conversation until they both could relax, and she would, he hoped, make an initial determination of interest. Then they could begin the complicated rituals of courtship with at least one woefully inadequate in that department. They got on well and she gave him her phone number before leaving.

She lived in Brooklyn, which seemed to him a long way from

Manhattan and though he knew nothing about that borough then, he was determined to pursue her up to and including Brooklyn. He waited impatiently for Wednesday night to come.

Buddy, his best friend said, "Don't call before Wednesday night. It's too soon, makes you seem too anxious. Thursday night is too late if you want to do something for Friday. If they get the idea that you're stalling them, they get pissed off and turn you down when you call even if they want to go out with you. It's tricky. Sometimes they don't know what they want until they get on the phone. That's women." Buddy was two years older and had experience, so he deferred to him in these matters. Wednesday night came. He consulted with his friend again on the best time to call.

"Eight-thirty," he informed him. "Give them a chance to get home, take a hot bath and relax. After that they're ready. But don't leave it too late or their roommate may begin to kid them about it, say he's not going to call, he's going to stand you up etc. Like I said, women are funny. There's always a little jealousy, a little competition there. You call late, and she's upset you didn't call earlier, she may take it out on you just to prove something to her roommate, even though what she wants most in the world is to go out with you. I'm telling you; women are funny."

He didn't follow Buddy's logic but deferred to his experience and called promptly at eight-thirty. She answered on the second ring and seemed happy he had called. Everything seemed to be on track. They made a date for the Friday night. He had decided he would ride out to Brooklyn and pick her up as evidence of his commitment and obtained all relevant information. They went to the City Center ballroom and had a good time. She was easy to get on with, was a good listener and wasn't a big talker. They were beginning to feel very comfortable together and on the slow dances, as the night progressed, they began to get real close.

He remembered that ride out to Brooklyn as if it were yesterday. They had to take three trains and the last train very old with rattan seats. It groaned, rattled, and screeched its way to Flatbush as if in protest that it had not been retired by now and was sick, sick, sick of riding those rails day and night. He sympathized but had other things on his mind. It was crowded and when a seat became available, May sat down while he stood over her, hanging on to the strap as it bumped its way deep into the borough. He looked down at her, admiring her nice breasts, how she sat, and breathing in that mixture of woman and perfume that emanated from her and felt an overwhelming urge to take her in his arms and hold her tight. There was sexual tension between them, and she kept on giving him smiles and touching his leg, body, or arm. He cautioned himself not to be aggressive, to let things happen naturally.

Bobby's words came to him, "Relax, let them set the pace. They'll let you know when they want to do something. When they want to, they won't take no for an answer, believe you me."

They got to her apartment. She told him her roommate was away for the weekend. Then it happened like it was the most natural thing in the world, like it had happened a hundred times before. She took his hand and they walked into her bedroom, took off their clothes, jumped into bed and were in each other's arms. It was one of the most incredible nights, the prayers-come-true of a horny neophyte. He was overwhelmed by feelings of lust, desire and sexuality and engaged in an erotic marathon with a more than willing partner. He learned that night that women can be as sexually driven as men and that his preoccupation with sex was the normal biological urges of a nineteen-year-old. Halfway through, May got up and made them both sandwiches. They ate the sandwiches and chugged beer, sitting up naked in bed and talking casually, contentedly back and forth. Then they resumed their lovemaking.

It seemed to go on all night, though it lasted, probably, not more than four hours, for it had been three A.M. by the time they reached the apartment. They had finally fallen asleep, exhausted as dawn broke over Brooklyn. Later that morning they got up and ate breakfast at an old diner nearby, enveloped in an intimacy that only lovers can know. They returned to her apartment and made love again, this time less frenzied, more relaxed but just as satisfying.

He rode the trains back to Manhattan that evening a satisfied, fulfilled man. He was a man. In one night, he was transformed from an unsure, inexperienced nineteen-year-old to an accomplished lover. Hardly, but he was a different person. He had a girlfriend and an uninhibited partner in sex. When he got back to his apartment, Buddy looked at him, murmured 'U-huh,' and went back to watching T.V.

They were inseparable each weekend after, and he usually stayed over on Friday and Saturday nights. Her roommate had no objection to this arrangement. They had separate bedrooms and they respected each other's privacy. He played hurling in Gaelic Park on Sundays and, on those days, left early in the morning. Other times they spent the day walking in the park, sunbathing and eating out but sex was a constant.

Quentin Crisp wrote: The continued propinquity of another human being cramps your style after a time unless that person is somebody you think you love. Then the burden becomes intolerable at once.

Outside the bedroom, May was quiet and serious and as time went on, the lack of conversation between them began to irritate him. He would initiate a conversation or discussion only to see it sputter and die. That was her personality, was part of her, and if the relationship was to continue, he had to accept it. But it got so that he would breathe a sigh of relief when he boarded the train for Manhattan. By midweek, with his body screaming for sexual relief, he was on the phone to Brooklyn. Soon he was meeting her in the bar next to her apartment house and after a drink or two, they would retire to her bedroom.

He was always in a fever of desire when arriving there, but with his desires satisfied, was beginning to resent having to spend the rest of the weekend there. They continued the relationship for six months, but May was starting to drop hints about making the relationship more permanent and even mentioned the dreaded M word.

On the phone one night, she mentioned it again and he indignantly replied that he had no intention of getting married for a long time. She slammed down the phone and refused to take his calls for two weeks. By then, of course, he was willing to promise everything but marriage. They resumed their relationship, as neither one was willing to sever it then, but they both knew that it had changed. May was even quieter than before and one night she accused him of using her. He replied that she had gotten at least as much as he had out of the relationship. It was over and they both knew it.

It was his first steady girlfriend/sexual relationship, and he would always be grateful that it was overall a positive experience and grateful to the woman that shared it. It was a huge growing-up period for him and a good beginning in the complicated relationship between man and woman. Sexual relationships play such a large part in our lives, and it can be such a positive force - or not. Years later he would dwell on the good things in that relationship, the closeness they achieved for a while, the physical attraction, and the sexual experimentation they freely indulged in. At one stage, May shaved her genital area and he found this a big turn-on.

The first crush that one has for a member of the opposite sex is usually a very memorable experience. So, also, is our first serious sexual involvement. It sometimes sets the tone for other relationships that come after. The same could be said for same sex encounters, I imagine.

His first serious sexual involvement was with May, and it was a positive one of exploring, tasting and experimenting. He learned much about his own sexuality, with a woman who wasn't afraid to be open and inhibited. They both gave and received pleasure and both, he believed, matured sexually. But in the end, it was one-dimensional, based mainly on sexual attraction and sexual compatibility. A man and a woman need more than just good sex, more than just love. One has to like, admire, and respect another also.

Walter Lippmann wrote: Lovers who have nothing to do but love each other are not really to be envied; love and nothing else very soon is nothing else.

He wondered sometimes, where was she now, what was she doing and how her life had turned out. He thought how nice it could be, to meet now, years later, sit down, share a cup of coffee, and reminisce about their relationship; reminisce about life, sexuality and that amorphous entity called love. On more than one occasion, he sent a silent prayer to Heaven; May, wherever you are, you will always be a part of me. May the God of Good Fortune smile on you and yours forever.

Winter's End

At times in Spring, I sense a quietness,

- exhaustion even.

The struggle has been great – again.

Wind, snow and lashing seas have bent and bowed,

And lost – again.

It will never win.

Nor understand it never will.

Slink, crawl back to where you lie.

Lick wounds, mutter dire predictions

Wait, wait till next year.

Quarrels

His parents would quarrel constantly. For a while, he convinced himself that it was their way of loving, that it didn't mean much. Later when he saw them hug or kiss tenderly, he'd say to himself, see, I told you, you idiot, they really do love each other and you, big worry head, going around stooped over, as if carrying a huge weight on your shoulders, and you all of ten years old.

That was sixteen years ago. Images of that time enveloped him and soon he was back there, an angry and frustrated kid, listening to his parents argue. He's sitting in his room and the words punch through from below.

Pop: "I asked you not to use the checkbook until I had deposited my check."

Mom: "Why do you have to deposit your check? I can deposit it for you. Why do I have to wait around for days until you decide to cash it and deposit?"

Pop: "Because I work overtime, I can't always get to the bank right away."

Mom: "But you're never short of money, are you? I can deposit the check and hold out money for you."

Pop: "I have a right to cash my own check, don't I?"

Mom: "This is about power, isn't it, about you the wage earner keeping me dependent on you for money?"

Pop: "I like to cash my own check. You have a big problem with that, don't you? Get a job and then you get to cash your own check, okay."

It went on and on. It could be any subject. It might begin with the most innocuous remark. His mom went to school part-time, had been going for quite a while. His dad felt she should get a job and contribute to the family's finances, thereby easing the burden on him. The more he objected, the more determined she became, and she was no shrinking violet. The battle was joined and my mom was a formidable foe.

As time progressed, there was more conflict, more strident now with an edge to it. Hugs and kisses and tender moments became rarer. Conflict has a way of perpetuating itself, a vicious circle that feeds on itself, the onus on one to up the ante on the other.

Parents, do they have any idea how kids feel when they argue? He felt like a tennis ball between two ferocious racquets, being batted one way and then the other, or a shuttlecock in a fiercely contested game of badminton. Like the tennis ball or the shuttlecock, he was powerless, a victim of circumstances. He wanted to scream and curse, make them acknowledge his presence but even then, it would be momentary before they returned to their game. It was a game to them, and the name of the game was 'Piss me off and I'll piss you off more.'

He thought, do they know what this stupid game was doing to him? Do they know he would run to his room and pound his pillow in rage and frustration, while tears streamed down his cheeks? Do they know he would entertain wild schemes to burn down the house or cut himself with a razor; that surely would draw their attention, or would it?

What made it worse was that they had some good times together. For a while, they vacationed in Cape Cod. His dad and he would walk the dunes, attempting to push each other over the edge and he'd always let him win. When they went to the movies and he sat between them, he felt so secure. He would look up at his mom on one side and his dad on the other. His mom would squeeze his hand and his dad would wink.

He felt so secure, so loved. He wouldn't have traded that spot to be president. Through the turmoil that engulfed his family, he held on to this memory. It was like a rock that you cling to, in the middle of a raging river as the wind rips and buffets in its effort to hurl you into oblivion.

He thought, so what do I do? How can I get through to them that they have to stop? Some days were better than others. Some days he felt like an old bone that's been sucked on for ages, dried up and useless. He talked to his best pal Joey. Joey knew Billy was hurting', though he hadn't told him much. He felt ashamed to tell others, but he knew Joey knew cos he'd seen and heard them too. 'Like two dogs fighting over a bone' is how he described it and his parents used to be like that, too, but cooled down eventually.

Joey: "Billy, listen to me. I know you're hurtin'. They're your parents, for God sakes and you hate to see them fighting and arguing constantly. Why do they have kids if they want to act like that? Y'know what pisses me off? When they talk about their parents and tell us how wonderful they were, how this and how that. I feel like sayin', so what happened to you, what went wrong? Guess what, if I said that to them, they'd look at me like I had two heads. They can't make the connection."

Bill: "They don't deserve to be parents."

Joey: "Yeah, if I were in charge, I'd tell them if I see you fighting again, you don't leave the house for a week. That'd stop them real fast."

He said I should write a letter to them and tell them how I feel.

Joey: "Look, I been reading about this stuff. They call it 'conflict resolution.' They say you can't take sides, no matter how much they want you to. But you should write a letter addressed to both of them and tell them everything, how it's tearing your guts up to listen to them arguing."

Billy: "That's stupid."

Joey: "It sounds stupid, but it works."

But Joey was pretty sharp, so he figured maybe it was worth a shot. So, he wrote the letter.

He remembered the time and concentration he put into that letter. It was a short letter, not begging or pleading, but just telling them how frustrated and angry it made him to listen to their constant arguments. And they did stop. Things returned to normal, somewhat, for a couple of years. They were polite to each other, and he never heard them argue again like they used to. Once in a while a slammed door, but that was it. He thought something was lost, though, in that time of turmoil, that they could never recover, and they divorced seven years later. His dad remarried but his mom never did. Now he had a child of his own, a boy, and he would never witness parental confrontation; he and his wife had pledged to that. No child should have to experience it. When he saw parents argue in public and study their children, he could see in the face of the child all the frustration and anger he felt so many years ago.

Last Days

He lay on the bed and knew that he had just a little time left on this earth. He wondered, idly, what his next existence, if any, might be? But he believed in the indestructibility of the soul, that the soul was immortal, was tied inextricably to the Divine and that his soul would have an existence after this life. He wasn't fearful or uneasy about the journey ahead, he decided. He had done the best he could in the time allotted to him and he was ready to go on.

His body was old and worn out and he was unable to do the things that had brought him pleasure for many years. He walked painfully, for arthritis had ravaged his joints. He had trouble with his eyes; he had loved so much to read and had read all his life. That pleasure was now restricted, and he missed it. He occasionally bought audio books and while enjoying them, did not derive the same pleasure as the actual process of reading. He had enjoyed everything about reading; turning the pages, pausing, and thinking about what he had just read, rereading a page or two to clarify its meaning or its significance to the story, marking the page and abandoning the book until the time was right to pick it up and continue.

His children were successful and forging ahead with their own careers, with less and less time to spend with him. He understood this, would not have it any other way. He felt strongly that was the way it should be - that after graduating from college they should have the freedom to choose their own life paths. He was always available for advice or counsel, if asked, but they had to make their own decisions, own mistakes, for that was part of the process, too. His advice to them as they left for school was always the same:

"You must rely on your own judgement, your own set of values, your own strength of character. Whom you associate with, how late you stay out, how much studying you do is entirely up to you. Mom or I won't be there to guide you and your actions -good or bad, will always have consequences. College should not be all study. It's an exciting time in your life; first time away from home, making new friends, having new experiences but it should not be all partying either. You will begin to figure out what you want to do for the rest of your life. No matter what happens, we're here for you and love you."

They had all done well, though he had seen them off to college with apprehension grabbing his insides. They were only eighteen, with so much to learn and so many dangers and pitfalls out there. But they had the optimism of youth, the strength and vitality that he once had but not anymore. He and his wife had done a pretty good job of raising those kids, he thought, and his beautiful wife Jane, was with him all the way. He was sometimes surprised, as he studied the children, at their confidence and poise and overall niceness. No drugs and no pregnancies either, often problems in this day and age. Yes, he had a lot to be thankful for.

He had been so out of control at one stage of his life, drinking and staying out late and causing his wife untold misery. He had justified everything by believing that he earned good money and always provided for his family. He had finally come to his senses, and his wife seeing something redeemable in him, had forgiven him. After that he had settled down to being a good father and husband. He sometimes thought that someone was watching over him; that some Divine presence was keeping him out of harm's way; that someone was besieging heaven with their prayers on his behalf. He thought it must be his mother. In her spare moments, which were few and far between, he would often find her with the rosary beads in her hands, working the beads and mouthing the words silently. He was convinced that it was her prayers that had guided his life.

Prayers on someone else's behalf must be very powerful, he mused, though prayers seemed less and less an option in today's world. Chanting seemed more popular and that was alright, too, as he believed it to be a form of prayer. He felt very tired tonight, but calm and at peace. He awoke briefly and found his children around his bed. Why have they come, he wondered? It must be someone's birthday. They always tried to get together for a celebration. He could never understand why they celebrated them. He never remembered them and was always being prepped by his wife on upcoming birthdays. He wondered whose turn it was.

He tried to raise up and speak but it was such an effort. He smiled weakly and lay back. The bed was so comfortable. He would sleep for a while. The background noise subsided and everywhere was peace and calm. He was floating in a sea of tranquility. Worry, stress, old age, illness slipped away from him. He felt whole again. He found himself praying, "Our Father, who art in heaven, hallowed be thy name, thy kingdom come, thy will be done on earth as it is in heaven...."

Ping

He sat in his cottage, halfway up the mountain, self-sufficient as all hell. He lacked for nothing, it seemed. He grew his own vegetables, kept a few chickens, and milked a cow. Though the town was no more than three miles away down, he was rarely seen there.

He seemed to need no company. Distant, they described him, a loner. He had left from that same cottage as a young boy and gone away. After his parents died the cottage sat empty for a few years. One day the chimney was smoking, and he was back living there. Those who knew him as a boy – there were few left – came around and they chatted. He had been at sea; he told them and had lived in different places. He seemed unable or unwilling to reconnect with his childhood. He had changed and they couldn't put a finger on it. So, they left him alone and it seemed that was what he wanted. He didn't say what they wanted to hear, that he was glad to be back or there's no place like home. They wanted to hear that, those who had never left and then they'd say "Ha ha, ye all come back. Sure, there's no place like it."

I was walking up that way one day in the early afternoon when I passed his cabin. I hadn't walked that way since I was a small boy and though I knew of him, I had never met him. He was sitting on a small stool by the door.

"Nice day," he said to me and encouraged by this friendly comment, I replied

"That it is, that it is," and then "And how are things with you?"

"Divil a care," he replied, "why would I be complaining? Haven't I all I want here?"

"You have, boy, you surely have," I said, looking around and down towards the town and the bay stretched beyond it. "You surely have."

There was a pause and then he said, "Would you like a cup of tea?" and I replied right away, "I'm always on for a cup of tea."

"Good man you are," he said and gesturing towards the cottage, "come in, come in."

I entered, my eyes adjusting to the darker interior and trying to restrain my curiosity. The cottage was as neat as a woman would have it, cups neatly stacked and a nice fire burning. He busied himself by the fire and in a few minutes the tea was up with a plate of scones.

"Help yourself," he said, "don't be shy."

I laughed, "They can accuse me of a lot of things but never that." We ate in companionable silence, the only sounds the slurping of tea and the munching on the scones.

They think I'm a bit strange down there or unfriendly, I'd say, do they?" he asked, and I replied,

"Well, they do wonder, sometimes, if it's good to be alone, as much as you are."

"I like a good discussion as much as the next man. I have no time for gossip or conjecture and maybe little patience with it anymore. I'm content to be alone, and that surprises me. I always wanted company when I was younger" He gestured towards his books, "now I read and every book I read gives me stuff to think about, food for thought as they say. Because I have nowhere to go, and no desire to go anywhere - I've been everywhere - I have time to think about what I've read. Knowledge is a strange and fascinating mistress. The more I acquire, the more I want and so on. I have a curiosity about everything, when we rode the first horse, the pull of the moon and tides."

"You're mentioning some very serious subjects now," I said.

Abruptly he said, "Were you ever in love?

"Well, I'm married going on thirty-seven years..."

"But were you ever in love?" he insisted.

"I think so. We were mad to be married, I know that, Peg and I, she barely twenty and I a year older..."

"Well, I know I was in love," he said, an intensity creeping into his voice. "Most people never know real love. They throw around 'I love you,' and 'he loves me' with not a notion in their head of what it is." He was silent for a bit. "I was like that, too. Then I met Ping. Yeah, that's what I always and ever called her, my Ping. I met her in Hong Kong in 1953, in the library of all places. I don't know what drew me in there. I was reading little then. She was a waitress in a small restaurant near the docks. I was coming through Hong Kong a lot, then, mostly on oil tankers. I met Ping and on our second date, we were body and soul in love."

He sighed and stared out the window. "I signed off the ship and we moved in together. I was the happiest man alive. We never quarreled. How could I say or do anything that would make her sad? My soul was filled with her goodness and love. I'd look at her as she moved, ate, laughed, or cried and couldn't envision loving anybody like I loved her. Yes, she cried sometimes. Her family was in China and going through hard times. She was desperate to help but there was no way. Aside from that we had no worries. Then she got word that her mother was sick and soon after, that she was dying. She said she had to go to be with her mother. She crossed into China on September 7, 1955. I never saw her again. I searched for four years for any scrap of news of her whereabouts. Finally, I got good information that there had been an accident or ambush going in and she had died, forty years ago today." He paused again.

"It's a sad story you're telling me," I said.

"I suppose it is, but as the years pass, I realize how lucky I was. I had two long years with the one woman I could love unconditionally, the one woman in all the world that fulfilled me in every way."

"Are you saying there's only one woman we can be happy with?" I said.

He smiled, "Aw sure, there's a million of them that you'll be happy enough with. But there's only a few that will bring you real love and I think only one, total love. I found mine."

"Did you never think of marrying again, I inquired?

"Never," he said. "I had the best, and we'll be together soon again." I turned and looked at him and he returned my stare. "It won't be long now, she said."

He stopped talking, his body tensed, and his eyes locked to the window. A wind came up, sudden and sharp, unusual on this mild September day and the moaning had a human quality. I felt the atmosphere change and I held my breath for fear of disturbing or distracting. Long minutes passed and then, just as suddenly, the wind died.

"That's as good a cup of tea as I've ever had," I said as I left myself out, but he didn't answer.

Wet Season in Costa Rica

Rain inexhaustible falls.

Mist clings and penetrates

The drenched, green hills.

It is wet season in Costa Rica.

And I all alone, sit in a room

In an artist's colony.

And gaze at the fog-draped hills

I wait to be inspired.

Wracking my brain, willing the words

But they refuse, they will not come.

Dig ditches, build roads,

You are not a writer.

I see a bird, black, foot long

Perched on a branch.

Motionless, serene, a blank scape.

Where will he spend the night or meet another.

Where has he come from, going,

How was his day?

How can he balance with such perfection?

On such a slender branch.

Is he remembering, planning?

As dusk settles over the wet hill

And torrential rain eases

How to maintain such stillness, a sleep state,

As dusk turns to dark,

He fades from view.

As one with the browns and blacks

In this timeless scene.

Commitment

"If we get married..."

"You mean when we get married."

"I mean if..."

"But you've already agreed to marry me."

"I've agreed to marry you in six months."

"So."

"So, a lot of things may happen in six months."

"Like what?"

"Like what if one or the other contracts a life threatening or life ending disease. Is it fair to ask the other to honor a marriage commitment?"

"Well, in a situation such as you've described, both would have to be in total - and I mean total - agreement to marry.

"Okay, that sounds good."

"Is that it?"

"No."

"No?"

"There are other reasons, hundreds probably. If you or I fool around with someone else while engaged, that would be reason enough to break the engagement."

"Well, I have no intention whatsoever of fooling around. Do you?"

"No, but never say never."

"What's that supposed to mean?"

"I'm just saying that we don't always do what we intend to do, even with the best of intentions."

"Yes, but we have to make the commitment, don't we? We can't say I love you and won't fool around but be aware that I'm human and I might succumb to temptation. Is that what you want me to say?"

"No, of course not. It's right and proper to be enthusiastic and optimistic and committed to the relationship. That's how it should be."

"But?"

"But life has a way of deflating and disappointing us. I don't want to be disappointed again. I was so blind once."

"You happened to fall in love with or be attracted to a very mixed-up guy, someone who was not able to be honest with you for whatever reason. His mother abandoned him when he was very young. Isn't that what you told me? He possibly had some major problems to work through before committing to a relationship and he never did. His life may be a succession of failed relationships and it may have a lot to do with his mother abandoning him."

"I know. He was such a nice guy in many ways. I was not in love with him, though it could very well have happened if we had stayed together. But when he left without explanation, giving me no reason, I was angry and hurt."

"Of course, you were. Who wouldn't have been?"

"So, we take it a day at a time."

"Are you getting cold feet? Are you having second thoughts? Is that what this is all about?"

"No."

"But?"

"I'm as much if not more committed than I was when we first became engaged but..."

"There you go again with the 'buts'."

"But I want us to be completely honest with each other in this relationship. If I for some reason feel that the relationship is not right or meet someone that I feel very attracted to, and want to pursue it, I will tell you, must tell you and you must understand and accept. If on the other hand, you feel at any time, for whatever reason that you do not wish to make the commitment, I will expect the same from you."

"Of course, we have to trust each other. There is no real relationship without trust, except maybe a purely sexual one. Would you be interested in a purely sexual relationship?"

"Mmm, let me think about that."

"Why so serious tonight? Where's the fun-loving beauty I've come to know and love?"

"That's exactly what I'm talking about. I'm not always in a good mood and I may not always look my best and that's the commitment we're making, in good times and bad."

"Don't you think I know this? Do you think that I'm always confident and optimistic? Don't you think I have times when I feel insecure and need reassurance; when I lie awake at night, unable to sleep, curled up in a fetal position, sucking my thumb."

"The engagement is off, darling."

"Only kidding, only kidding."

"Goodnight. Love ya."

"Love ya."

Dream Journey

His mind returned to that night again. He was twelve years old, a restless, questing kid. It was the middle of July, and New York was experiencing one of those godawful heatwaves that descended on the city, without fail, each summer. It was a hot, muggy night - hazy, hot, and humid, the three h's as the weathermen described it - and he lay in his narrow, single bed tossing and turning, hoping the night would proceed quickly and maybe, just maybe, dawn would bring some relief. But there was no relief, this night in this hot, sweltering apartment. The window was open, but it meant nothing, as nothing stirred outside.

They lived on the fifth floor of a fifth-floor walkup, the sun pounded on the roof all day and, all night, the roof released its heat to the apartment. Why couldn't they move to the suburbs, like some of his friends had done, or rented in an elevator building, or even rented on a different floor, any floor but the fifth.

Bathed in sweat, he gazed out the window and watched idly as a string of lights gently floated in the window. Wow, pretty, he thought. They seemed of the purest light, but easy to look at. He studied them intently, admiring their fluid movement. Suddenly, his body chilled. Holy shit, what the hell were they? He thought, I'm not dreaming, am I? He blinked and shook his head, but they remained there, and he felt the first small beginnings of fear through his body.

The lights kept coming until there were about twelve in all, and now they began to line up around his bed in some sort of precise and intricate order, that they, only, seemed to know. A trickle of sweat slowly descended between his shoulder blades and suddenly, everything was deathly quiet. All the street noises that had permeated the night, minutes before, ceased. He was afraid to move, breathe even. He felt that he was in some kind of suspended animation and that the next few minutes would impact on his life forever.

He studied the lights intently, but now, suddenly, he wasn't afraid anymore. In seconds, something had changed in the room. Nothing physical, for the room remained the same. His bed, the scarred desk and chair that creaked every time he moved on it, were there, the wardrobe in its usual place, opposite his bed, cheap and looking it. His father had moved it into his room when they got a new one for their room -- a new one, but just as cheap. But there was a definite change in atmosphere. Everything had slowed down and was quiet, as if a warm blanket had enveloped the room. A faint, almost non-existent, droning noise was filling his mind with delicious sensations of feel-goodness. He was suffused with an unbelievable feeling of peace and tranquility. It was like he was lying on a bed of the softest material imaginable.

His mind was empty of all discord, his senses were alive, and he lay there, unafraid. Something gently touched his eyelids and closed his eyes. He felt himself beginning to lift off the bed and float in midair. He did not try to open his eyes or resist. He began to accelerate and felt himself travelling at tremendous speed.

Finally, after an indefinable time, he began to slow down. He opened his eyes and looked around. In the distant, he could see a group of people, conversing and moving about, all dressed in long white robes. They turned, as he approached, and he recognized his father and mother and, oh my God, there was his grandpa, whom he had loved so much. They came towards him, and his grandpa threw his arms around him and lifted him up in the air, all the time communicating to him how happy he was to see him, how tall he had gotten and how handsome he looked. He noticed his father held his mother lovingly, his arm around his waist. He had not seen this in a very long time.

They communicated together for what seemed a long time, though nobody spoke. Nobody spoke but all understood. His father expressed regret for his past actions and showed him where he had succumbed to despair. He gently admonished him never to despair.

They all communicated to him how much they loved him and that they would always be near him, watching and protecting, throughout his life. He had never known such a feeling of love, of giving and receiving, and he wanted to stay in this place forever. But he knew, it was not his time.

Later, they gently disengaged, and he again felt himself floating in mid-air, before beginning to accelerate, this time in the opposite direction. He watched the waving figures of his mother and father and beloved grandpa recede in the distance but felt no sadness. Hours later, he woke up, his mother gently shaking him. He surprised her when he threw his arms around her neck and hugged her. He was not usually that demonstrative. The heatwave had broken, and a cooling breeze poured through the open window. Though his father was at that time drinking heavily, Billy tried very hard to be solicitous of his father, and his father, sensing this, reached out more to his son. His father died the next year. Billy never told anyone of his journey.

He got up from the chair and called out to his son, "Billy, how about a little baseball, me and you?" He heard his son call, "I'm coming, Dad." His son was eleven years old and loved baseball. He walked out onto the back lawn, his son racing ahead. He stopped for a minute and gazed up into the sky. He sent a prayer skywards before his son's impatient voice intruded on his thoughts, "Let's go, Dad, I'm waitin'."

Cabin in the Woods

When I was younger, I had this dream – of a house I would like to, someday, own. Of course, there are no kids, no wife, no job I have to have – I am financially secure. I can go where I want to go, put down roots when I find the ideal location, ideal climate, environment. This is what I dreamed.

The house would be a log cabin, essentially one large living room with high ceiling, lots of wood and glass with a large fireplace. The living room is the center piece of the cabin. The bathroom would be separate and spacious, large shower, no bath. My bed would be a fold down bed, that when not in use, would fold into the wall. There would be a very large couch in front of the fireplace, also adaptable as a bed. The kitchen area would be in one corner of the room with a countertop, seating, and all appliances necessary. The cabin is sturdily built. It is raised six feet above ground. There is a small deck attached to the back. It is surrounded by trees, but for the front, which allows for an unobstructed view of the lake.

There is a radio but no TV. There are lots of books. Here in this tranquil place, I do some of my most productive writing. I write every day, long days, no TV, no radio, only the sound of silence. My writing becomes better and better, richer in every way. Whether I am published, or not, is of no consequence. I am doing what I want, what

I am meant to do, and, some day, my words will, hopefully, inspire and give hope to others.

The pretty little lake is about one hundred yards away, and I have a beautiful view of it from the cabin. The cabin is one of many dotted about the lakeside, but on account of the abundance of evergreens, are not easily seen, one from the other. Yet none are so isolated that they can't be reached in a few minutes. My cabin is practically maintenance free; the ground outside is mostly a carpet of pine needles, and no fence or railing surrounds the property.

I visualize waking up early in the morning and taking a long walk in the woods. I return to the cabin and make breakfast. I take breakfast out on the deck or by the large picture window looking out on the lake. Times, I listen to the morning news and contemplate the scene.

The sun is beginning to rise in the sky. It's going to be a hot one. The sky is blue, fluffy white clouds drifting slowly by. A hawk circles in the sky. There is a flash of brown in the undergrowth at the edge of the forest. A fox, maybe? The wind ripples the surface of the lake. Where the trees grow close to the edge, the scene is reflected in the water. Something breaks the surface -- maybe some trout, though they usually clear the surface, or maybe an otter. There is a host of other possibilities. It is another perfect day.

What are my plans for the day? None really. I have no plans. I have no commitments, no deadlines. I will read and later stroll by the lake. I may stop and study some natural phenomenon, some unique work of nature that grabs my attention for the moment. There is always something interesting. I may study it for an hour or even a day. I'm working on increasing my powers of concentration and - time I have plenty of. Later I'll take a leisurely swim in the lake. I'll read some more.

In the afternoon, I'll requisition my bike and cycle into town, two miles away. It's not really a town, just a collection of shops: diner, grocery store, post office, hardware, library, gas station and Chinese take-out. I'll chat with the grocer who is a friend of mine, and who always has time to chat. Interesting, too. I'll take my groceries and peddle back slowly, the wind in my face and the sun on my back. Life is good.

I'm reading the one hundred best books ever written and am about halfway through the list. Then I have poetry books to read, historical novels, autobiographies, various diaries. The list goes on and on, enough to last a lifetime. I continue with my writing. I write religiously every day but not at the same time. Sometime during the day, I will feel the urge to write, without fail.

In the evening, if it turns cold, I'll light the fire. I may invite some friends over. Or if I prefer some solitude, I'll spend the evening alone. The community is made up of writers and artists. We come together periodically, to discuss our work and how it is progressing. But privacy is valued, so no dropping in unannounced. It is the perfect place to write, to paint, to pursue artistic endeavors. Most residents are intelligent and educated. Most residents have come to this beautiful place to fulfill long-held aspirations in the various arts. Most residents, including me, live long and happy lives.

I like to travel, too. I leave my cabin about three or four times each year and visit interesting and unique places all over the world. I'm always excited as I leave for a new travel adventure, but always I enjoy returning to my cabin. I think of it as home. When I visualize it, sitting in the midst of the evergreens, near the sparkling lake, snug and warm in the winter, cool and airy in the summer months, why, I just get the warmest feeling inside me. I must be the luckiest person on the face of the earth.

Cause: Effect

I arrived in the U.S. as an emigrant from Ireland, in November 1960. I felt at home here from the beginning and thought I might like to spend the rest of my life here. I'm still here some sixty years later. Why did I come to the United States? Because I expressed a desire to do so, but even more important, because my aunt was willing to sponsor me. That was the catalyst.

My wanting to come would have come to naught if my aunt had not agreed to sponsor me. Just that act set me on a radically different life path than I would have had, had I stayed in London where I was then employed, or in Ireland if I had decided to return there.

I think our lives are made up of a series of what I would call 'random decisions,' most of which are usually out of our control. They point us in very different directions, sometimes, from what we envisage.

I remember when I was in Secondary School in Ireland, my father approached me about working in the local creamery, where he was employed. There was an opening as an Apprentice Fitter and he had already spoken to the manager, Mr. Foley. The job was mine if I wanted it. This was a highly desirable position in my town where jobs were scarce, for not alone would I have a job, probably for life, but I was also learning a trade.

The creamery, even then, was expanding into cheese-making,

milk powder, chocolate crumb and yogurt production. I turned it down because I did not want to leave school. I had dreams of travelling and though I was not sure what I wanted to do then, I knew that I did not want to spend the rest of my life in the town where I grew up.

When I did finish Secondary School, my mother sat me down, one day, and asked me what I wanted to do or where I wanted to go. I mumbled something about not being sure. She told me that there was a family friend living and working in Rhodesia, now Zimbabwe, and she would write to him and inquire whether he would consider claiming me out there.

I thought this was a great idea and I was immediately excited at the prospect of emigrating to this strange hot country in Africa and possibly spending the rest of my life there. I lived in hope for a few weeks until our friend replied that he would be unable to claim me. I was disappointed as the idea of going out there had really grabbed my imagination.

I sometimes wonder what my life would have been like if I had emigrated there. I imagine it would have been radically different. The act of declining to claim me out to Rhodesia sent my life in another direction.

After graduating Secondary School, I went to London and got a job as a bus conductor. I took some tests there, also, and was offered an entry level position in the British Civil Service. I decided against taking it as it meant making a commitment to live in London, and I wasn't happy living there. I longed for something else, and I was not sure what.

My mother was disappointed, I think she liked the idea of having one of her children working for the British Civil Service, and she believed, rightly, that it could be a job for life. And I wonder, again, what my life would have been like had I committed to that position.

I came to the United States and eventually got a job with the Transit Authority of New York City. But I was still dissatisfied and dreamed of something more exciting. I took the N.Y.C. Police Officer and Fireman tests and passed both with flying colors, but was rejected for medical reasons. I had had a bleeding ulcer. If I had been eligible for both, I would have chosen the police officer position, and I wonder how my life would have turned out. These occupations, because they are so much of a person's life and consume so much of a person's time, change our personalities in different ways, making us possibly cynical, arrogant, angry, cruel, uncaring; or loving, confident, happy and accepting. I wonder how being a police officer would have fashioned me?

Soon after taking the above tests, I took a test for Border Patrol Officer, passed the test but was rejected after the interview. This job would have entailed my moving either to the border areas of Canada or Mexico. I'm sure my life would have been so much different there.

If I had a magic wand, I would wave it and demand that I see an accelerated version of how my life would have been in all of these different situations. Of course, life is a series of random choices, either ours or someone else's. If we marry one and not another, our lives will be different. If we had taken a chance with that business opportunity that sounded so good, or married rich and not good looking, or rich and good looking. If we had been badly injured in that car accident from which we walked away, miraculously, unharmed.

But we cannot spend our lives wondering what if, or what might have been. We have to deal with the cards that have been handed to us. We have to do the best with what we've got and as a wise man once said: "Keep your nose clean and trust in the Almighty." But Rhodesia (Zimbabwe) still sounds intriguing!

Global Warming

Sick, stick-like figures glide through failing light

Shadow, substance, shape changing.

Fog licks and clings and the drip, drip

Of liquid, loud as drums, reverberates.

I sense impending doom, life-force diminished

A world with end, planet drained, toxic, spent

A last, great effort failed, the final, shuddering expiration at hand.

Homeless Person

When I first saw her, it was November in Manhattan. Winter was on its way, a cold wind sweeping through the canyons. She might have been a homeless person – or maybe not. She wore boots; not the in-fashion hikers many women prefer, but work boots, heavy and worn down at heel. Her dark brown woolen dress and black tweed overcoat reached down to her boots, giving an impression of being too big, that it had been given to her or bought cheap at a used clothes outlet. A black felt hat completed the outfit, tilted back carelessly, rakishly on auburn curls that danced and glinted in the sun. A pair of thick woolen socks were glimpsed occasionally over the tops of the boots as she strode along and she wore a long black scarf that matched the felt hat, wrapped round her neck, one end thrown over her left shoulder and the other trailing in front to her waist. On another occasion, she wore the exact same outfit, except the scarf was scarlet red and on still another day the scarf was a mixture of yellows and blacks.

Was this some kind of statement, the latest in avant-garde, elements of high fashion mixed with hand-me-down; or a woman who had seen better days. At times she would stop abruptly, but perfectly balanced so that people following close behind had trouble avoiding her, turn to the store window and check out her image, tilting her head in various poses, oblivious to all around her. Pulling back her overcoat she would twist and turn concentrating on the image reflected. Just as abruptly, she resumed her journey.

I followed her, one sunny morning in early Spring, warmer than usual, as she headed towards Central Park. She carried a large bag as usual. It seemed heavy as she switched it from hand to hand. She walked purposefully, posturally correct with long strides, not like a homeless person, shuffling, bent over. No, it was more like a busy-upscale-Manhattanite-on-her-way-to-a-facial stride, or to shop at one of the fashionable boutiques on Madison. She entered the Park and proceeded to a rock outcropping by the lake with that same sure step. I sat as close as possible without intruding. She placed her bag on the ground and removed her overcoat, revealing a powder-blue collarless sweater and carpenter style blue denim work pants replete with extra pockets. I could see her form and shape more clearly now, could see that she had a good figure and was much younger than I had thought. She was probably in her thirties.

She looked my way and for the first time I saw her face clearly. Her face was youthful and unlined, not the face of a homeless person. It was a face that had been cared for, had not suffered the rigors of New York winters outdoors. She proceeded to do some stretching exercises, took cream or lotion from her bag and applied it to her face. Next, she took a large towel, spread it out and lay down facing the sun. But she never removed the felt hat. I wrestled with this mystery; a socialite dressing down, a mentally challenged individual,

426

a nervous breakdown waiting to happen, a writer. I went on my way pondering the vagaries of human nature.

Huckleberry Finn

Ernest Hemingway wrote that "All modern American literature comes from one book by Mark Twain called *Huckleberry Finn*." I tend to agree with him. H.L. Mencken wrote that the discovery of *Huckleberry Finn* was "the most stupendous event of my whole life." By writing *Huckleberry Finn*, Mark Twain defined American literature, or at least what it would be from that time on. He cast off the European model and the English influence and struck out on a bold new path.

By writing it, he was also swimming in uncharted waters and had no idea how it might be received. Who would be interested in a story of uncivilized, poorly educated, backwoods people in one of the former colonies? But it was what he knew. He couldn't write of London or Paris or for that matter, New York, or San Francisco. He knew nothing of these places. He had to write of what he knew.

He wrote something so totally different and fresh that American literature would never be the same again and in doing so, he charted a new course for American writers. It was okay to write about this new country and this new country had a million stories. The country itself, was a story in the making - newly born and taking it's first, timid steps toward order and democracy. But no, not timid. America never did anything timidly. It was always full speed ahead and to heck with the begrudgers.

Exciting if traumatic events were taking place in America: the trek west, the Indian wars, the problem of slavery, homesteading, cattle drives and cowboys, oil strikes, the gold rush and infamous and famous outlaws and lawmen. These were all distinctly American happenings. America was the new frontier, and the Europeans were fascinated.

Their countries were settled, order had been established and their social order was rigid. It was difficult, if not impossible for the poorer masses to gain access to higher education. The few universities were for the rich and titled. The poor and uneducated stayed poor and uneducated. The stories from America were of cheap land, magnificent mountains, fertile valleys, broad rivers, endless forests.

In this novel, Mark Twain created a character, Huck, who could be both tough and tender, rarely lost his sense of humor and was the envy of every boy who had to wash unfailingly each morning and go to school unfailingly each day. he embodied that spirit of independence, the frontier spirit that was synonymous with America in those early years and is, still, to an extent today. Gosh darn it, he even smoked a pipe. Huck was, what we would call today, a free spirit and free spirits had a lot more space then than now.

Mark Twain, whose real name was Samuel Clemens, was for a time a steamboat pilot and grew up beside the Mississippi, in Hannibal, Missouri. He was familiar with the river and all the characters that lived and passed through there, the good, the bad and the ugly. He must have had a fascination with the various dialects of the area: the Mississippi negro, the backwoods Southwestern dialect and the 'Pike County' dialect. This dialect adds inestimably to the story.

Huckleberry Finn is such a uniquely American story, and it projects the sense of freedom, of opportunities and maybe of naivete of the country. Huck is a curious mix of innocence and shrewdness. He's resourceful, courageous, and kind. He has a strong sense of fair play, of what's right and what's wrong. Jim, the slave, who is helped by Huck to escape, is a kindred spirit in his basic goodness. Huck recognizes this in Jim, and they become firm friends. Nowhere in the story does Huck agonize over Jim's status as a slave. It is just a fact of life in this place at this time. Huck is not out to change the world, but neither will he accept injustice easily. He reacts to events on a basic, even primitive level. His pappy is beating him, so he resolves to escape. The idea of stealing or making a raft seems like a 'capital' idea so he resolves to do it. Neither does he agonize over having a father who beats the tar out of him for little or no reason. He does not worry about tomorrow or the day after or what happens when he gets to the river's end. He'll cross that bridge when he gets to it. It was this kind of spirit that the emigrants, the gold diggers, the homesteaders, and the cowboys had to have. Get by today and when tomorrow comes, get by tomorrow. Nobody knew what tomorrow would bring so why worry about tomorrow.

Huckleberry Finn is full of wonderful characters but again they are uniquely American characters: the Grangerford and Shepherdson clans feuding and killing each other and Colonel Grangerford's son Buck who befriended Huck and was killed by the Shepherdsons, the 'king' and the 'duke' - two of the most unforgettable characters that have ever appeared in literature, his friend Tom Sawyer, the Wilks family and of course, Jim the slave.

Mark Twain was a distinctive American voice writing on distinctive American subject matter. This culture though still in its infancy, had little to do with European culture for nowhere in Europe were conditions as they were in America at this time. America was a raw, evolving, lawless land in constant flux. Most of the population was to be found in the major cities and there were vast areas of the country barely populated but for the native Indians.

Communication systems were primitive. It took weeks for news to reach some areas. Cattle rustling and stagecoach robberies were common and hustlers and flim-flam men - like our acquaintances the duke and the king in this story - abounded. Mark Twain allows us to peek into this time and brings it to life with a great story and wonderful dialogue.

Listen to Twain's words: "I never felt easy till the raft was two miles below there and in the middle of the Mississippi. Then we hung up our signal lantern and judged that we was free and safe once more. I hadn't had a bite to eat since yesterday, so Jim he got out some corn dodgers and buttermilk, and whilst I ate my supper we talked and had a good time. I was powerful glad to get away from the feuds, and so was Jim to get away from the swamp. We said there warn't no home like a raft, after all. Other places do seem so cramped up and smothery, but a raft don't. You feel mighty free and easy and comfortable on a raft. Two or three days and nights went by; I reckon I might say they swum by, they slid along so quiet and smooth and lovely. It was a monstrous big river down there -- sometimes a mile and a half wide; we run nights and laid up and hid daytimes. Soon as night was most gone, we stopped navigating and tied up -- nearly always in the dead water under a towhead; and then cut young cottonwoods and hid the raft with them. Then we set out the lines. Next, we slid into the river and had a swim; then we set down where the water was about knee-deep, and watched the daylight come. The first thing to see, looking away over the water, was a kind of dull line -- that was the woods on t'other side; then a pale place in the sky; then more paleness spreading around; then the river softened up and warn't black anymore, but grey; and by and by the mist curls up off the water, and the east reddens up, and the river; then the nice breeze springs up, and comes fanning you, so cool and fresh and sweet to smell on account of the woods and the flowers; but sometimes not that way, because they've left dead fish laying around; and next you've got the full day, and everything smiling in the sun, and the songbirds just doing it!"

Later he writes "Sometimes we'd have that whole river all to ourselves for the longest time. Yonder was the banks and the islands, across the water; and maybe a spark -- which was a candle in a cabin window; and sometimes on the water you could see a spark or two -- on a raft or a scow; and maybe you could hear a fiddle or a song coming from one of them crafts. It's lovely to live on a raft. We had the sky up there, all speckled with stars, and we used to lay on our backs and look up at them and discuss about whether they was made or only just happened. Jim, he allowed they was made, but I allowed they happened; I judged it would have took too long to *make* so many. Jim said the moon could 'a' *laid* them; well, that looked kind of reasonable, so I didn't say nothing against it, because I've seen a frog lay most as many, so of course it could be done."

This was fresh and original writing. It signaled a breaking away from the stilted formal writing that passed as good literature before. Writing works when the reader becomes involved, when emotions are stirred, when the story comes alive. If we're transported to that time, walk side by side with the character and feel their happiness or pain then that is good writing. Twain was able to do this and more.

Huckleberry Finn is Mark Twain's masterpiece. He was a product of the river and its environment and brought it alive for his readers. He stated that "the face of the river, in time became a wonderful book that... "told its mind to me without reserve, delivering its most cherished secrets as clearly as if it had uttered them with a voice." Mark Twain was born in 1835 and his experiences growing up in Hannibal, Missouri - going to school, playing, fishing, fighting and swimming - was the raw material for *Huckleberry Finn*. He died in April 1910 his reputation as a distinctive American voice and a giant of American literature firmly established.

Huck Finn 2

Throughout this story, Huck demonstrates that he possesses some remarkable qualities in one so young. We will discuss these qualities. The primary quality must be his resourcefulness. Whether he was born with it or whether he was forced to develop it to survive; we'll never know. It may have been a combination of both. Without doubt he was intelligent though with little formal education but because he had to fend for himself from an early age, he developed a knowledge of life and what it took to survive way beyond his years.

There are numerous incidents throughout the story that highlight his resourcefulness. When the river would begin to rise, he collects firewood and pieces of log rafts floating down and sells them to the woodyards. One of the more notable incidents was when he made up his mind to escape from his father. His father beat him and treated him badly and he determined to leave him. When he sees an abandoned canoe floating down, he swims out and retrieves it, but instead of handing it over to his pap he hides it in a small creek and covers it with vines and a bunch of willows. He plans his escape meticulously and plans it so everyone, including his father, is convinced he's been shot, and his body dumped in the river. He shoots a pig and spreads its blood throughout the cabin, gets an axe and breaks the down the door and removes the food and supplies from the cabin. The evidence suggests that he's been attacked and killed, his body dragged to the river and disposed of.

He lights out for Jackson's Island after escaping from his father. He sets up camp, sets out his traps, catches a catfish and cooks himself supper. Later he explores the island, discovers a cave and moves into the cave with his friend Jim, the slave, who has run away from the Widow Douglas. When a frame house floats by, they get on board, make the canoe fast and wait until light so they can see what they may be able to salvage and what might be useful to them on their trip down the river. Beside some clothes "we got an old tin lantern, and a bran-new Barlow knife, and a lot of candles, and a tin candlestick, and a cup, and a ratty old bedquilt, and a reticule with needles and pins and thread and such truck in it, and a hatchet and some nails, and a fishline with some hooks on it, and a roll of buckskin, and a dog collar, and a horseshoe. And so, take it all around, we made a good haul." On the way back to the island, Huck makes Jim lie down in the canoe as by then it was broad daylight and "if he set up people could tell he was a nigger a good ways off." Five nights below St. Louis, in the middle of a major storm, in the middle of the night, Huck spots a wreck "a steamboat that had killed herself on a rock." Going on board appeals to him as an adventure "it being away in the night and stormy, and all so mysterious-like, I felt just like any other boy would 'a' felt when I seen that wreck. I wanted to get aboard of her. Jim, the slave is reluctant, but Huck persuades him. They come across a band of robbers and of course Huck wants to get closer to find out what's going on. In the meantime, their raft has broken loose, and these robbers are also murderers and are armed. Ever resourceful Huck locates the robbers' boat and steals it from under their noses and they are able to make their escape with the robbers' loot which had been stowed in the boat.

Huck and Jim drift down the river and every night Huck slips ashore and buys some meal or bacon and sometimes "I lifted a chicken that warn't roosting comfortable." Mornings before daylight he slipped into cornfields and 'borrowed' a watermelon, or pumpkin, some corn or things of that kind. Was he resourceful? He was resourcefulness personified.

Being just a boy, Huck can't resist playing a joke on his friend, Jim every once in a while.

When they're separated going down the river, he searches for Jim all night and eventually locate him asleep on the raft. He makes fast his canoe and lies down "under Jim's nose on the raft, began to gap, and stretch, and I says, 'Hello, Jim, have I been asleep? Why didn't you stir me up'?" He convinces Jim that it was all a dream, being separated and lost in the river, but when Jim sees the leaves and rubbish and the smashed oar, he realizes that Huck has been pulling his leg and he's upset, coz' he's been so worried about him "En when I wake up en fine you back ag'in, all safe en soun', de tears come, en I could 'a' got down on my knees en kiss yo' foot, I'm so thankful. En all you wuz thinkin' 'bout wuz how you could make a fool uv ole

Jim wid a lie." When Huck realizes how upset Jim is, he apologizes and resolves never to play no more mean tricks on his friend.

Another quality of his is his openness or initial trust until proven otherwise. Though he can be shrewd and conniving, his first instinct when meeting new people or situations is take them at face value. He is not by nature, suspicious or distrustful. He takes the 'king' and 'duke' on board his raft. They're in trouble and his instinct is to help them. Though they immediately reveal how they've been getting by and the various scams they've been involved in, Huck believes the younger one when he claims he's the Duke of Bridgewater and accedes to his wishes to be called "Your Grace" or "Your Lordship", wait on him at dinner and do any little thing for him he wanted done. Huck states, "Jim's eyes bugged out; and I reckon mine did too," when the 'duke' tells them "By rights I am a Duke."

When the other, in turn, informs them he is the Dauphin, "the wanderin', exiled, rightful King of France" Huck is equally impressed and accedes to his wishes to be called "Your majesty," get down on one knee to speak to him, wait on him first at meals and don't set down in his presence 'til he asked them. "So, Jim and me set to majestying him, and doin' this and that for him, and standing up till he told us we might set down." Huck soon figures out that this pair is no king or duke but "lowdown humbugs and frauds," but he realizes it is to his advantage not to let them know at this time, that he's seen through their scam.

He has a very keen sense of right and wrong according to his sense of values. Though he'll steal to lie or survive, he treats people as he would expect to be treated. He respects people's feelings. When he meets the Wilks family, he's very taken with Mary Jane "Mary Jane was red-headed and she was most awful beautiful, and her eyes was all lit up like glory." When 'the harelip' begins to question him about England and accuses him of lying, Mary Jane comes to his defense and Huck ruminates "This is a girl that I'm letting that old reptile rob her of her money." And when her sister Susan also jumps to his defense "Says I to myself, and this is another one that I'm letting him rob her of her money." When he finds Mary Jane crying in her room over the fate of the slaves and the fact that the children are to be separated from their mother, he resolves to do something about it and tells her the truth about the scam being perpetrated by his companions. He reckons "she had more sand in her than any girl I ever see. I haven't ever seen her since that time that I see her go out of that door; but I reckon I've thought of her a million times, and of her saying she would pray for me; and if ever I'd 'a' thought it would do any good for me to pray for her, blamed if I wouldn't 'a' done it or bust."

Jim, the slave is betrayed by the 'king' for forty dollars. Huck is convinced that God is angry with him for helping Jim escape from a poor old woman "that hadn't ever done me no harm." He decides to write her a letter telling where she can find the slave. But after he's written it, he begins to recall the happy times he spent with Jim as they made their way down the river - "and we a-floating along, talking and singing and laughing ......him standing my watch on top of his'n, so I could go on sleeping...how he would always call me honey, and do everything he could think of for me." This is a huge moral dilemma for Huck, the toughest he's encountered. Whichever path he chooses, he's damned. If he does not reveal the whereabouts of Jim to the Widow Watson, he's breaking God's law and if he does, he's betraying Jim. He wrestles with this for a while but decides to tear up the note and not reveal the slave's whereabouts, though he feels he's condemning himself to hell: "I sort of held my breath, and then says to myself, "All right, then, I'll go to hell..." This represents the conflict between organized religion and values of the community he comes from and the feelings and instincts he's developed in his travels. And he goes with his instincts.

He is not enthusiastic about Tom Sawyers scheme to free Jim, the slave, and the circuitous route taken. He empathizes with Jim's predicament and feels it's wrong to prolong his agony. This is the one incident in the book that rings false to me. The reason is, I think, that up to this we are in complete sympathy with the main character, Huck, and his friends. We cheer them when they're triumphant and feel sorrow when they're vanquished. They're decent and honorable and fighting bad characters and evil forces that try to bring them down. In this incident we have Huck and his friend, Tom Sawyer, the 'good' characters being cruel and uncaring, though mostly it's Tom's doing. All through his journey, Tom has survived with principles more or less intact. We've been with him when he's wrestled with his conscience, and he's made the right decisions - mostly. But here he's assisting Tom in a cruel hoax on Jim and we, the readers, are disappointed. We feel he has not done the right thing. He should have confronted Tom and told him "Now looky here, Tom Sawyer, it ain't right to be treatin' Jim like this. Jim here is a friend of mine an' we bin through thick an' thin t'gether. I know ev'ry second he spends locked up is an ag'ny for him and we should be doin' our dadblamed best to git him out as quick an' as easy as we know how. And that's what I'm a gonna do. And if you ain't with me, you're agin me, Tom Sawyer, and that's all I'm a gonna say on it."

Another quality of Huck's, much to be admired though unusual in one so young, is his total familiarity with, and lack of fear of, the outdoors. He seems more at home and content in the woods and on the river; not just content but transformed. The wilderness brings out the best in him. It is as if he welcomes the challenge of surviving and has no doubt whatever of his ability to meet this challenge. When he escapes from his pap he hightails it to Jackson's Island where he's all alone for three days and three nights before he stumbles across Jim, the slave: "the next day I went exploring around down through the island. I was boss of it; it all belonged to me, so to say, and I wanted to know all about it. I found plenty strawberries, ripe and prime; and green summer grapes, and green razzberries, and green blackberries was just beginning to show. They would all come handy by and by, I judged." When he hooks up with Jim, they discover a cave and move into it and soon after a violent storm strikes the island. There's thunder and lightning and heavy rain, wind that bends the trees down and deepest blackness and brightest light. What is Huck's reaction to all this? "Jim, this is nice," I says. "I wouldn't want to be nowhere else but here. Pass me along another hunk of fish." He has no fear of nature or of natural disasters, but civilization makes him uneasy.

Finally, there's maybe his most endearing quality, his optimism. His indomitable and optimistic spirit is a constant throughout his journey. We feel that no matter how many impossible situations he gets himself into, that he'll be able to extricate himself, somehow, someway. He extricates himself from the Widow Watson, escapes from his pap, outwits the 'duke' and the 'king' and helps Jim escape. He triumphs because he never despairs, or if he does, it is only while he catches his breath and he's off again. That's why we love him. We want to be like him, have his spirit, his optimism. We want to float down the Mississippi with him, lie under the stars and wonder how they came to be, smoke a pipe at ten years old, and scramble out the window in the dead of night and meet our best friend.

Is Huck somewhat of an odd character, anti-social even? He does not like civilization and its trappings. He does not like school, cares little about being able to read or write, chafes under the stewardship of the Widow Douglas - though he's got a room and a bed and three squares a day. But she exacts a price for these comforts. She expects him to dress proper, eat proper and pray proper. He's a young boy who has not had many good experiences with family or father. He's naturally wary of authority and finds contentment outside -- in the woods and by the river. He also has a talent for surviving there; not just surviving but living comfortably. He is not anti-social, if anti-social means harmful to the welfare of people and his good deeds far outnumber his bad throughout his travels. Huck harbors no grudges and carries no anger in his heart. He's too busy gettin' on with his life, tryin' to make a livin' and doing the best he can.

What would Huck say if some 'educated' college professor accused him of being anti-social? Let's ask him.

"Huck, some of those fancy college professors back east have been analyzing you and your story and they're coming up with some wild and woolly theories. Some theorize that you may have anti-social tendencies, that this desire to run away constantly may be a manifestation of some deep-seated trauma in your psyche, an inability or fear of dealing with people and, rather than stay and deal with it you flee. Your reply?"

"Now, looky here, Professor, you all so hung up on this dadblamed psychology nonsense that you can't see the trees for the forest. I ain't nothin' but a poor uneducated Southern boy and if you hadn't spent so much time with your nose in a book and studyin' in them Ivy colleges - which got your mind messed up, you would have seen just that long time ago. I ain't sayin' I'm dumb, 'cos you and I know I ain't. I bin in tight spots and I was always able to figger somethin' out. But I sure as heck ain't anti-social neither and never was. I help my fella man and even says a prayer to the almighty to keep me on the straight and narrow path. And I think he hears me coz I ain't never strayed too far. And that ain't no lie I'm tellin'. So put your crazy suspicions in your back pocket coz what you see is what you get. We gotta take people at face value, we gotta trust each other coz we're all we got. We gotta trust the carpenter to build th' house and build it right, don't we? And we gotta trust th' gunsmith to make a good gun, and the ferry-boat cap'n to steer that boat proper, the teacher to teach the kids good and the farmer to grow good vittles, don't we? What we are and what we achieve, it all depends on trust, professor. Dadblamed, but that's the first thing they should have taught you in that fancy college. You got to get with the program, profess' and no wonder the country's messed up. You suppose to be the best and the brightest but you sure ain't actin' like it. No sirree, all that psychology stuff you spoutin'. Makes me think maybe us common folks, huntin' and fishin' for a livin', should be in charge and runnin' the country. Couldn't do no worser."

How would Huck survive today in America -- in Westchester County? He would have neither the open spaces nor the freedom of that earlier age. His skills as a survivor in the great outdoors would be of less importance than they were in that earlier time. But somehow, I believe Huck would have adapted and adapted quite well. Man has survived because he has been able to adapt so well over thousands of years. In every age and every culture there are different challenges to meet, obstacles to overcome and stresses to deal with. Huck was the prototype of the modern, successful man -- resourceful, adaptable, realistic but optimistic with a can-do attitude. Huck would have made out fine wherever he ended up, thank you. It's been proven in studies that optimistic people, even those unrealistically optimistic, are more successful that pessimists. Huck is the eternal optimist, like the country that bred him.

From the opening statement from Huck, "You don't know about me without you have read a book by the name of The Adventures of Tom Sawyer." We're with him as he takes us along on his adventures. We're not just uninvolved spectators for Huck confides in us like we've been friends for a long time. We're sharing this adventure together and he just tells the story more or less as it happened. He ain't tryin' to make himself look good and he ain't glossin' over the times when he maybe should have acted better. He's tellin' us the plain, unvarnished truth and we love him for it. He deals with his travails as they arise, and he doesn't always win. He does the best he can, and he moves on.

There is a sense of America in these qualities of Huck. These are qualities most admired by Americans and in turn by others as distinctly American. The qualities of optimism, resourcefulness, friendliness and maybe even the idea that they are a chosen people or that God has seen fit to bless them with many advantages seem an American 'thing'. Were the seeds of America's future greatness planted by the qualities that Huck possessed and others like him; Huck with his innocence, optimism, friendliness, righteous indignation, and never-say-die attitude.

Are there other motives in Twain's story of Huck Finn? Is there a greater significance in this simple tale? Is it just a simple tale? My feeling is that there are no other motives. Though it is a simple tale, it deals with slavery and slavery is a complex subject. Twain has to walk a fine line between creating a story that has universal appeal and portraying slavery as neither evil nor good. The prevailing thinking at that time was that slavery was not necessarily evil and that blacks would never be the equal of the white man. If the book were an outright condemnation of slavery, it might never have been published. In that Southern society violence and bigotry were commonplace. Was Jim, the slave portrayed favorably? Too favorably for most Southerners, probably. Did Huck display a condescending attitude to Jim? Was Jim given too many human, too many intelligent qualities? Did some consider that it was too accepting of slavery? How did blacks feel then about this story, about Jim's portrayal, about slavery's portrayal? How would they consider the story today? Did Twain envision the day when slavery would be viewed as what it really was; the subjugation of a race of people by another and the process of dehumanizing the subjugated to make it more acceptable. Today, the characters change but the scenario is repeated. It is an ongoing story on our planet; one race or segment of society feeling superior over the other.

There is a lesson in this story of Huck's adventures and as we travel the woods and river with him and admire his fortitude, resourcefulness and all the other qualities he possessed and we've discussed, we are left with a distinct impression that if we all had a little more of Huck's philosophy and outlook, dadblamed it but this world jes' might be a better place. An' thass what I believe.

The Fate of the Boy Soldier, John Condon

The Irish War Effort in World War 1

On the eve of World War 1, one of the greatest wars known to man, "the British army found itself grievously unprepared for large-scale warfare." (Ireland's Unknown Soldiers – Terence Denman) However, the imminent outbreak of this war also heralded a gigantic surge of jingoism as each nation wanted to prove itself and engage in the international battle. Thousands of young men flocked to join the army in pursuit of money, adventure, and pride.

Over two hundred thousand Irishmen, both Nationalist and Unionist enlisted to serve in the British Army. Many of the Nationalists hoped that by doing so, they were fighting for the freedom of small nations and that they would speed the Home Rule cause.

John Condon, a young Waterford boy, was one of the thousands to sign on. He was to become the youngest Allied soldier killed in action in the Great War.

John Condon was born in 1901 to John and Mary Condon in Waterford City. The 1911 Census confirms their residence as a two-bedroom tenement at number 2 Thomas's Avenue, fondly known as Wheelbarrow Lane.

During his childhood, John spent much of his time with his older cousin, Nicholas Condon. According to Nicholas's surviving son, the two boys had been known locally as "the Condon twins," such was their closeness. He also added that John and his father were always 'looking for a bit of adventure.'

It was during one such 'boyhood adventure' that the two boys stowed away on the Claddagh, a Waterford Steamship Company Steamer to Liverpool. After failing to secure employment there, John returned home while Nicholas enlisted in the York and Lancaster Regiment. John was soon to follow his cousin into the army.

Back in Waterford, the local M.P. John Redmond was pushing a huge campaign encouraging 'young men of fighting age' to enlist in the British Army. According to Dr. Jim Stacey, a Waterford historian, 'virtually every family in Waterford had a member in the war' (Nationwide) The Condon family was no exception.

Private John Condon, No. 6822 signed on in 1914, aged thirteen. He gave his age as seventeen and was assigned to the 2nd Royal Irish Regiment, 12th Brigade, 4th Division. An article in a local paper, Waterford Today, reported that his recruiting officer, J. Conway noted on John's file that he was 'sober and honest.'

Once enlisted, John went to the barracks in Clonmel to train as a member of the reserve force. Within a matter of months, the war was raging and British Forces at the front were suffering colossal casualties. Unbeknownst to his family, John was shipped out to France on December 16th, 1914. In April of 1915, he was posted to the front in an area known as the Salient in Southern Belgium.

On April 22nd, 1915, the Germans launched the Second Battle of

Ypres. They had succeeded in breaking through the Allied lines and John's unit was called up fill the gap. During their merciless advance, the Germans had secured a hill at Bellevarde Ridge. This left the Allies with no choice but to engage in a dangerous and perilous battle.

Despite the odds stacked against them, the Allies were slowly regaining territory. Fearful of being captured, the Germans released a batch of lethal chlorine gas on May 24th, 1915. John Condon died that day, a young boy-soldier of fourteen years on Malftrap Farm on Flanders field, where he and some comrades had sought sanctuary from the toxic gas. (Age 14 – The John Condon Story, Geert Spillebeen).

When John's body was found almost a decade later, he was identified solely by a piece of leather boot with his number stamped on it. He was laid to rest in Plot LVI, Row F in Poelcalelle Cemetery in Belgium. In 1922, Pte John Condon was decorated with the British War Medal and the Victory Cross, proving himself to be a hero regardless of his age.

Manhattan Random

I wanna get something straight, okay? I'm a live-and-let-live kind of guy, okay? Don't show no discrimination on account of race, religion, or national origin. Don't bother me and I won't bother you. You're okay until you prove otherwise. If you prove otherwise, I shrug my shoulders and move on. We can't all be good guys. As I said, a live and let live kind of guy. But I'm human. I do get annoyed.

So, a couple of weeks ago, I'm strolling down Varick Street in lower Manhattan, going nowhere, just enjoying the city. I like walking and I like the city, especially on a nice day in May. A nice sunny day in May, in Manhattan, hard to beat, you don't want to be anywhere else. This, to me is God's country. I turn the corner, the corner of Worth onto Varick and I get hit with an avalanche of sound. This guy is carrying a boombox, the sidewalks vibrating. He confronts me, says something to me. I can't hear a word he's saying so I cover my ears and point to the box. He turns it down and I tell him I can't hear him. So, what does this asshole say?

"I have a right to play it loud, this is America" This is a grade A asshole.

So, I say again slowly, "I couldn't hear you."

"Oh, oh, right. Look, man, I was looking for some change, okay?" he tells me.

I look at him. He's overweight, hasn't missed a meal in many moons, carries a substantial belly. The t-shirt he's wearing is three sizes too small and riding high on his body, his bellybutton one of those protruding types.

I say, "you don't look hungry?"

"So what?" he says, "whattaya think I am, a bum?"

"So, why'd you stop me," I say?

"Batteries, man. I need batteries for my box. They eat up batteries," he replies in an

accusing tone as if I got something to do with it.

"Don't play it as much," I tell him, "they'll last longer."

"Look," he says, "if you don't wanna give me something, that's fine, but don't lecture me, okay, don't lecture me. If you wanna give me something, fine, if you don't, I may not like it, but I'll understand. We need to understand the relationship here, okay?"

I let that one pass. "Ever think about getting a job?"

"A job," he says, his lips compressing, "a job and let corporate America suck me dry? No way, man, no way. They eat you up and spit you out. They don't care about the little guy. They work you till you can't work no more and then they cast you aside. That ain't for me."

I interrupt him. "'Under what circumstances would you work?"

"Are you in the Government?" he asks suspiciously.

"Nope, just a poor slob who goes to work every day."

"Bought into it, ha?" he says.

"Bought into what?" I say.

"Work hard, pay your taxes, success, the American dream, all that happy horseshit - poor slob is right. I ain't fallin' for that crap."

So, I ask again, "under what circumstances would you get a job?"

"Well," he says, "I like music, y'know. That's my forte, if you know what I mean, music, composin', promotin', writin'."

"Why don't you get a job in the music industry?" I ask.

"I may," he says, "but right now I'm exploring, letting ideas percolate."

"How long you been letting ideas percolate?" I ask.

"Oh, eight, nine years, I guess. You can't hurry it, has to happen in its own time on its own terms. That's where dudes make the mistake."

"How long more?" I say.

"I dunno, man but I'll know when it happens."

"I wish you luck, but I got no money for batteries," I say.

"I spend ten minutes tellin' my story, explainin' what I'm about," he tells me, "opening myself up to you, and you say no?"

"Get a job and explore on the side," I tell him as I walk away.

"Tight ass," he snarls, turns up the volume and walks away.

Parents

I've been thinking about my parents. If I were to classify or label them, what classification or label would I attach to them? I loved my parents, but most children do. It is a natural thing to love our parents, for as babies and growing up, we depend on them, turn to them, and expect to be fed, clothed, and loved by them. We also expect discipline from them. We rely on them to set parameters, to scold us when we step out of line and to register their approval when we are good.

But how would I classify my parents? Were they ideal parents? If ideal means hugging me regularly, fussing over my homework assignments and being involved in my extracurricular activities, then they were not ideal. My father never hugged me. My parents rarely attended my sporting endeavors and neither fussed over nor took any part in my homework assignments. Were they loving parents?

Love has so many different meanings to so many different people. Were my father and mother visible presences in my life? Yes, very much so. Was it generally a household of contentment, a place to where we could retreat, a warm safe refuge from the often-harsh reality of the world? Yes. My parents' love was not a demonstrative, highly visible kind of love, but all it takes is a gesture, a look, a smile, a pat on the head, a touch on the shoulders for a child to recognize love. Even without anyone of the, a fore mentioned, a child will still recognize love. I knew, as sure as the sun shines in summer, that I was loved, and it was sufficient unto itself.

Were my parents rich? No. Did it matter? No. Did rich automatically mean good - or bad? Being rich or poor has little to do with love or for that matter being a good parent. To know that he, or she, is loved is the most important ingredient in a child's life and even extreme poverty can be dealt with if the child knows this.

There are other labels we can attach to parents: indulgent parents, financially irresponsible parents, hard luck parents, sick parents or what might be called medically compromised, in the new vernacular. Then there is the flower child, the pessimistic and the pie-in-the-sky, eternally optimistic, dysfunctional, alcoholic, drug-addicted, welfare, single parents and living with the in-laws' parents.

Parents are essentially people and people come in all varieties. Most people want to be good parents, but not everyone has the discipline and patience necessary to be successful. The alcoholic parent is fighting his or her addiction to alcohol while trying to support and give guidance to the family. Likewise with the drug-addicted parent.

The indulgent parent is afraid to instill discipline in his children yet knows that lack of discipline has complicated his life. The flower-child parents are living in an era that has passed them by and by trying to relive an era where drugs and promiscuity were rampant, they may be putting their own children at risk. Parents who are sick or who have medical problems throughout their lives constantly fight a battle to stay ahead of bills, remain employed and attend to their families' needs. Financially irresponsible parents also fight a constant battle to stay ahead of bills, often living from day to day, and the stress this involves.

But children are extremely resilient and though the parents might have problems of their own to deal with, it does not mean automatically that they will make poor parents. If the parent recognizes that he has a problem and avails himself of the services available and if he wants to do the right thing for his child, then there's an excellent chance of success.

But in this age of job insecurity, two-parent wage earners, homelessness, unmarried teenage mothers, children having children, gangs, easy availability of drugs, self-centered or emotionally insecure parents and all the other stresses of modern society, there is no doubt that children are more and more at risk every day. Where once these phenomena were the exception, now they are the rule. The two-parent nuclear family is becoming rarer.

Personal responsibility needs to be fostered, the idea that we are our brother's keeper, and that cruelty and indifference to one, diminishes all. Parents, good parents, have a crucial role to play.

Priorities

He got out of his car and slammed the door. 'Why am I still working here,' he thought? 'I don't hate the job, but I don't like it either.' At times he disliked it intensely and at other times, he thought 'It's not bad really, it pays reasonably well, the hours are okay, vacation time sucks but the medical coverage is excellent.' So, for the umpteenth time, he argued the pros and cons of this job, as he proceeded slowly towards the entrance and felt that familiar sense of irritation and dissatisfaction.

He approached the door, and as he opened it, heard the familiar strains of the Salve Regina pouring out of the speakers, which are placed strategically inside the facility. He hears again Father Sheridan's murmur, "if it's the Salve Regina, it must be Friday." They always finish mass on Friday with this hymn. He didn't know this, don't know one hymn from another but Father knows. He's a patient in Rose Hill Nursing Home. He receives Communion every morning. So, they have to set him up, first thing every morning. They straighten out his bed, set up the crucifix on a white cloth draped over the bedside table. On each side of the crucifix, they place a burning candle in a red glass but if there's oxygen in the room, the candles are not lit. "There ye go, 'foostering' around again," he tells us, as we straighten out the bed. He has a lot of Irish expressions.

He is also blind in both eyes, so he usually asks, "what kind of a day is it?" So, he'll describe the day as in, "It's about twenty degrees, no wind so it does not feel cold, blue skies, going up to a high of about forty-one degrees. It will be sunny for most of the day but clouding up later. He might wax a little poetic, "there's a lone hawk hovering menacingly in the sky."

"Hovering menacingly, I like that, m-m-m, very descriptive," he murmurs.

"Yes Father, I thought it was quite nice myself," and he continues "there's a squirrel frantically rushing about trying to remember where he buried those darn nuts, it seems like a lifetime ago, and getting more and more frantic by the minute. He's probably saying, 'I should have made a map, I should have made a map. My wife was right, my wife was right.'"

"Jimmy, you have a fertile imagination."

"Father, is that the best you can come up with? - fertile."

"Yes, let's leave it at that, there's much worse than fertile."

So, they banter back and forth.

A few minutes later, the Administrator, Sister Mary Rose, and Father Adrian come down from the chapel and administer Holy Communion to Father.

As already said, he has conflicting feelings about the job. One day, everything goes beautifully, and he may say, "I can deal with this for another four years." Four more years equals ten years' service equals a pension. But then there is some unpleasantness with the administrator and he's saying, "what am I doing here, at my age? I have to take this crap. Put your thumb and forefinger together as close as possible, without touching. That's how close he's been to quitting a half dozen times or more. But his innate cautious nature takes over. So, he argues with himself, and the argument goes like this.

"I can't take it anymore. I don't need this. No job is worth this aggravation."

"Easy, easy, big guy, just relax. Don't get upset. You know when you're in the right. She has a bug up her ass and is taking it out on you. She has the problem, not you."

"She's my supervisor, not my goddamn superior. She talks to everybody like they're lower than whale s..."

"It was just your turn today. It'll be somebody else's tomorrow. Everybody agrees that there's something medically wrong there. One minute, she's as sweet as sweet can be, the next, she's a raging lunatic."

"Over what? The pay phone rings, somebody wants Dougie. I go to call Dougie. "Jim, Jim, is that a phone call for Dougie?"

"Yes, Sister."

"Jim, you know we don't receive phone calls here, unless it's an emergency. You should have informed them of that and hung up."

"But Sister …"

"Jim, you should know better. Haven't you been told that there are no personal calls taken here?"

"Sister, I have never taken a phone call for Dougie, not in five years, so I figure it might be important."

"No Jim, no. I know who that is. He's been calling a lot lately"

"I didn't know, Sister . . ."

"That's our policy, Jim, inquire if it's an emergency and if it's not, hang up."

So now, he's upset. His insides are churning. If she could read his mind, she'd run and lock herself in her room and fear for her life. He visualizes a dozen different violent deaths for her. Ten minutes later, they pass in the hall, and she says in the sweetest most angelic voice, "Oh, hi Jim, how is everything going?" She must know how he's feeling, because it's showing in his face. That's why he thinks we're dealing with a classic paranoid/schizophrenic or is it manic/depressive? Ward is convinced she forgets to take her medicine, on occasion, - many occasions. He knows she's had confrontations with the other sisters. They hear these things through the grapevine. And Ward is her favorite whipping boy. He walks out of here sometimes and I'm not sure if he's going to cry, get drunk or commit suicide.

"I know, I know. But remember how we've talked about not being influenced by outside events. If we are, we're like a ship tossed around with no direction. We can regulate two things, our own lives, and our reactions to others. We cannot regulate other peoples' lives. But we can control our reactions to their actions. We must, otherwise we're subject to the whims and outbursts of every Tom, Dick, and Harry. That's an awful way to live your life."

(Sigh) "Yeah, you're right, but if she just loosened up a little, it could be so nice around here."

The job could be nice. He liked the hours, seven to three. They got their lunch, and they got paid for their lunch hour plus two fifteen-minute breaks. Rose Hill is a home for the terminally ill with cancer. He's never had a problem with the patients and feel he's of some comfort to them, that he makes a difference in their lives. But supervision stinks. They are total control freaks. They've even opened mail addressed to the staff, which is mail tampering and is illegal.

Also, it's a good situation in other ways. It's located about ten miles from where he lives, and a huge improvement over having to drive into the city, which was what he had to do in his previous job.

Sometimes he tries to visualize a bigger picture. What I'm doing with my life, what I want to do, where I want to be in ten or fifteen years. He'll have earnest conversations with his wife about future plans, their financial situation, should they move, sell their house? If they sell, should they rent? Should they move South?

In three years, their youngest son, Benjamin, would finish college, hopefully. Then they would have to make decisions. His wife wanted to be near their children, all who lived and worked in and around the New York area. He liked New York but hated those winters. So, he's considering spending some of the winter months down South. Down South where? That's another decision to be made.

For now, he thinks about this job of his. Will the sisters turn over a new leaf? Will they advance enough in their spirituality that they become kinder and more tolerant? Will he stay the course if they don't, or make an offering of his suffering for sins past? Will he learn to be more tolerant of the sisters and the stress involved in running a facility such as this, the long hours they work, the lack of free time - one day a month? More to come, stay tuned.

Snow in August

It snowed in August that year, the year of our Lord 2000. Strange happenings had occurred all year. Temperatures soared in February to eighty degrees.

Flowers began to bud and blossom. Birds and animals moved frenziedly about, out of control, their biological clocks out of sync. As suddenly as this heatwave had occurred, it disappeared. Blossoms wilted, birds flew listlessly about, and animals appeared shell-shocked, confused, and disoriented. Huge snowstorms followed and later, in endless procession, strange black clouds drifted across the sky. The sun disappeared, as if it had left our galaxy for another.

Newspapers were full of catastrophes all year, floods and fires, earthquakes, mud slides and sinkholes. A strange flu-like sickness affected millions, leaving them weak and vulnerable and killing many elderly. It baffled scientists. Violent and irrational behavior prevailed world-wide and quiet, decent people turned mean and ornery. It was the worst of times.

The world was on edge, on the verge of insanity as mayhem and murder prevailed. The planet seemed headed for disintegration. Churches and synagogues filled to overflowing and prophets, in their thousands, emerged to predict the end of the world order, the imminent coming of the Messiah, destruction for the wicked and redemption for the chaste and God-like.

The summer was a strange one too, wet and damp. People were edgy, abrupt, and rude. They scurried about, suspicious and avoiding others. There were four major air crashes and three major train collisions that year. The Premier of France was assassinated, the Eiffel tower was bombed, and scientists informed us that New York City was sinking rapidly, due to a newly discovered major fault-line in the earth's crust. The early nineties of booming stock markets, decreasing Government deficits and tax cuts were a distant memory.

There were sightings of strange disc-like objects in the skies. People claimed to have been abducted by space aliens. A meteorite crashed into the earth's surface in the Australian desert, creating a hole the size of two football fields. People in their thousands streamed there each day to see and pray at the site. Nasa proclaimed that we should accelerate space research, that this could be the beginning of the end of planet earth.

Then suddenly on December 21, it ended. Normalcy returned. It was as it had been before. People reverted to normal behavior, the weather became seasonal and optimism and good spirits returned. Oh yes, New York City stabilized. The experts were not sure what had caused it to sink and argued among themselves.

Within a short time, this time of turmoil was forgotten by all. It had been too traumatic, too scary for people to understand or deal with. It was again the best and worst of times.

I was six years old then. I asked my grandmother, blinded in an accident since she was sixteen years old, what it all meant. She turned her sightless eyes to me and replied, "For a little while, God stopped loving us."

Summer

How people perceive the different seasons - and specifically winter and summer-has always fascinated me. I myself hate winter and love summer and as the years progress, my opinions become more entrenched.

How can anyone like winter? I remember receiving my fuel oil bill this past winter. The figure jumped out and smacked me, and left me weak and panting, doubled over and trying to regain equilibrium. The thought entered my mind again. How can anyone like winter?

People wax lyrical over winter. They describe scenes of pristine snow, little boys and girls sledding with their fathers, skating on the village pond where a great bonfire blazes in the background, marshmallows roasting on an open fire, while chatter and laughter rings through the air.

They describe rosy cheeks, carol singing, ski trips to exotic places, snowball fights, families safe at home where a blazing fire lights up the living room or den, mom and kids sipping hot chocolate, and dad partaking of a hot toddy. Then there's Christmas shopping, socials, dances and club meetings that seem to proliferate throughout the season, not to mention football and tailgate parties.

But the winter I know is far different. I have lived in this area for thirty-five years and have seen my share of cruel, wicked, mean, and nasty winters. They are not all bad, but the problem is that we never know, so we go through this "wonderful" season with head down and apprehension gripping our hearts. For the truth is, nobody really knows when the next big one is about to happen. For all of the advancements in science, satellites and computers, weather forecasting has little changed these past fifty years. I remember winters where the ground froze to thirty-nine inches depth, where we had twenty-three storms and eighty inches of snow. My back ached from shovelling and my eyes glazed as I surveyed new mounds of snow where a few days before my driveway, steps, decks and pathway had been shovelled and swept clean after many hours of tortuous, spirit bending, mind numbing, soul destroying manual labor.

I remember driving home from the Bronx on the Sawmill River Parkway with one lane open from Hawthorne to Mount Kisco. There were cars abandoned in the other lane all the way, and these had been buried by the snowplows keeping the one lane open. If I had not been lucky enough to get behind a snowplow for the last couple of miles, I doubt if I would have made it.

If the same plow had not exited at Mount Kisco, I doubt if I would have been able to exit there. The side streets had not been plowed, so I had to park downtown and walk home through snow drifts that sometimes reached to my chest.

I remember dead batteries and frozen pipes, treacherous driving conditions, wind chills of thirty below, trees and power lines overloaded with snow and ice crashing onto roads and parkways. Commuter trains and buses were also affected resulting in restricted service and irate commuters. And of course, let us not forget flooding. But that is not a winter-only phenomenon.

And what of summer? Ah, summer, that season of sun and fun. As spring turns in to early summer, we begin to emerge from our cocoon, shed layers of clothing and survey winter's damage. We've put on weight because when we are cold, we eat, when we are stressed, we eat, and somehow, when we are buried under layers of clothing who know or who cares. So, we look with dismay at our out-of-proportion bodies and again curse winter.

But summer is upon us and like our fellow denizens of this beautiful, complicated planet, we are suddenly gripped with a fever of activity. We clean house, work out, cut grass, dig garden, work out, clean gutters, paint and replace winter's damage and work out. We begin to take back our property, street, neighborhood. We go for walks, bicycle rides, or jog. We spend time outside on our deck, have barbecues, invite, and visit friends.

We soak in the sunshine, swim in the pool, or visit the ocean, walk, or jog the beaches. Driving is not a hassle anymore, so we visit interesting places and enjoy new experiences. Slowly the scars of winter heal. Our spirit is renewed, refreshed, and reawakened. We are living life again, not just surviving. We are in control, or somewhat.

Am I prejudiced where both seasons are concerned? Probably. Do I see the glass half empty where winter is concerned and half full for summer? I prejudge winters and summers to come because of my experiences with winters and summers past. I like everything about summer and easily deal with extreme heat. Summer touches my spirit. Winter's onset makes me nervous, uneasy. I hope that we'll survive relatively unscathed, but I won't enjoy it. Scenes of snow and rosy cheeks leave me cold. And those fuel bills....

Cat That Ran Away

You read about the cat which was missing for five years in California and then was found in New York? The cat had a chip under his skin and that's how they identified him. I was watching the newscast closely to see the cat's reaction to being back home. He wasn't happy.

Think about it. The cat stays away for five years, travels across the country to get as far away as possible from 'home.' Whatever or wherever home was, it wasn't where he wanted to be. He knew the chip was there and tried to keep it hidden. He did – for five years. Then, then some nosy son of a gun – or daughter of a gun - discovers it.

"Daddy, mommy, there's something under pussy's skin."

"Oh my god, it's a chip," and I can hear Pussy, drawing a deep breath, saying

"Well, memories are made of this. It was a good run and reckon all good things must come to an end."

Imagine the family's reaction. "He's back, he's back, thank God Almighty, praise the Lord, our kitty's back. God directed him home."

God didn't direct him home. It was the chip, dummy. Did they stop to think, why couldn't he find his way home? How come he kept moving in the opposite direction?

They might not have been bad people, but maybe they were

unimaginative and boring and dull, and he was bored out of his skull. Maybe he's a cold weather cat and couldn't take that sunshine, sunshine, bullcrap all year-round weather in Lala land. Maybe they smothered him, restricted his freedom, kept him indoors too much, restricted his access to other cats, who knows? Maybe he was just looking for some cat companionship, for friendship, cat friendship, leading to... more than just friendship? Romance?

Animals are similar to humans in many ways. We all crave a deep and lasting relationship. Maybe his favorite song was Me and Bobby Mc Gee, by Janis Joplin? Maybe he did meet his Bobby McGee somewhere out on the open road, and maybe Bobby shared the secrets of his soul. He knew, intrinsically, the only way to, maybe, experience this kind of life-changing event, was to take to the open road. My guess is he had more than one life-changing experience out there on the open road. His Bobby Mc Gee stayed for a while and then moved on. That's how Bobby was, and is. He was sad to see her go but he knew Bobby was not for long-term relationships.

Though he missed her, he would be forever grateful for their time together. It had changed him in so many ways. He had experienced true love for the very first time and it was all he had ever heard or read about. Yes, dummy, cats read – though they prefer if humans don't know. The less they know about feline capabilities, the better off they are, both feline and human.

But it is romantic striking out on one's own with just the fur on your back, no baggage, no backpacks, just as you came into the world. Who could resist?

"Where you headed for?"

"Dunno."

"How far have you come?"

"Dunno."

"Aren't you just a little bit afraid?"

"Nope."

"Wow, I really admire your, your courage."

Of course, he didn't want to be back. He was riding high in April, May, June, and July too - right across the continent, gaining skills and confidence as he travelled. He was self-sufficient, eating mice and nuts, fresh meat, sleeping under the stars, his natural instincts honed to a near perfection, always, always, on guard for bigger predators – and of course for even more Bobby Mc Gee's, so he could share even more secrets of his soul.

Maybe he had to outfight or outrun some of the big cats. Now he's back home, eating cat nuggets out of a bag. He's not happy and he's not gonna be home long. This story is not finished.

Abbeyside

There is a place, beyond the sea

A special, special place, to me

A holy place of history

By broad Atlantic Sea.

(Chorus) Oh Abbeyside, by surging tide,

You're with me day and with me night

Where're I go, on sea or shore

You are my shining light.

I long to be, embraced by thee

To stroll your streets, A cuppa tea

The Pond, the Strand, the Friars Walk

The pub, the pint, the talk.

(Chorus) Oh Abbeyside....

Augustine is our patron saint,

Came wandering for the love of God

Peregrinatio pro Dei amore

That's how we came to be

(Chorus) Oh Abbeyside....

Your sons and daughters roam the earth,

To Far East shores and to the West

But always, always in their hearts

Love burns so true for you

(Chorus) Oh Abbeyside….

Some day when home from deck and mast,

In Alice's, I'll raise a glass.

play Pitch-and-Toss, and Forty-Five,

And from that bridge I'll dive

(Chorus) Oh Abbeyside….

To hang around the Poor Man's Seat

With boyhood friends, a special treat

We'll talk of days gone by and more

The Scouts, the teams, the score

(Chorus) Oh Abbeyside….

And then one day, my journey o'er

They'll carry me through that old door

I'm where I've always yearned to be

I'm home at last and free.

(Chorus) Oh Abbeyside….

Made in United States
North Haven, CT
21 December 2022